American Free Verse

American Free Verse

The Modern Revolution in Poetry

by Walter Sutton

A NEW DIRECTIONS BOOK

ACKNOWLEDGMENTS

Grateful acknowledgment is made to the editors and publishers of books
where some of the excerpted material quoted in this volume first appeared
or from whom permission to reprint has been obtained.

Atheneum Publishers, David Higham Associates, Ltd., and Hart-Davis,
Ltd. (London) for "When I Go There," from *The Lice* by W. S. Merwin
(Copyright © 1966 by W. S. Merwin. "When I Go There" appeared orig-
inally in *Poetry*).

Harcourt Brace Jovanovich, for portions of E. E. Cummings's *Poems,
1923–1954* (Copyright © 1954 by E. E. Cummings) and *95 Poems* (Copy-
right © 1958 by E. E. Cummings).

Harper & Row, Publishers, and Faber & Faber, Ltd. (London), for por-
tions of "Ariel," from *Ariel* by Sylvia Plath (Copyright © 1965, 1966 by
Ted Hughes).

Holt, Rinehart and Winston, and Jonathan Cape, Ltd. (London), for
portions of *Rivers and Mountains* by John Ashbery (Copyright © 1964 by
John Ashbery).

Indiana University Press, for "Forsythia," by Mary Ellen Solt, from
Concrete Poetry, edited by Mary Ellen Solt (Copyright © 1968 by His-
panic Arts, Indiana University).

The Macmillan Company, and Faber & Faber, Ltd. (London), for
portions of "The Fish" and "Propriety" by Marianne Moore, from the
Collected Poems (Copyright 1935, 1951, by Marianne Moore).

New Directions Publishing Corporation, and Faber & Faber, Ltd. (Lon-
don), for portions of Ezra Pound's *Personae* (Copyright 1926 by Ezra
Pound) and *The Cantos* (Copyright 1934, 1937, 1940, 1948, © 1956, 1959,
1970, 1971 by Ezra Pound; Copyright © 1969, 1972 by the Estate of Ezra
Pound).

New Directions Publishing Corporation, Laurence Pollinger, Ltd., and
MacGibbon & Kee, Ltd. (London), for portions of William Carlos Wil-
liam's *Collected Earlier Poems* (Copyright 1938 by New Directions Pub-
lishing Corporation), *Collected Later Poems* (Copyright 1948, 1949 by
William Carlos Williams), *Paterson* (Copyright 1946, 1948, 1949, 1951, ©
1959 by William Carlos Williams; Copyright © 1963 by Florence Wil-
liams), and *Pictures from Brueghel and Other Poems* (Copyright 1954 by
William Carlos Williams).

New Directions Publishing Corporation, Laurence Pollinger, Ltd., and
Jonathan Cape, Ltd. (London), for portions of Denise Levertov's *The
Jacob's Ladder* (Copyright © 1961 by Denise Levertov Goodman) and
With Eyes at the Back of Our Heads (Copyright © 1959 by Denise Lever-
tov Goodman).

Contents

Foreword

UNLIKE more general discussions of American poetry, this book concentrates on the origins and growth of the powerful free verse movement from its beginnings in the Romantic revolution to the present. I hope that it may offer complementary testimony to the vitality and imaginative resourcefulness of American poetry, especially in the twentieth century.

Emphasizing both theory and practice, the following chapters discuss representative figures and groups of poets from the beginning of the nineteenth century, through the revolutionary modern period, in which free verse was established as a dominant mode, to the contemporary postwar years, which have produced a rich variety of poetic interests and achievements. One point, implicit in what follows, should perhaps be made explicit here: although the modern movement in the arts was broadly international, the free verse movement in English has been a predominantly American phenomenon.

I am grateful to James Laughlin and Hayden Carruth for thoughtful readings of the manuscript and helpful suggestions. My greatest debt is to Vivian R. Sutton, my closest critic and reader.

Portions of the following pages have appeared in somewhat different form in *Contemporary Literature, Criticism, The Minnesota Review, The Journal of Aesthetics and Art Criticism, American Poetry*, ed. Irvin Ehrenpreis (1965), and *Sense and Sensibility in Twentieth-Century Writing*, ed. Brom Weber (1970); I am indebted to the editors for permission to reprint.

W. S.

1. The Romantic Revolution

THE FREE VERSE MOVEMENT in America was part of a larger international revolution that broke the mold of Victorian and academic conventions in all the arts. Led by the American and English Imagists in poetry and by the Vorticists, Cubists, and other abstractionists in the arts, the rebels called for a total repudiation of the past. The violence of their rejection can be seen in the rallying cry of the Vorticists in the July 1914 issue of their short-lived London journal *Blast*: "BLAST / years 1837 to 1900 / Curse abysmal inexcusable middle-class / (Also Aristocracy and Proletariat)."

For all their intransigence, the moderns were rooted, more deeply than they would admit, in the English and American Romantic revolution of the late eighteenth and early nineteenth centuries. The movement was extremely complex, with many strands of influence, many attitudes, and not a few contradictions and inconsistencies. Yet it is possible to identify certain tendencies in Romantic poetic theory and practice that have special importance for the modern revolution in poetry. Among these was the abandonment of neoclassical fixed forms (like the heroic couplet) and genre distinctions in favor of organically determined functional forms. The general revolt against the authority of the past encouraged the rejection of established poetic diction and the promotion of a more particularized and idiomatic language representing the individual perception of the writer. Contrary to the teaching of Dr. Johnson's Imlac, the Romantic poet *was* expected to number the streaks of the tulip.[1] The organic impulse, which developed largely as a reaction against neoclassicism and its doctrine of imitation, persisted into the twentieth century and supplied the foundation for theories of functional form in all the arts.

The tradition of free verse in English also has roots that reach much further back into history. The conventions of Anglo-Saxon alliterative verse as seen in *Beowulf* and *The Seafarer* (which Pound later translated) were carried forward into the Middle English period by Chaucer's contemporary, the poet of *Piers Plowman*. Although alliterative verse did not survive as a distinct form, many of its features were absorbed into the main stream of poetry in English and provided a resource for later poets as diverse as Swinburne, Hopkins, and Pound. In the seventeenth century, the combined influence of the continuing Protestant Reformation (with its strain of nonconformism) and the classics was especially important. The King James Bible (1611), based largely on Tyndale's sixteenth-century version, provided beautifully cadenced free renderings of Hebrew poetry, especially the Psalms, that were to leave their mark on the work of generations of poets. Sixty years later, John Milton (whom William Carlos Williams was to celebrate as a revolutionary "Communist" among earlier poets) appealed to the example of "monostrophic" Greek verse to justify the irregular and surprisingly "free" verse of the Chorus in *Samson Agonistes* (1671). But it is the pre-Romantic work of the eighteenth century that gave the strongest impetus to the impending revolution.

[1] In Chapter 10, "Imlac's History Continued. A Dissertation on Poetry," in Samuel Johnson, *The History of Rasselas* (1759).

In the emotive power and expansive freedom of James Macpherson's Ossianic verse of the 1760s and William Blake's prophetic books of the 1790s and the century's turn, one feels the surge that was to break the restraints of social and artistic forms. It is significant that in his later poems Blake also deified the creative imagination.

Fellow travelers of the same path, the nineteenth-century Romantics elevated the imagination as a spontaneous creative force and in so doing displaced the eighteenth-century requirement of analytic wit as the test of poetry.[2] The sensuous image, the product of the imagination, became more important than the logical sentence as the approved medium of poetry. As presentational rather than discursive language came to be thought essentially poetic, poetry of statement gradually sank to the status of an inferior subspecies. It is this view that helps explain Matthew Arnold's reference to the works of Pope and Dryden as classics of English prose.

The Romantic devaluation of wit was part of a general reaction against rationalism. The political revolutions of the eighteenth century had been generated in a spirit of enthusiasm for reason as the key to individual and social perfectibility, but by the end of the century a rebellion of the heart against the head was well under way. Most but not all Romantics shared an anti-intellectual animus against science and proclaimed intuition a surer guide to truth than reason.

As they broadened their work to accommodate a fuller range of experience, the Romantics carried forward the process of literary democratization. Literature was to be for the whole society rather than for a supposedly superior class or coterie. The main thrust of the age was toward the opening of literature, especially poetry, to greater possibilities of subject and form.

The leading English and American champions of this new freedom were William Wordsworth and Ralph Waldo Emerson. In the preface he wrote for the second edition (1800) of *Lyrical Ballads*, Wordsworth vigorously defended the poems he and Coleridge had published in the first edition of 1798. Looking

---

[2] See the discussion of Coleridge below, pp. 153–54. Wit and irony enjoyed renewed favor in the twentieth century, but without lessening the importance of the imagination; see below, pp. 154–55.

back, one finds it hard to appreciate the newness of this poetry, so radical for its time, and to understand how Wordsworth's poems of common life could have provoked such censure from conservative critics. As a sophisticated theorist who fought for his principles, Wordsworth skillfully countered the main objections to his language. He explained that he was deliberately avoiding conventional diction in favor of "a selection of language really used by men." He denied that there was any essential difference between the language of prose and that of poetry, pointing out that many of the most effective passages of poems would be "strictly the language of prose, when prose is well written."

Wordsworth also worked to liberate poetry from neoclassical metrical restraints. Although he did not write anything resembling free or experimental verse by modern standards, he exerted great influence on his own and later times by turning back to the simpler and looser forms of the popular ballad stanza and, in longer poems, of blank verse.

He saw the poet as a civilizing influence and a spokesman for humane values but not as a seer possessed of mystical powers. He was rather "a man speaking to men," though a man of superior sensibility. To Wordsworth, as to Aristotle, poetry was "the most philosophic of all writing," having as its object "truth, not individual and local, but general, and operative; not standing upon external testimony, but carried alive into the heart by passion." His view of the poet's role was more humanistic, and modern, than that of Coleridge,[3] Emerson, and other more mystical Romantics.

Wordsworth was sensitive to the relation of poetry to its changing social environment. Despite the deepening conservatism of his later years, he looked back fondly at his youthful enthusiasm during the early years of the French Revolution, when the dream of reason and equality seemed about to be realized, not in Utopia, "But in the very world, which is the world / Of all of us,—the place where, in the end, / We find our happiness or not at all!" "Bliss was it in that dawn to be alive," he exclaimed, "but to be young was very heaven!"

---

[3] For the effect of Coleridge's ideas on modern theory, see below, p. 154.

A kindred but unqualified enthusiasm marks Emerson's call, in "The American Scholar" (1837), for a new poetry to express the qualities of life in a new, open society: "If there is any period one would desire to be born in, is it not the age of Revolution; when the old and the new stand side by side and admit of being compared; when the energies of men are searched by fear and by hope; when the historic glories of the old can be compensated by the rich possibilities of the new era?"

Emerson recognized the essential traits of the Romantic movement and pointed out their connection with political and social changes, with special interest in the new importance attached to the common life: "The same movement which effected the elevation of what was called the lowest class in the state, assumed in literature a very marked and as benign an aspect. Instead of the sublime and beautiful, the near, the low, the common, was explored and poeticized." Turning his back on the exotic, the poet was to seek the meaning of "the meal in the firkin, the milk in the pan, the ballad in the street."

In *Nature* (1836), Emerson first formulated the Transcendentalist theory that he was to elaborate in essays published over the following twenty or thirty years, but without any significant change in outlook. In all his writing, Emerson celebrated the imagination as a power of mystical perception. In "The Poet," the imagination is described as "a very high sort of seeing, which does not come by study, but by the intellect being where and what it sees." Through this power, which resolves the subject-object dichotomy and man's alienation from the world of natural objects, the poet was to Emerson an "integrating seer," even a "liberating God" who could show man the divine fact amid appearances. The highest function of poetry was, accordingly, to provide a transcendental stairway to the stars of ideal truth.

Emerson's idea of poetic form is more modern in temper. In "The Poet," he articulates his notion of organic form in terms that retain freshness and force despite his Transcendentalist assumptions: "For it is not metres, but a metre-making argument, that makes a poem,—a thought so passionate and alive that, like the spirit of a plant or animal, it has an architecture of its own, and adorns nature with a new thing. The thought and the form are equal in the order of time, but in the order

7

of genesis the thought is prior to the form." He elaborates by saying, "The poet also resigns himself to his mood, and that thought which agitated him is expressed, but *alter idem*, in a manner totally new. The expression is organic, or, the new type which things themselves take when liberated." In a passage anticipatory of the modern idea of poetic metamorphosis and perceptually determined form, Emerson speaks of the poet as one who "turns the world to glass, and shows us all things in their right series and procession. For, through that better perception, he stands one step nearer to things, and sees the flowing or metamorphosis; perceives that thought is multiform; that within the form of every creature is a force impelling it to ascend into a higher form; and, following with his eyes the life, uses the forms which express that life, and so his speech flows with the flowing of nature."

With his recognition of variability and complexity, Emerson's idea of form anticipates some of the most sophisticated theory of the present century. But admirable though it is, it was not enough to free his own verse from the often mechanical rhythms of conventional tetrameter and pentameter lines which he himself found oppressive. Occasionally, however, the compelling rhythm of passionate thought does break the mold of convention to create an architecture of its own. In the gnarled verses of the "Ode" to W. H. Channing, the irregularity of meter and line length and the combination of short lines and dwarfish images work together to intensify the poet's tone of indignation:

> The God who made New Hampshire
> Taunted the lofty land
> With little men;—
> Small bat and wren
> House in the oak:—
> If earth-fire cleave
> The upheaved land, and bury the folk,
> The southern crocodile would grieve.

But the *idea* of organic form was a favorite theme. In "The Snow-Storm," a blank verse lyric, the north wind, the creative principle in nature, is imaged as a "fierce artificer," careless of "number or proportion," who functionally shapes his fantastic forms, "white bastions with projected roof / Round every wind-ward stake, or tree, or door," and, retiring:

> Leaves, when the sun appears, astonished Art
> To mimic in slow structures, stone by stone,
> Built in an age, the mad wind's night-work,
> The frolic architecture of the snow.

Emerson also gave voice to the cultural nationalism of a young republic eager to challenge Europe in the arts. His essay "The Poet" rises to an appeal for a poet who might do justice in theme and form to the "incomparable materials" of American life in a period of unparalleled expansion:

> I look in vain for the poet whom I describe . . . . We have yet had no genius in America, with tyrannous eye, which knew the value of our incomparable materials, and saw, in the barbarism and materialism of the times, another carnival of the same gods whose picture he so much admires in Homer; then in the middle ages; then in Calvinism. Banks and tariffs, the newspaper and caucus, Methodism and Unitarianism, are flat and dull to dull people, but rest on the same foundations of wonder as the town of Troy and the temple of Delphi, and are as swiftly passing away. Our logrolling, our stumps and their politics, our fisheries, our Negroes, and Indians, our boats, and our repudiations, the wrath of rogues, and the pusillanimity of honest men, the northern trade, the southern planting, the western clearing, Oregon, and Texas, are yet unsung. Yet America is a poem in our eyes; its ample geography dazzles the imagination, and it will not wait long for metres.

Neither Emerson nor America had long to wait. It was only a decade later that Walt Whitman issued the first edition of *Leaves of Grass* (1855). Much of the long poem that came to be entitled "Song of Myself" seems an expansion of Emerson's brief celebration of the variousness of American life in "The Poet." Most important, it was Whitman who broke the molds of conventional rhyme and meter to launch the modern free verse movement.

2. Walt Whitman: Pioneer of the Modern

ONE OF THE MOST convincing proofs of the effect of poetic theory on practice can be seen in the impact of Emerson's essays on Walt Whitman, who later testified, "I was simmering, simmering, simmering; Emerson brought me to a boil." The preface to the 1855 edition of *Leaves of Grass* reverberates with echoes of Emerson's essay "The Poet." Whitman subscribed to Emerson's idea of the poet as a self-sufficient seer and reinforced his theory of organic form: "The rhyme and uniformity of perfect poems show the free growth of metrical laws and bud from them as unerringly and loosely as lilacs or roses on a bush, and take shapes as compact as the shapes of chestnuts and oranges and melons and pears, and shed the perfume impalpable to form."

Emerson's call for a poet who might do justice to the American experience struck a responsive chord in Whitman. As a radical Jacksonian Democrat of Quaker descent, he outstripped his mentor and infused his work with an uncompromising equalitarianism. Emerson's assertion that "America is a poem in our eyes; its ample geography dazzles the imagination, and it will not wait long for metres" was taken up by Whitman: "The United States themselves are essentially the greatest poem."

But Whitman did more than echo Emerson. He found the measures that Emerson sought. A true innovator, Whitman was the first nineteenth-century poet to realize in free verse the Romantic idea of organic form. More sympathetic to science and democracy than Emerson or most of his contemporaries and more receptive to all kinds of experience ("Through me forbidden voices"), the celebrator of the years of the modern stands at the head of the modern free verse movement.

Conscious of the fact that he was breaking the conventional mold of English verse, Whitman referred to his compositions as songs, carols, or chants rather than as poems. In "Starting from Paumanok," he introduced the word *ensemble* to suggest the complexity of poetic order. When he wrote, "I will not make poems with reference to parts / But I will make poems, songs, thoughts, with reference to ensemble," he was thinking more of natural or cosmic unity than of prosody. Yet his words, taken in or out of context, are also consistent with his poetics. If the "ensemble" is identified with the poem, the statement reveals an interest in the organic unity of the whole composition rather than in such "parts" as rhyme or meter, which Whitman regarded as only two of many aspects of form. In context, the lines express his insistence that he was singing not just of a day "but with reference to all days"—that he was interested not simply in particulars but in particulars as manifestations of the unity of man and nature in a larger scheme. The word *reference* is a reminder of Whitman's belief that the value of his poems lay not in their words as a unique object or artifact (in the modern sense) but in the world of shared experience evoked by their language. It was his habit to identify his poems with their human and natural subjects and to value the subjects more highly than the words. In "So Long!" he says, "Camerado, this is no book, / Who touches this touches a man." In "A Song of the Rolling Earth," he sees "little or nothing in audible words" in the face of "the unspoken meanings of the earth. . . ." He

11

repeatedly stresses the organic features of poetic form, but his organicism, unlike that of some later critics,[1] assumes the openness of the poem and the identification of its formal elements with the shared experiences of its readers.

Anyone confronting the problem of analyzing the often bewildering complexity of the formal patterns of Whitman's free verse poems must be aware of the inadequacy of the idea of "parts" such as rhyme or meter or conventional stanzaic organization. The poems are, rather, "ensembles" or complexes with interrelated patterns of organization that together comprise a "form" only partially apprehended by any one reader.

Although the patterns are interrelated, they can be identified with one or more of four kinds or dimensions of form: sound, syntax, event (including images and actions), and meaning. *Sound* patterns embrace such devices as rhyme and meter (often overemphasized in the analysis of conventional verse), alliteration, assonance, euphony, dissonance, cadence, or onomatopoeia, depending on the nature of the poem. *Syntax* has to do with the grammatical relationship of the elements of the poem. It may be involved with the dimension of sound, as when parallel constructions provide rhyming effects, and it is necessarily involved with questions of meaning. The poem's sequence of *events* includes all the imagined happenings represented by its words: actions, thoughts, feelings, dreams, sense impressions— which together supply the foundation and fabric of its fictive world. *Meaning*, which is both conceptual and emotive, exists on two distinguishable levels. On the plain-sense level, the events of the poem have meaning in terms of the world of the work. On the level of metaphor, the events are charged by the reader and invested with meanings and values supplied by his larger experience of literature and life. The metaphorical level includes the argument and theme of the poem, however these may be defined, and the individual images and events through which they are developed.

Some such idea of interrelated patterns is necessary for an understanding of the organization of Whitman's free verse poems in *Leaves of Grass*. Of these, the longest and best known— untitled in the first edition of 1855, called "A Poem of Walt

[1] See below, pp. 152–55.

Whitman, an American," in 1856, and known since the edition of 1881 as "Song of Myself"—displays many but not all of the devices employed in later and more complex poems like "Out of the Cradle Endlessly Rocking," "When Lilacs Last in the Dooryard Bloom'd," and "Passage to India."

In its final version, "Song of Myself" reveals many recurrent organizing devices. The most obvious are the syntactical. The use of grammatical parallelism and of the sentence or paragraph as a containing unit comparable to the conventional stanza is consistent throughout the poem and contributes to its formal unity. Both devices can be seen in the first sentence-stanza of section 31:

> I believe a leaf of grass is no less than the journey-work of
>   the stars,
> And the pismire is equally perfect, and a grain of sand,
>   and the egg of the wren,
> And the tree-toad is a chef-d'œuvre for the highest,
> And the running blackberry would adorn the parlors
>   of heaven,
> And the narrowest hinge in my hand puts to scorn
>   all machinery,
> And the cow crunching with depress'd head surpasses
>   any statue,
> And a mouse is miracle enough to stagger sextillions
>   of infidels.

The passage illustrates several effects of Whitman's parallelism. When syntax is related to meaning, it can be seen that grammatical parallelism is an especially appropriate form for a poet with a democratic equalitarian outlook. Furthermore, Whitman's equalitarianism is pantheistic and religious as well as political. The relation of syntax to sound is clearest in the pattern of repeated "And the's." This initial parallelism, reminiscent of the verses of the King James Bible, is well suited to Whitman's conception of the poet as a seer and prophet who would proclaim the gospel of the democratic society of the future.

Alliteration and assonance are among the most obvious devices of sound, which also include rhythm and measure. Al-

13

though "Song of Myself" begins with a perfectly regular iambic pentameter line ("I celebrate myself and sing myself") and although certain lines and passages approach metrical regularity, most of the verses are irregular and, in anticipation of the Imagist proviso, observe the sequence of the musical phrase rather than that of the metronome.

Identifying himself with a multitude of aspects of American life, in the manner suggested by Emerson in "The Poet," Whitman brings together a great variety of images and characters, such as the contralto, the carpenter, the farmer, the lunatic, the printer, the quadroon girl, the machinist, the squaw, and others presented in section 15. Besides these apparently unrelated particulars, several dominant, even archetypal images serve as keys to Whitman's controlling viewpoint and his work as a whole. One is the grass itself (section 6), identified with the principle of life in the nature cycle and with the impulse toward creative expression in the poems as individual "leaves of grass." Another is water, or the sea (sections 17, 22), like the grass a symbol of the life force, embracing as a womb-tomb image (both "cradle" and "unshovelled graves") the terminal experiences of all living things. The image of the journey (32, 44, and following sections) represents the progress not only of man but of the physical universe. It encompasses the process of evolution, directed toward a goal of perfectibility in which man's divine potential is to be realized in a meeting with the "great Camerado" who waits at the end. It is also the progress of a free nation along the "open road" that leads to democratic community and brotherhood. For the individual, as for the boy disciple who accompanies the poet, it is the journey of life and the quest for truth.

These key images and events are not interrelated except as the reader recognizes that they are all part of the experience of the poet, who confidently identifies himself with all mankind ("And what I assume you shall assume") and introduces himself in section 24 as:

Walt Whitman, a kosmos, of Manhattan the son,
Turbulent, fleshy, sensual, eating, drinking and breeding,
No sentimentalist, no stander above men and women or apart
    from them,
No more modest than immodest.

The characterization tallies with the portrait of Whitman in workman's clothes that faces the poem in the first edition. The persona of the poet as a common man and seer who identifies himself with all aspects of life helps to explain the apparently fragmented and discontinuous sequence of events in "Song of Myself." But the device is not entirely satisfactory because it does not require any relating of the particular aspects of experience. There *is* a selection of details, as there must be in art, but the rationale of the selection cannot be ascertained. For all the wealth of image and incident, the reader is left with a sense of diffuseness and lack of firm control.

This looseness is emphasized by contrast as one turns to "Crossing Brooklyn Ferry," first published in 1856 as "Sun-Down Poem." Its images and events all relate to a single experience and a single setting: the crossing of the East River by ferryboat, with a view of the river and harbor and of Brooklyn and Manhattan. Within these limits, or within this frame, the sensuous images of the opening sections of the poem (1–3) establish a sense of verisimilitude. The soaring gulls, the ships with the flags of all nations, the hills of Brooklyn, the light on the water, all attest close observation of a coherent scene and contribute to a sense of the unity of the experience, both for the individual crossing and for crossings separate in time. The image of the crossing or transit metaphorically suggests the life of the individual and the lives of separate generations. For the separate images reflecting the varied experience of the voyaging poet are all subordinated to the image of the ship which traverses the river (of time) from gate to gate (birth and death) and supports the universality of the crossing described in the poem.

By appealing through sensory images to a sense of shared experience, Whitman affirms a bond of *community* among individuals of the same generation and between himself, as poet, and later generations:

> It avails not, time nor place—distance avails not,
> I am with you, you men and women of a generation,
>   or ever so many generations hence,
> Just as you feel when you look on the river and sky,
>   so I felt,
> Just as any of you is one of a living crowd, I was one of
>   a crowd. . . .

15

Beyond the identity of experience there is, for the Romantic poet, the recognition of a unity of soul, or life stuff, among all men:

I too had been struck from the float forever held in solution,
I too had receiv'd identity by my body . . . .

The harbor images are invoked again in conclusion, but in a more exalted mood, as the poet's feeling of alienation is resolved by the assurance of the identity of soul as well as the community of experience. His confidence is reinforced by the assertion of the unity of body and soul, for Whitman, unlike the orthodox Transcendentalist, regards physical nature as a "necessary film," without which the soul cannot be known.

The introduction of a set of images relating to a single experience, the speculation upon their meaning, and the re-evocation which resolves the dualism of body and soul, time and eternity, constitute a new development in Whitman's technique, one that suggests the influence of music upon his conception of form. The method serves to interrelate effects within the dimensions of sound, syntax, and meaning as well as of image and event. The principle is comparable to that of rhyme if it is recognized that in a broad sense rhyme involves the repetition and resolution not of sounds alone, but of grammatical units, sense impressions, and ideas. The repetition of the harbor images involves auditory rhyme through sonic repetition, visual rhyme through the images that the repeated words evoke, and conceptual and emotive rhyme through the associations of the words and images. All contribute to the central theme which they sustain and develop. William Carlos Williams's observation, in "The Orchestra," that "it is a principle of music to repeat the theme" applies also to poetry.

"Out of the Cradle Endlessly Rocking," first published in 1860 as "A Word Out of the Sea," is a complex, carefully integrated poem. It introduces, as a new device, a set of three images—boy, bird, and sea—through which Whitman develops his theme by means of a dramatic colloquy. (A similar triadic pattern, but with less dramatic tension, appears in such later poems as "When Lilacs Last in the Dooryard Bloom'd" and

"Passage to India.") There is also a recurrence and resolution of image patterns, as in "Crossing Brooklyn Ferry." A further musical device, inspired by opera, is the use of the arias or bird songs of fulfillment and frustration, which provide interludes of lyric expression of the feelings aroused by the poem's events and interpreted through its narrative and dramatic structure.

The arias function in all dimensions of form: in sound, as their lyric intensity enhances the emotional charge of the verse; in syntax, as they are set off in relatively self-contained italicized units that complement the mood and counterpoint the events of the rest of the poem; in event, as they present images from nature—the heavy moon, the sea pushing upon the land—to express the inner feelings of love and frustration; in meaning, largely emotive but also metaphorically expressive as the male bird's songs of "lonesome love" and the "throbbing heart" bring home to the boy, the "outsetting bard," an awareness of the relation between suffering and art, of the fact that for him poetry is to be a sublimated expression of thwarted love.

The poem opens with a reminiscence of an experience in which the poet, as a child, saw a pair of mockingbirds nesting on the beach. The impression of love fulfilled is heightened by the brief "two-together" aria. The disappearance of the female and the grief of her mate, expressed in the longer aria, introduce the boy to the knowledge of loss and frustration which the maturing poet comes to recognize as the basic motive of his work.

The first section brings together images relating to the childhood experience, now interwoven into a symbolic fabric that reaches beyond the original context of the events:

> Out of the cradle endlessly rocking,
> Out of the mocking-bird's throat, the musical shuttle,
> Out of the Ninth-month midnight,
> Over the sterile sands and the fields beyond, where the child
>   leaving his bed wander'd alone, bareheaded, barefoot,
> Down from the shower'd halo,
> Up from the mystic play of shadows twining and twisting as if
>   they were alive,
> Out from the patches of briers and blackberries,
> From the memories of the bird that chanted to me,

17

From your memories sad brother, from the fitful risings and
    fallings I heard,
From under that yellow half-moon late-risen and swollen as if
    with tears,
From those beginning notes of yearning and love there in the
    mist,
From the thousand responses of my heart never to cease,
From the myriad thence-arous'd words,
From the word stronger and more delicious than any,
From such as now they start the scene revisiting,
As a flock, twittering, rising, or overhead passing,
Borne hither, ere all eludes me, hurriedly,
A man, yet by these tears a little boy again,
Throwing myself on the sand, confronting the waves,
I, chanter of pains and joys, uniter of here and hereafter,
Taking all hints to use them, but swiftly leaping beyond them,
A reminiscence sing.

The remembered details are interwoven in a poetic context.
The weaving process, in which the voice of the bird is a "musi-
cal shuttle," is suggested by devices of syntax and sound. The
repeated introductory prepositions—*out of, over, down from,
up from*—support the sense of the converging movements of an
interweaving. The sound pattern is rich in devices that interrelate
the individual words. Assonance, alliteration, and internal rhyme
are combined in such sequences as *rocking-mocking, beyond-
wander'd, bareheaded-barefoot*. Sound and sense also interact
in such a phrase as "the mystic play of shadows twining and
twisting as if they were alive."

The main theme of the poem is foreshadowed as the poet
identifies himself with the bird, his "sad brother," and sees in
the experience of frustration the awakening of his own sense of
vocation, the "thousand responses" of his heart and the "myriad
thence-arous'd words." Finally, there is the realization that the
ultimate release from tension (partially resolved through art)
is death, "the word stronger and more delicious than any,"
whispered by the old crone, the sea. The poet is the "uniter of
here and hereafter" (Emerson's "integrating seer"). The speaker
is conceived as "taking all hints to use them, but swiftly leaping
beyond them," as the images from the reservoir of memory

become charged with thought and feeling in the poetic, or metaphoric process.

A reading of the complete poem sustains the impression of a complex formal organization that can be only suggested here. All devices of sound are supported by the rhythm of the verses, beginning with the irregularly stressed but strongly rhythmic opening lines with their intermingled trochees and dactyls, appropriate to the movements of both the sea and a loom:

$$- \cup \cup - \cup \mid - \cup \cup - \cup$$
$$- \cup \cup - \cup \cup - \mid \cup - \cup \cup - \cup$$
$$- \cup \cup - \cup \mid - \cup$$

The initial parallelism in itself introduces a feature of regularity comparable to that provided by end rhyme.

Of the syntactical devices, besides the parallelism (which also provides a sonic effect), the sentence stanzas afford a periodic control for the individual lines as well as a pattern for the expression of meaning. The experiences of childhood, as they are ordered in memory, support the awakening sense of poetic vocation. Patterns of meaning exist on the plain sense level in the dramatic treatment of the child's experience, and on the level of metaphor in the disclosure of the meaning of art and the role of the poet. The theme encompasses not only maturation, as the child is introduced to the experiences of love and death, but also a deeply regressive motive, as the stress of frustration turns the poet's thoughts first to the idea of art as sublimation and then to the recognition of death as a welcome final release. The emotional burden of the verse is intensified by the boy's empathic responses to the bird's songs of love and grief and by the exaltation that accompanies his discovery of his vocation.

The organization of "Out of the Cradle" easily refutes the blanket indictment of "formlessness" sometimes leveled against Whitman's poetry. In this poem, he achieves a detachment and a distancing of subject through the device of the three related figures who as dramatic characters participate in the development of the theme. The figures of the boy, the bird, and the sea are introduced, the significance of their roles is revealed, and the conclusion resolves the colloquy as the bird's cries of unsatisfied love and the message of death whispered by the sea are fused with the poet's "own songs awakened from that hour."

Among simpler poems, some of the most successful are the vignettes of the Civil War in *Drum-Taps*, first published separately in 1865 and later incorporated into *Leaves of Grass*. "Cavalry Crossing a Ford" presents a picture of an observed event:

> A line in long array where they wind betwixt green islands,
> They take a serpentine course, their arms flash in the sun—
>   hark to the musical clank,
> Behold the silvery river, in it the splashing horses loitering
>   stop to drink,
> Behold the brown-faced men, each group, each person
>   a picture, the negligent rest on the saddles,
> Some emerge on the opposite bank, others are just entering
>   the ford—while
> Scarlet and blue and snowy white,
> The guidon flags flutter gayly in the wind.

The poem imagistically conveys the color and other sensuous details of a military scene. In its detachment and objectivity, the pictorial effect is comparable to that of a camp sketch by Winslow Homer. Though there is some movement and sound, the pause at the ford provides a relative stasis that enables the observer to focus the scene and compose its details. Visual imagery is the most conspicuous formal element, but the poem is not purely imagistic. The serpentlike column and the brown faces relate the men to primitive nature. The scene in general conveys a sense of fitness, grace, and competence. The flashing of arms and the clanking of equipment suggest the impersonality and efficiency of the war machine. Through association and suggestion, this brief glimpse of campaigning succeeds in conveying an impression of adjustment to nature, of excitement and color. The metaphorical meaning seems not deliberately developed, however. It rises spontaneously from a treatment focused on visual experience.

Another poem of observation is "An Army Corps on the March":

> With its cloud of skirmishers in advance,
> With now the sound of a single shot snapping like a whip, and
>   now an irregular volley,

The swarming ranks press on and on, the dense brigades
     press on.
Glittering dimly, toiling under the sun—the dust-cover'd men,
In columns rise and fall to the undulations of the ground,
With artillery interspers'd—the wheels rumble,
     the horses sweat,
As the army corps advances.

This poem displays much the same concern for sensory detail, the same association of human and physical nature. But there is a difference in the quality of the impressions, in keeping with the difference of subject. Instead of stasis, there is confusion and movement. The individual forms do not stand out but are absorbed in the masses: "cloud of skirmishers," "swarming ranks," "dense brigades." Although visual images predominate, sound is also important. In the third verse, the regular iambic rhythm and the incremental repetition of the parallel clauses ("The swarming ranks press on and on, the dense brigades press on") reinforce the sense of a remorseless forward motion of a mass that obliterates the identity of its constituent members.

"A Sight in Camp in the Daybreak Gray and Dim" reveals a more poignant experience and a fuller metaphoric development:

A sight in camp in the daybreak gray and dim,
As from my tent I emerge so early sleepless,
As slow I walk in the cool fresh air the path near by the
     hospital tent,
Three forms I see on stretchers lying, brought out there
     untended lying,
Over each the blanket spread, ample brownish woolen blanket,
Gray and heavy blanket, folding, covering all.

Curious I halt and silent stand,
Then with light fingers I from the face of the nearest the first
     just lift the blanket;
Who are you elderly man so gaunt and grim, with well-gray'd
     hair, and flesh all sunken about the eyes?
Who are you my dear comrade?

21

Then to the second I step—and who are you my child and
  darling?
Who are you sweet boy with cheeks yet blooming?

Then to the third—a face nor child nor old, very calm, as of
  beautiful yellow-white ivory;
Young man I think I know you—I think this face is the face
  of the Christ himself,
Dead and divine and brother of all, and here again he lies.

The three figures suggest the ages of man, while the identi-
fication of the third with Christ invites the ideas of sacrificial
suffering and the Christian Trinity, which Whitman typically
supplants with a triadic secular image of three soldiers who
have died in a common struggle. The "brownish woolen blanket,
/ Gray and heavy blanket" is the earth, the anonymous nature
into which the forms are sinking. Lifting the blanket, the poet
penetrates the veil of flesh, of nature, to recognize the divine
potential of man. The syntactical arrangement (the recurrent
pattern of "I . . . stand, / Then . . . ," / "Then . . . I step . . . ,"
/ "Then to the third . . . ," followed respectively by "Who are
you . . . ?" "and who are you . . . ?" and "I think I know
you . . . .") integrates the verses, suggests a symbolic progres-
sion, and develops a suspense resolved by the recognition of
the third encounter.
  This brief poem is more complex than the two others because
of the interrelatedness of its images and meanings. The symbol
of the human victim of war as a Christ is clearly indicated,
although it is not as fully developed as the sacrificial figure of
Lincoln in the long elegy "When Lilacs Last in the Dooryard
Bloom'd."
  An even more intimate connection of image and meaning can
be seen in "The Dismantled Ship," composed late in Whitman's
life and published first in 1888:

In some unused lagoon, some nameless bay,
On sluggish, lonesome waters, anchor'd near the shore,
An old, dismasted, gray and batter'd ship, disabled, done,
After free voyages to all the seas of earth, haul'd up at last and
  hawser'd tight,
Lies rusting, mouldering.

As in "Cavalry Crossing a Ford," there is a direct presentation of visual imagery without any direct statement of meaning. Yet the imagery of this poem is immediately recognizable as metaphoric, suggestive of the pathos of old age, its sense of futility and desolation. The images of ship, voyage, harbor—although they may well reflect direct observation—are traditional metaphors or symbols that carry a burden of associations accumulated through centuries of use. Moreover, the image of the ship had been employed by Whitman to symbolize a life-quest in both "Crossing Brooklyn Ferry" and "Passage to India," and the reader is struck by the constrast of tone in the treatment of this central image between the confident outsetting of the latter poem ("Sail forth—steer for the deep waters only, / Reckless O soul, exploring, I with thee and thou with me. . . .") and the somber end of the voyage in "The Dismantled Ship."

A greater formal complexity than may be evident in a casual reading can usually be found in even relatively simple poems. In "The Dismantled Ship," which seems primarily imagistic, patterns of sound and meaning are functionally interrelated. The long vowels and the interrupting consonants retard the tempo to support the sense of the sluggishness of age. The long, deep vowels of "unused lagoon," "lonesome," "shore" contribute to the tone of melancholy. They are "dark" vowels in the spectrum of mood as well as sound. The alliteration of g's and d's, the onomatopoeia of *batter'd*, and the harshness of the a sounds all reinforce the sense of the line, "An old, dismasted, gray and batter'd ship, disabled, done." Images become metaphorically charged through the relation of "dismasted" to the impotence of age and of "nameless bay" to the problem of identity as life draws close to its source in nature.

Whitman's free verse poems demonstrate that poetic form is an open rather than closed system, susceptible always to redefinition and further development in the shifting perspective of the reader. The form of a work is a potential of its verbal structure. Although it may be discussed from various viewpoints, no analysis or interpretation can be commensurate with its complexity, however simple it may appear at first reading. Any analysis which presents itself as systematic and definitive is false to the nature of the poem and a belittling of it, perhaps to the temporary advantage of the critic.

Whitman is a fitting representative of the idea of open and relative form because he never regarded his poems as complete but revised them from edition to edition of *Leaves of Grass*. Although he wished them to tally with the world of nature, he recognized their limitations as verbal abstractions—as art. Yet he also recognized their peculiar power—that as poetic ensembles they relate to the larger scheme in ever-changing ways and that they are inexhaustible to interpretation.

In viewpoint, as basic an aspect of form as metrics, Whitman remains the most revolutionary of American poets. The spirit of radical equalitarianism that animates his work challenges his readers with a vision of democracy that America has yet to approach in actuality. In this and other respects Whitman has fulfilled his own conception of the poet (in the 1855 preface) as one who brings his readers to no terminus but leads them on a continuing quest for the meaning of the forms of art and the common life expressed through them: "Whom he takes he takes with firm sure grasp into live regions previously unattained . . . thenceforward is no rest . . . ."

3. Interchapter:
The Later Nineteenth Century

ALTHOUGH WHITMAN lived on in Camden until 1892, his hope
for "poets to come" who would justify his and Emerson's
prophecy of a new American poetry was not realized in his
lifetime. The years following the Civil War, which saw the
beginnings of modern American fiction in the work of Mark
Twain, Henry James, and William Dean Howells, were an age
of prose, and until the final decade of the century, when the
poems of Emily Dickinson and Stephen Crane appeared, the
period was barren of new developments in poetry.

The decline of American poetry in the late nineteenth cen-
tury was in part a result of the shift in the literary climate from
romanticism to realism and the extension of public education,
which created a large audience for the serialized fiction of popu-
lar authors. Prose eclipsed poetry, with its more specialized and
demanding conventions and its smaller audience. The poetic

theory of the Romantics seemed irrelevant to the rising generation, and no new theory of consequence took its place. Earlier interest in the American epic gave way to speculation about the "great American novel." The novel came into its own during these years, and the best and most representative American criticism and theory were focused on fiction. Henry James's "The Art of Fiction" first appeared in 1884, and the essays and reviews that Howells had been writing for *Harper's Monthly Magazine* were collected under the title *Criticism and Fiction* (1891).

In differing ways, James and Howells managed to transform and transfer to the novel and novelist many of Emerson's and Whitman's ideas about the nature and function of poetry. In *Criticism and Fiction*, Howells argued that the American novelist, like Whitman's American bard, should champion the values of democracy: "The arts must become democratic, and then we shall have the expression of America in art." In "The Art of Fiction," James, like Emerson and Whitman, rejected traditional distinctions between form and content or idea and eloquently urged the principle of organic unity:

> This sense of the story being the idea, the starting point, of the novel, is the only one that I see in which it can be spoken of as something different from its organic whole; and since in proportion as the work is successful the idea permeates and penetrates it, informs and animates it, so that every word and every punctuation point contribute directly to the expression, in that proportion do we lose our sense of the story being a blade which may be drawn more or less out of its sheath. The story and the novel, the idea and the form, are the needle and the thread, and I never heard of a guild of tailors who recommended the use of the thread without the needle, or the needle without the thread.

Among poets, Sidney Lanier produced the only theory of comparable interest. In *The Science of English Verse* (1880), Lanier developed the argument that time rather than accent is the dominant factor in poetic rhythm. Based upon an analogy with music and employing musical notation to indicate the duration of sonic units in verse, Lanier's theory was a serious attempt to investigate the problem of metrics from a fresh perspective. Though it effectively demonstrates the truth of the variability of time in verse measures, the theory, like Lanier's own practice, lies outside the main line of development of modern poetry.

Only two poets, whose overlapping lives spanned the long stretch from the beginnings of American Romanticism to the end of the century, attempted new directions in verse; and the work of both is closer in temper to the twentieth than the nineteenth century. They were Emily Dickinson (1830–86), who wrote in self-imposed isolation in her Amherst, Massachusetts, home, and Stephen Crane (1871–1900), who during his brief life devoted most of his energies to the writing of prose notable for its poetic qualities of compression, rhythm, and vivid imagery. Though separated in age by more than a generation, the two were contemporaries in publication. The first of Emily Dickinson's posthumous volumes, *Poems*, appeared in 1890; it was closely followed by *Poems: Second Series* (1891) and *Poems: Third Series* (1896). Crane's two slim volumes of free verse are *Black Riders* (1895) and *War Is Kind* (1899). Although neither poet seems to have been interested in theory or criticism, their work reveals many of the qualities of modern verse influenced by the tradition of organic form.

Written in almost childishly simple patterns—ballad stanzas and rhymed tetrameter quatrains—Emily Dickinson's poems are remarkable for their precision, vivid imagery, and effective use of approximate and slant rhyming. Rather than traditional ballads, however, it seems to have been the homely hymns of her Protestant heritage that provided the metrical model for her poems.

Her outlook, conditioned by the Transcendentalism of the New England of her childhood, nevertheless encompasses a peculiarly modern sense of alienation that emerged in the closing decades of the nineteenth century. Emily inherited the Emersonian idea of nature as illusion, but behind the veil there lay for her not the beneficent Oversoul but the abyss of an unplumbed self to be confronted with fear and courage. And yet, with an individualism as uncompromising as Emerson's, she insisted upon the sovereignty, if not self-sufficiency, of the single separate person. In "The Soul selects her own Society— / Then —shuts the Door—" she concludes:

27

> I've known her—from an ample nation—
> Choose One—
> Then—close the Valves of her attention—
> Like Stone—

The sonic solidity of the final *Stone*, with its long *o*, reinforces the *One* which is the object of the soul's choice. The complex image of the machinelike, heartlike, clamlike valves exemplifies Emily Dickinson's talent for developing unexpected apt metaphors reminiscent of the best in the metaphysical tradition.

A similar sense of absolute finality is enforced by the homely and seemingly inevitable images of a poem on the death of a housewife:

> How many times these low feet staggered—
> Only the soldered mouth can tell—
> Try—can you stir the awful rivet—
> Try—can you lift the hasps of steel!
>
> Stroke the cool forehead—hot so often—
> Lift—if you care—the listless hair—
> Handle the adamantine fingers
> Never a thimble—more—shall wear—

In lighter moods, there are poems like that on the hummingbird, which, were it not for its metronomic regularity, might seem written in anticipation of the Imagists' prescriptions for a precise rendering of the "thing," whether subjective or objective, with no superfluous word or detail:[1]

> A Route of Evanescence
> With a revolving Wheel—
> A Resonance of Emerald—
> A Rush of Cochineal—
> And every Blossom on the Bush
> Adjusts it's tumbled Head—
> The mail from Tunis, probably,
> An easy Morning's Ride—

[1] See below, pp. 33–34.

There is even, in the "Resonance of Emerald," the peculiarly modern kind of synesthetic imagery favored by the French Symbolists and later poets like Eliot who began writing under their influence.

The poems of the younger Stephen Crane are at once more radical in form and more modern in outlook. In its conciseness and metaphoric originality, his work is sometimes like that of Emily Dickinson, whose poems were brought to his attention by William Dean Howells. But Crane wrote in free rather than regularly measured verse, and some of his poems are reminiscent of Whitman's. An example for comparison and contrast is the title poem of his second book of verse, *War Is Kind*, which ironically celebrates the relief from suffering provided by death. The theme recalls the passage in "When Lilacs Last in the Dooryard Bloom'd" in which Whitman looks back on the "debris of all the slain soldiers of the war" and sees that they, unlike the living, have been freed from suffering. Like Whitman, Crane employs parallel structure as his basic organizing device. His verse is typically more economical and compressed, however, as in his opening stanza:

> Do not weep, maiden, for war is kind.
> Because your lover threw wild hands toward the sky
> And the affrighted steed ran on alone,
> Do not weep.
> War is kind.

Unlike Whitman, whose pantheistic faith provided an optimistic view of death, Crane treats the subject with a distinctively modern irony:

> Swift blazing flag of the regiment,
> Eagle with crest of red and gold,
> These men were born to drill and die.
> Point for them the virtue of slaughter,
> Make plain to them the excellence of killing
> And a field where a thousand corpses lie.

For Crane, as for Whitman, death provides an escape from the tension of existence. But to the more modern poet, the escape is not a return to the immortal sea of spirit, but a descent into the void precipitated by man's murderousness. Crane's ironic mode enforces a sardonic moral condemnation of war lacking in Whitman, who, buoyed by his cosmic optimism, was capable of saying, "What blurt is this about virtue and about vice."

Some of Crane's satiric poems also reveal a flair for the kind of paradox favored by a later generation. In one of these,

> A newspaper is a collection of half-injustices
> Which, bawled by boys from mile to mile,
> Spreads its curious opinion
> To a million merciful and sneering men,
> While families cuddle the joys of the fireside
> When spurred by tale of dire lone agony.
> A newspaper is a court
> Where every one is kindly and unfairly tried
> By a squalor of honest men . . . .

Even more remarkable for its indignant irony and novel imagery is the poem which begins:

> The impact of a dollar upon the heart
> Smiles warm red light,
> Sweeping from the hearth rosily upon the white table,
> With the hanging cool velvet shadows
> Moving softly upon the door.

The synesthetic effects of the imagery suit a society corrupted by materialism, in which the "outcry of old beauty" is "whored by pimping merchants." The conclusion moves toward an unusual, and modern, use of the image of "hats" to point up the precedence of superficialities and conspicuous consumption over social ideals among a people enslaved by greed:

> Silly rich peasants stamp the carpets of men,
> Dead men who dreamed fragrance and light
> Into their woof, their lives;
> The rug of an honest bear
> Under the feet of a cryptic slave
> Who speaks always of baubles,
> Forgetting state, multitude, work, and state,
> Champing and mouthing of hats
> Making ratful squeak of hats,
> Hats.

In the temper and technique of poems like these, Crane, even more than Emily Dickinson, was a pioneer in advance of his age. But the inventive genius that both displayed in the poetic Sahara of their time was not to find proper soil for full growth and flowering until the beginnings of the modern revolution in the decade of the First World War.

4. The Modern Revolution

LIKE THE EARLIER Romantic revolution, the modern movement
had its beginning in a time of social and political upheaval as
the monarchies of Europe crumbled during the decade of the
First World War. Less violent than the war-borne changes but
no less profound in effect was the revolution wrought in man's
view of himself by the rise of modern science. Darwinism had
already cast man out of his garden world and into a jungle
struggle for survival. The new physics of the new century un-
dermined the solid foundations of his universe. The depth
psychology of Freud and other explorers of the unconscious
destroyed the rational foundations of his inner world and ex-
posed a seething realm of animal drives and impulses. Yet all
these changes, threatening though they were to modern man's
self-esteem and sense of security, helped to usher in a period of
innovation and brilliant achievement in literature and the arts.

Responsive to their constantly changing environment, the arts produced a number of intense revolutionary movements—all displaying a tendency toward fragmentation and a counter-impulse toward some pattern of coherence in the midst of confusion and violent change. They included, among others, Expressionism, Cubism, Futurism, Imagism, Vorticism, Dadaism, Surrealism. Each had its day and declined, but each also contributed in one way or another to the development of modernist aesthetics and expression.

Of these movements, Imagism was most important to the development of the new poetry and its supporting theory. Under the leadership of Ezra Pound and T. E. Hulme, the Anglo-American Imagist movement developed in the prewar years as a reaction against the subjective impressionism and decadent Romanticism of the Victorian era. The Imagists, whose other moving spirits included H. D. (Hilda Doolittle), Richard Aldington, and F. S. Flint, called for a new poetry to be distinguished by a classical hardness and precision, objectivity, economy of language, and freedom of form. While their base remained in London, they found a valuable American outlet in Harriet Monroe's *Poetry: A Magazine of Verse* (Chicago, 1912–), for which Pound acted as foreign editor and which he characteristically used as a platform from which to launch his own ideas.

The March 1913 issue of *Poetry* contained not only Pound's famous definition of the image as "that which presents an intellectual and emotional complex in an instant of time" but also a succinct yet comprehensive statement of the principles of the new movement. These three "tenets," as Pound called them, appeared under the name of F. S. Flint, although Pound later said that he and Richard Aldington and Hilda Doolittle had agreed upon them as early as 1912:

   I. Direct treatment of the "thing," whether subjective or objective.
   II. To use absolutely no word that does not contribute to the presentation.
   III. As regarding rhythm: to compose in sequence of the musical phrase, not in sequence of the metronome.

Both the definition and the tenets place a premium on concentration, objectivity, and presentational immediacy. The Imagists were generally agreed, in theory at least, upon the need of a "classical" firmness and restraint to counter the wordiness of Victorian poetry and the subjective "mushiness" of the Impressionist tradition.

But despite their professions of classicism, the Imagists were solidly in the Romantic tradition in their concern for a sensuous language that would express a sense of the "thing" and in their theory of free functional form, which, although new in formulation, was actually an extension and further development of the organic theory of the Romantics. They did, however, supply a timely and extremely influential rationale for the modern free verse movement: the three principles set forth in their tenets are in effect a capsule poetics for functional organic verse. Imagism was not only a school of poetry. Its principles, extended in other essays by Pound, Hulme, and Flint, represent an important movement in criticism—one which led through the new emphasis on structure encouraged by Pound and Eliot and their followers into the New Criticism of the 1940s.

Antedating Imagism and not completely divorced from it was the older tradition of Symbolism, which also had roots in Romanticism. It emerged as a modern movement in the work of the nineteenth-century French Symbolist poets and through them influenced twentieth-century writers, including Yeats and the younger Joyce and Eliot. Reacting against science and rationalism, the Symbolists stressed the il- or a-logical quality of poetic language and the integrity of the poem as a symbolic structure impervious to rational analysis. Charles Baudelaire had looked back to Poe as an inspiration, and Poe had insisted that poetry had nothing to do with logical truth. In this aspect, the Symbolist movement represents a quest for certainty in the modern world—one in which the poetic symbol was regarded as an absolute not only rivaling but surpassing the truths of science.

As Edmund Wilson explains in *Axel's Castle* (1931), the Symbolist felt that he could express his unique sensibility only through a special language which depends upon symbolic images rather than direct statement: "Symbolism may be defined as an attempt by carefully studied means—a complicated association of ideas represented by a medley of metaphors—to communicate unique personal feelings." Wilson's view is more secular than that of the earlier English historian of the movement, Arthur Symons, who points to its mystical orientation in his description of Symbolism in literature as "a form of expression, at the best but approximate, essentially but arbitrary, until it has obtained the force of a convention, for an unseen reality apprehended by the consciousness." In both viewpoints, there is a recognition that the Symbolist (unlike the more objective Imagist) distorts and manipulates his perceptions in the interest of personal feeling.

In the perspective supplied by Wilson and Symons, Symbolism can be seen to have a strongly subjective if not visionary tendency unlike the Imagists' impulse toward hardness and clarity in expression. The idiom of the Symbolist resisted normal syntax and tended toward the language of the unconscious (with its dream imagery) or of the undifferentiated stream of consciousness. The extreme of the tendency manifested itself in Surrealism.

Among young modern poets, T. S. Eliot was most deeply influenced in his early work by the French Symbolists. He is very close to the tradition in such poems as "The Love Song of J. Alfred Prufrock," "Gerontion," and *The Waste Land*, in which normal syntax and transitional passages are violated for the treatment of "unique personal feelings" through a "medley of metaphors" or sequence of apparently dissociated images. There is also the suggestion of a stream-of-consciousness technique in all these poems, especially in the musings of the repressed Prufrock. The general effect of fragmentation and dislocation stands in contrast to the cameolike precision of imagery favored by the Imagists and realized in some of their verse, most fully perhaps by H. D. in "Oread" and other poems of *Sea Garden* (1916) and by Ezra Pound in the Chinese poems of *Cathay* (1915) and *Lustra* (1916).

The impact of both Imagism and Symbolism on twentieth-century poetry has been great. Without the innovations generated by these movements and the influences exerted not only through explicit theory but also through the practice of poets, it is difficult to imagine how the work of such strongly individualistic modern poets as Ezra Pound, T. S. Eliot, William Carlos Williams, Hilda Doolittle, Wallace Stevens, E. E.

Cummings, and Marianne Moore could have come into being.

In one respect, the modern revolution was less sweeping than that of the Romantics. In reacting against a Romanticism gone decadent in the verbiage and sickly rhythms of much Victorian poetry (Swinburne was a favorite target), many of the modernists invoked the conventional spirit of classicism. Unlike Emerson and Whitman, who had found the burden of the past galling, Eliot and those who followed his example were defenders of orthodoxy who sought to identify themselves with sustaining traditions of one kind or another.

In the early essays collected in *The Sacred Wood* (1920), Eliot assumes the role of mediator between the forces of permanence and change. "Tradition and the Individual Talent" affirms the normative influence of an existing body of literature but gives scope to innovation by recognizing that the existing order is itself changed and modified by the introduction of each new work. By its very nature, however, a moderate position such as Eliot's, which ostensibly recognizes the equal claims of tradition and innovation, tends to resist revolutionary change, even though Eliot's early poetry introduced radical innovations in technique. It is perhaps a substantiation of his thesis that many of the conventions he introduced in *The Waste Land* and other early poems quickly became established features of the new *tradition* of modernism.

Prerequisite to an understanding of the relation between the individual talent and tradition is the "historical sense," which Eliot considers indispensable to anyone who would be a poet beyond his twenty-fifth year and which "involves a perception, not only of the pastness of the past, but of its presence." It is something that compels a poet to write "not merely with his own generation in his bones, but with a feeling that the whole of literature from Homer and within it the whole of the literature of his own country has a simultaneous existence and composes a simultaneous order." This ingrained sense of tradition is a classical and humanist component of modernism that distinguishes its representatives, especially Eliot, from Romantic rebels against the past and champions of original inspiration like Wordsworth, Emerson, and Whitman.

The same essay sets forth Eliot's idea of an "impersonal theory" of poetry and art. According to this view, an individual poem must be judged not on its own terms, as a unique expression, but by the standards of the "tradition" in which it takes its place (and which it alters). The poem is not self-expression, the direct statement of the personal emotions of the author; it is rather an impersonal formulation of common feelings and emotions which need not even be experienced at first hand. Poetry is thus "not a turning loose of emotion, but an escape from emotion; it is not the expression of personality but an escape from personality." Consistent with these ideas is Eliot's preference for dramatic rather than lyric poetry.

"Hamlet and His Problems" introduces a term that was to become widely adopted by the supporters of the impersonal theory: "The only way of expressing emotion in the form of art is by finding an 'objective correlative'; in other words, a set of objects, a situation, a chain of events which shall be the formula of that *particular* emotion; such that when the external facts, which must terminate in sensory experience, are given, the emotion is immediately evoked." Whether or not Eliot's term was used, the idea of the objective correlative was accepted by most of the modern poets and by the New Critics, and by mid-century the standard of impersonality was firmly established as a test of poetic quality.

In another essay, "The Metaphysical Poets" (actually a review of H. J. C. Grierson's edition of seventeenth-century metaphysical poetry), Eliot remarks that in the seventeenth century, with the civil wars and the rise of science, a "dissociation of sensibility" had set in, a separation of thought and feeling from which modern culture has ever since suffered. Although later poets have been inclined in one direction or the other (toward abstract thought in the eighteenth century; toward feeling in the nineteenth), they have not been able to fuse these differing experiences as the metaphysical and earlier poets had. They have not been able, like Donne, to "feel their thought as immediately as the odour of a rose."

The idea of the "dissociation of sensibility" was useful to Eliot because it supported both his revival of the metaphysical tradition and his own poetic techniques. The kind of metaphysical conceit that Eliot developed in his own early poetry, like the comparison of the evening sky to "a patient etherized upon a table" in the opening of "Prufrock," suggests that the split might

37

be relieved, if not healed, by a new kind of metaphysical poetry. The idea also provided an explanation of the kind of conflict from which Eliot's poetic characters, like Prufrock and Gerontion, suffered as victims of modern culture. Moreover, it supplied a basis for attacking that culture from a conservative position that looked back to an idealized past that was thought to have existed before the regicide of Charles I and the decline of the Church of England, before the rise of science and popular government, before the emergence of a vulgarized mass society.

Eliot's idea and term have recently been subjected to critical reassessment. In *Romantic Image* (1957), which devotes a chapter to the subject, Frank Kermode points out that the idea is neither original with Eliot nor historically true. Furthermore, any informed reader knows that to be successful a writer must project in his work the sense of his own unified sensibility, as in Pound's recognition of an intellectual *and* emotional complex presented by the image, even though he may be treating a conflict or split within the personality of a neurotic character like Prufrock. But these facts have not lessened the appeal of the idea of dissociation to many who have found in it nourishment for a nostalgia for the past and an alienation from the present.

Although Eliot, like his contemporaries, rejected his immediate, Victorian past, his poetic theory and criticism fostered a conservative regard for older tradition.

But there were also outright rebels among the new poets. It is possible to see two strongly contrasting strains in the modern movement, each with its own adherents or "party." In keeping with the spirit of Imagism, one group has insisted upon complete freedom of individual expression through the development of experimental free verse poems. Ezra Pound, William Carlos Williams, Marianne Moore, E. E. Cummings (in much of his work), and other poets influenced by Imagism constitute what might be called the radical wing, or the party of free experimentation. The other, more conservative party, preferring traditional themes and measures, embraces Frost (whom Pound was unable to win over to free verse), the later Eliot, and Eliot's followers, including the Southern "Fugitive" poets and the younger poets of the Middle Generation.

The difference between these groups is significant though not absolute. Pound belongs with the intransigents despite his interest in "making new" the literature of the past through creative translation. Despite the startling "newness" of his early poetry, Eliot belongs with the conservatives because of his social and political views, his traditionalism as a critic, and his movement toward greater conventionality in form—a shift that can be seen when the *Four Quartets* is compared with the earlier *Waste Land*. One thing that becomes clear when these groups are distinguished is that Pound and Eliot stand at the head of differing traditions in modern poetry and that within each there has been an interaction of poetic theory and expression.

A few poets, like Wallace Stevens and E. E. Cummings, have combined traditional and experimental modes in their work, and some, like Cummings and Frost, have argued against the relevance of criticism to poetry. But most modern poets of any account have been deeply affected by the critical thought of their time. Even Robert Frost, whose most obvious subjects seem far removed from the lamp of theory and from the principal interests of the modern movement, cannot be exempted.

Frost was somewhat older than most of the new poets, and his style was already substantially formed when Ezra Pound helped him find an English publisher and belated recognition. Conservative in his choice of metrical patterns, his only concession to innovation seems to be the introduction into his traditional measures of the counterpoint of idiomatic New England speech rhythms. For the most part, Frost has been regarded as a middle-of-the-road Yankee poet whose restrained enthusiasm for nature is balanced by a humanistic concern for accepted norms of social behavior and responsibility.

But such a view ignores Frost's sophisticated awareness of the aesthetic climate of his time, and his responsiveness to it. Although Frost was not officially an Imagist, Imagism helped to prepare the ground for his acceptance, and his work has affinities with its tenets. There is in his poems from the beginning a concern for the evocative image that can release "an intellectual and emotional complex" within a concentrated span, if not an "instant of time." This quality, which Frost stressed in his description of himself as a "synecdochist" who uses a part to suggest the whole, can be seen in such shorter poems as "The Pasture," "The Runaway," and "Spring Pools," in which a disarming simplicity and fidelity to experience conceal from the too casual reader the extent to which the language is charged with complex metaphorical implications. Also, despite his preference for conventional verse patterns, Frost is like the Imagists in the economy and precision of his language and in his endorsement of the values of functional organic form in a poem like "The Ax-Helve":

> He showed me that the lines of a good helve
> Were native to the grain before the knife
> Expressed them, and its curves were no false curves
> Put on it from without. And there its strength lay
> For the hard work.

The same kind of organic determination is recognized in the more qualified prose statement of "The Figure a Poem Makes":

> The figure is the same as for love. Like a piece of ice on a hot stove the poem must ride on its own melting. A poem may be worked over once it is in being, but may not be worried into being. Its most precious quality will remain its having run itself and carried away the poet with it. Read it a hundred times: it will forever keep its freshness as a metal keeps its fragrance. It can never lose its sense of a meaning that once unfolded by surprise as it went.

Wallace Stevens, five years Frost's junior, was also late in taking his place among the modern poets. It was not until 1923, when he was in his forties, that he issued *Harmonium*, his first book of verse. Although his urbane and cosmopolitan manner distinguished him from the rural New Englander, he shared with Frost an impulse toward the order of traditional rhyme and meter. He was more receptive to the new influences, however, and many of the poems of *Harmonium* are in free forms that reveal his aesthetic preoccupations. Even when he was working close to traditional norms, Stevens's poems display an impressive range of functional variation and adaptation of convention, as in "Peter Quince at the Clavier." Stevens's technical virtuosity is everywhere evident in this poem, especially as he modulates tone and rhythm from section to section of the piece. In Part II, as Susanna bathes in solitude and walks upon the grass just before the intrusion of the elders, Stevens intensifies the effect of fragile beauty and tremulousness of mood by alternating three- and two-stress lines with masculine and feminine endings:

Upon the bank she stood
In the cool
Of spent emotions.

. . . . . .

She walked upon the grass,
Still quavering.
The winds were like her maids,
On timid feet,
Fetching her woven scarves,
Yet wavering.

Within the lifework represented by *The Collected Poems of Wallace Stevens* (1954) and *Opus Posthumous* (1957), two general types of poems are discernible. In his more gaudy and sensuous poems, Stevens focuses upon the physical realities of the quotidian world ("The arrant spices of the sun") in an effort to convey the effect of the vibrant immediacy of the world of the senses. In his more reflective poems, Stevens explores, in meditation, the metaphysical problem, seductive but finally insoluble, of the relation of the reality of the imagination and of art to the reality of experience. Although the two categories are useful as representing distinguishable emphases in Stevens's work, they are somewhat illusory. Often poems which seem initially to be concerned with a precise rendering of a sensuous object (in the manner of physical Imagism) reveal an underlying preoccupation with some aspect or another of the same basic problem of reality.

"Study of Two Pears" is ostensibly an effort at presenting faithfully (and "purely") the poet's perception of a still-life arrangement of two yellow pears on a green cloth. Throughout the poem, Stevens concentrates on the sensuous and formal aspect of the objects, ignoring their qualities as domestic fruit (their pearness) and disclaiming any symbolic cultural associations. They are, however, identified at the outset as instructive:

1

Opusculum paedagogum.
The pears are not viols,
Nudes or bottles.
They resemble nothing else.

2
They are yellow forms
Composed of curves
Bulging toward the base.
They are touched red.

In the same manner, Stevens proceeds with his objective consideration of the spatial forms ("round / Tapering toward the top") and colors ("various yellows, / Citrons, oranges and greens") of the arrangement. The somewhat intrusive concluding comment, "The pears are not seen / As the observer wills," reveals an underlying pedagogic motive. Stevens wishes not simply to "present" his perception (whether of a painted still life or of actual pears on a table does not matter) but also to convey the idea that art is an abstraction and that this sensuously pure and disinterested mode is the proper manner of perception for the artist and viewer. There is also the modern Objectivist implication that the arrangement, or work of art, is an autonomous entity, a reality in itself, not to be manipulated or distorted by the subjective preoccupations of the viewer.

In contrast to this purist view, the artist speaker of "The Man with the Blue Guitar" begins with the assertion that "Things as they are / Are changed upon the blue guitar" of imaginative perception and artistic projection. Despite strivings for an absolute reality beyond limited human perception, there is an emphasis upon the value of the metamorphosis of art as reality is transformed and humanized by the "blue" imagination. It is thus "poetry" rather than objective reality (or "things as they are") which is the "subject of the poem"—another way of saying that the "world" of the poem is the world of the imagination. The rival claims of the imagination and the physical world continue to supply the central tension and conflict in Stevens's later meditative poems, with the most satisfactory solution, perhaps, suggested by the observation in "An Ordinary Evening in New Haven," that "The poem is the cry of its occasion, / Part of the res itself and not about it."

With some dazzling exceptions, the metrical form of the later poems tends toward a greater regularity, and sometimes even monotony, than that of Stevens's earlier work. When he does not write in blank verse, divided sometimes into couplets or short stanzas, he most often uses quite regular but varying lines of four, five, and even more stresses, in contrast to the shorter

42

verses of many of the earlier poems. One late poem which expresses the detached indifference of life at "so much more than seventy" is entitled "Long and Sluggish Lines," a phrase that recalls the tone and tempo of Whitman's poem of old age, "The Dismantled Ship."

A substantial problem of interpretation arises from the fact that although Stevens attempted to use poetry as a means of exploring and resolving a basic philosophical problem, often developing lines of rather systematic argument, he also believed that one of the virtues of poetry was an essential irrationality. As he said in a poem entitled "Man Carrying Thing," "The poem must resist the intelligence / Almost successfully," and, in the more well-known "Asides on an Oboe," "final belief / Must be in a fiction." For Stevens, of course, from the beginning to the end of his career, the "supreme fiction," or essential ordering principle, was poetry, which projects not a statement about the nature of reality but an integrated aesthetic image of the poet's perception of his world.

In his belief in the integrity and autonomy of the poem and his innovative use of free forms and functional variations of established conventions, Stevens was working in the spirit of his time as a contributor to the modern movement inaugurated by Pound and the Imagists.

The dominant mood of the war and postwar years was revolutionary and experimental. In Chicago, where Harriet Monroe's *Poetry* upheld the cause of Imagism in its early years, there was a wartime renaissance. Besides featuring the work of the Imagists and their American associates, the magazine helped to introduce new "Chicago poets" like Vachel Lindsay, Edgar Lee Masters, and Carl Sandburg.

The experimental tradition was fostered by a number of *avant-garde* little magazines, including *The Little Review, Others*, and *transition*. Committed to the spirit of innovation, they provided an outlet for poets as original and various as Williams, Pound, and Stevens, and for the experimental writing of Gertrude Stein. In these magazines, the practice of the newer poets was supported by essays and manifestoes setting forth the creeds of a whole series of post-Imagist movements including Dadaism, Surrealism, and Objectivism. The general spirit of experimentation fostered an unusual number of gifted, highly individualistic American poets.

43

In less obvious ways, popular culture, and especially popular music and jazz, contributed to the modern movement. At the same time that Imagism was being promoted by Ezra Pound from his base in London, Vachel Lindsay of Springfield, Illinois, at home in the Midwest that Pound could not abide, was establishing a reputation as a writer and public declaimer of poetry that drew upon the rhythms and other primitive qualities of religious revival music and jazz. In "General William Booth Enters into Heaven," the title poem of a volume published in 1912, Lindsay wrote verses to be sung to the tune of "The Blood of the Lamb," a favorite selection of Salvation Army bands. In "The Congo" (1914), subtitled "A Study of the Negro Race," he combined the incantations of savage voodooism, the catchphrases of jubilee revivalism, and the fantasy and cakewalk rhythms of the minstrel show in an effort to project a sense of the primitive vitality and spontaneous expression of Negro life and culture. In his primitivism and his effort to renew the rhythms of American poetry, Lindsay was working in the spirit of the modern revolutionaries despite his lack of contact with the international *avant-garde*.

Lindsay also helped to introduce the younger Negro poet Langston Hughes. The stripped laconic verses of Hughes's first book of poems, *Weary Blues* (1926), echo the rhythms of jazz and the idiomatic language of the blues. The title poem portrays a jazz piano player and his song:

> Droning a drowsy syncopated tune,
> Rocking back and forth to a mellow croon,
>   I heard a Negro play.
> Down on Lenox Avenue the other night
> By the pale dull pallor of an old gas light
>
>   .   .   .   .
>
> Thump, thump, thump, went his foot on the floor.
> He played a few chords then he sang some more—
>   "I got the Weary Blues
>   And I can't be satisfied.
>   Got the Weary Blues
>   And can't be satisfied—
>   I ain't happy no mo'
>   And I wish that I had died."
>
>   .   .   .   .

Although the poems of Lindsay and Hughes lack the conciseness of diction and the metrical freedom of Imagist poetry, their rhythms and diction were innovative. Admired by Left-Bank Parisians and expatriates as well as Harlem sophisticates, the syncopated rhythms of jazz and the slangy, idiomatic lyrics of a wide range of popular songs inspirited and leavened the work of the moderns. Even Eliot, among the most staid of modern poets, lightened the anxiety-ridden verses of the "Game of Chess" section of *The Waste Land* with a satirical snatch of a "Shakespeherian Rag." And William Carlos Williams paused in the middle of an essay on Pound's *Cantos* to praise the direct and idiomatic language of the popular song "Button Up Your Overcoat."

The more conservative trend within the modern movement was represented by *The Fugitive* (1922–25), published in Nashville, Tennessee. This magazine, given over largely to poetry, although some criticism was included, was the organ of the Southern "Fugitives," a group that numbered John Crowe Ransom, Allen Tate, Donald Davidson, Merrill Moore, and R. P. Warren among its members. The Fugitives shared many of the rebellious attitudes of the 1920s toward the social and aesthetic standards of the past. They proclaimed themselves "in tune with the times in the fact that to a large degree in their poems they are self-convicted experimentalists." Fundamentally, however, most of the Fugitives were traditionalist in temper and more sympathetic to the Old than the New South, with its industrialism and bourgeois leveling. When Ransom called for a program that would be "in manners, aristocratic; in religion, ritualistic; in art, traditional," he was echoing Eliot's description of himself as "classicist in literature, royalist in politics, and Anglo-Catholic in religion."

More than in other little magazines of the period, the metrical patterns of the verse published in *The Fugitive* tended to follow traditional models and the experimentation of the poets to take place within conventional limits, as in Merrill Moore's ingenious sonnets and Ransom's ironic variations on traditional types like the elegy and the ballad. (Both "Bells for John Whiteside's Daughter" and "Captain Carpenter" first appeared in the magazine.) A champion of conventional rhyme and meter, Ransom attacked *The Waste Land* for its fragmentation and neglect of traditional ordering devices. The younger Allen Tate, who had early come under Eliot's influence and who was the one editor sympathetic to free experimental form, defended Eliot's poem in the magazine, arguing that "aberrant versification" is sometimes a necessity for the modern poet.

Although *The Fugitive* introduced and helped to establish a number of new poets, it is perhaps more important that its editors came to form the nucleus of the New Criticism of the late 1930s and the 1940s. The principal members of the movement included Ransom (who in 1941 issued a book of essays entitled *The New Criticism*), Tate, R. P. Warren, and Cleanth Brooks, who had also been Ransom's student at Vanderbilt. Others not from the South who became identified with the group were R. P. Blackmur and Yvor Winters.

Despite Ransom's objections to the form of *The Waste Land*, he and his fellow New Critics favored and carried forward many of Eliot's ideas and attitudes, including his social and political conservatism, his classical traditionalism, his interest in Symbolist and especially metaphysical poetry, and his impersonal theory of art supported by the idea of the objective correlative.

Eliot's example and influence, reinforced by the developing theories of the New Critics, helped to produce a conservative reaction in outlook and method among younger poets of the Middle Generation, who began their careers in the 1930s and early 1940s.[1] During these years, which coincided with the rise of totalitarianism abroad and the development of wartime disillusionment, the more radical and revolutionary experimental tradition instigated by Ezra Pound was largely neglected. Supported by William Carlos Williams, who did not come into his own as an influence until the period of the Second World War, it was to experience a resurgence among the postwar poets of the Third Generation.[2] In the meantime, during the years between the wars, the major free verse writers of the modern generation—Ezra Pound, William Carlos Williams, Marianne Moore, E. E. Cummings—produced a body of verse that was to vindicate Whitman's prophecy of a revolutionary new American poetry.

[1] See below, Chapter 11, "The Conservative Counterrevolution."
[2] See below, Chapter 12, "The Revolution Renewed: Contemporary Poetry."

5. Ezra Pound: Early Poems and *Mauberley*

EZRA POUND, who was to become the most active leader and promoter of the modern revolution in poetry, left the United States at the age of twenty-two after a one-semester career as a teacher of Romance languages at Wabash College. Departing Crawfordsville, Indiana, which had seemed to him the sixth circle of desolation in "the most Godforsakenest area of the Middle West," he crossed the Atlantic on a cattle boat early in 1908. Stopping in Venice, he arranged for the printing of his first collection of youthful verse, *A Lume Spento*. The summer of the same year found him in London, which was to be his home and base of operations for more than a decade. He quickly took his place in the literary life of the city, and in 1909 his first commercially published book of verse, *Personae*, was issued by Elkin Mathews. Favorably received by critics who recognized an authentic new lyric voice, it was promptly followed by *Exultations*, published in the same year.

The word *personae*, which Pound also chose in 1926 as the title of his collected verse other than *The Cantos*, is a key to the understanding of his motive and method from the beginning. Since *personae* originally designated the character masks worn by the actors in classical drama, Pound's usage reveals his preference for a dramatic poetry in which the writer does not speak in his own person but assumes instead an identity with a poet or personage of the past or with an imagined character. It is likely that the term was suggested by the dramatic monologues of Robert Browning, which Pound admired in his youth, when Browning's reputation was at its height. In 1864, Browning had published a collection of his poems, including among others "Abt Vogler," "Caliban upon Setebos," and "Rabbi Ben Ezra," under the title *Dramatis Personae. Personae* was an equally appropriate title for a collection of Pound's early work, which consisted largely of translations or imitations of the verse of earlier poets, especially the late medieval troubadours of southern France.

This early interest in the convention of the mask was soon reinforced by Pound's introduction, in 1913, to the papers of Ernest Fenollosa, whose essay on the classical Japanese Noh plays Pound edited and published under the title *Noh—or, Accomplishment* (1916) and subsequently reissued in *The Classic Noh Theatre of Japan* (1959).

The idea of the *persona* or mask has further implications for Pound's poetry because it suggests a means of achieving impersonality of expression. Pound's *persona* actually anticipates Eliot's "objective correlative" as a "set of objects, a situation, a chain of events which shall be the formula" of a particular emotion.[1] The word *personae* also had a psychological meaning for Pound, who recognized the assumption of masks as an expresssion of a search for identity—a compelling theme in modern literature. In the early essay "Vorticism" (1914), Pound describes his own quest for selfhood and "sincere self-expression" in his early poems: "I began this search for the real in a book called *Personae*, casting off, as it were, complete masks of the self in each poem. I continued in long series of translations, which were but more elaborate masks." The translations,

[1] See above, p. 37.

so important for Pound's development, came to include, besides the work of the early French and Italian poets, other poems from classical Greek and Latin, Anglo-Saxon, German, and Chinese. The range of technical devices that Pound drew upon and adapted in these poems represents a search in which appropriate expression is necessary to a sense of identity. The mask or persona assumed by the poet may be understood in the broadest possible way: it embraces his choice of subject and language, his distinctive viewpoint, and the very rhythm of his speech. In surveying earlier literatures and adapting their conventions to his own ends as he speaks in the person of the troubadour, the Anglo-Saxon seafarer, the Odyssean wanderer who came to comprehend all these roles and more, Pound combined the Confucian principle of "making it new" with a demonstration of the interaction of tradition and the individual talent.

Three periods or stages can be distinguished in Pound's development as a poet, with *Mauberley* as a transitional work that links the second and third. The first consists of the early translations from the troubadour poets. Pound later came to see these poems as exercises in an outworn mode. This is the period, from about 1908 until 1912, that he had in mind when at the beginning of *Mauberley* he referred to the "dead" E. P. as one who, "for three years, out of key with his time," strove to resuscitate a dead art.

The second stage, beginning with the publication of *Ripostes* (1912), saw Pound's emergence as a practitioner and prophet of modernism in poetry and the arts. During and just before the First World War, he was an active promoter of Imagism in poetry and, through the Vorticist movement, of similar principles in painting, sculpture, and the other arts. He also found a new interest in Chinese poetry when he assumed custody of the papers of Ernest Fenollosa, the pioneer American historian of Oriental art. This period of intense concern for new techniques that might advance the craft of modern poetry ended in the convulsion of war, which brought a profound disillusionment with Western civilization to Pound and a whole generation of young writers. In 1920 Pound left London, where he said he had smelled decay in the streets, for the Continent, settling in Rapallo on the Italian Riviera in 1924 after a few years in Paris.

Hugh Selwyn Mauberley (1920), which Pound described as

"distinctly a farewell to London," introduces new themes of social- and self-satire in its attacks on the decadence and cultural sterility of England. It also introduces the third and last stage of Pound's development as he turned from the aesthetic preoccupations of his earlier poetry to the social concerns of *The Cantos*, which were already under way. Pound thought of this continuing work as an epic or "a poem including history"—or, more informally, as "the tale of the tribe" of Western man. Aside from several prose works, an opera on the life of François Villon, and translations from Confucius, most of Pound's energies went into the composition of successive groups of *The Cantos*, beginning with *A Draft of XVI Cantos* (1925).

The very early poems of *A Lume Spento, Personae*, and *Exultations* reveal Pound's youthful enthusiasm for the courtly tradition and the intricate verse forms of the wandering French and Italian poets of the late Middle Ages. Their chief weakness lies in their archaic language and attitudes, which often seem posed and false in a twentieth-century poet. Pound himself later dismissed the poems of *A Lume Spento*, in an edition reprinted in 1965, as "A collection of stale creampuffs." But even with the handicap of outworn personae, Pound scored successes in making new the idiom of the past. In "Cino," in which he speaks in the voice of a poet of the "Italian Campagna 1309, the open road," there is an effort to express the reckless spirit of the vagabond poet through an irreverent, slangy distortion of classical epithets: " 'Pollo Phoebee, old tin pan, you / Glory to Zeus' aegis-day . . . ." Cino's imagined song ends on an imagistic, almost modern note:

> I have sung women in three cities
> But it is all one.
>
> I will sing of the white birds
> In the blue waters of heaven,
> The clouds that are spray to its sea.

Pound also worked in intricate metrical forms which proved to be of little use to him as a modern poet, except perhaps as a language exercise. In "Sestina: Altaforte," a troubadour celebration of the virtues of war that begins "Damn it all! all this our South stinks peace," the same end words of the six-line stanzas are repeated, in varying combinations, in the six stanzas of the poem, which are rounded off by a three-line seventh stanza in which four of the end words (*music, crimson, clash, peace*) are brought together:

> And let the music of the swords make them crimson!
> Hell grant soon we hear again the swords clash!
> Hell blot black for alway the thought "Peace"!

The poem is impressive as a metrical tour de force, but its heroics seem grotesque if not ludicrous in a modern perspective. The sestina pattern, which was invented in the twelfth century by Pound's favorite, Arnaut Daniel, was also used by D. G. Rossetti and other nineteenth-century poets who influenced Pound's youth. The effect here, however, is archaic.

The contrasting influence of the modern revolution—the result of association with fellow Imagist poets and with abstract artists like Wyndham Lewis in painting and Henri Gaudier-Brzeska in sculpture—emerges in some of the poems of *Ripostes* (1912). The blank verse "Portrait d'une Femme," a Browningesque yet modern vignette, depicts the emptiness and sterility of the life of a cultured woman, surrounded by an exotic assortment of objects of art: "Your mind and you are our Sargasso Sea, / London has swept about you this score years / And bright ships left you this or that in fee. . . ." Despite her acquisitions, often the "fee" of casual alliances with cultured lovers, the lady is without a sense of identity or fulfillment: "No! there is nothing! In the whole and all, / Nothing that's quite your own. / Yet this is you." This subject and theme, anticipatory of Eliot's hollow men and women, appear again in *Mauberley* in the figures of the "Conservatrix of Milésien" and the Lady Valentine in the eleventh and twelfth poems of the first sequence.

Ripostes also discloses the beginnings of Pound's shift to free verse and toward abstraction. Both can be seen in "The Return," which Yeats described as having the quality of a brilliant improvised translation at sight from an "unknown Greek masterpiece":

> See, they return; ah, see the tentative
> Movements, and the slow feet,
> The trouble in the pace and the uncertain
> Wavering!

Yeats was disturbed by the obscurity of meaning in the poem, in which the subject is not identified. Although the "they" of the poem may most likely be the shades of Greek warriors returning from the underworld, neither this fact nor the metaphorical significance of their "return" is clearly established:

> Haie! Haie!
>   These were the swift to harry;
>   These the keen-scented;
>   These were the souls of blood.
>
>   Slow on the leash,
>   pallid the leash-men!

The fact that the figures once were "souls of blood" and now are pallid supports a reading that could identify them as ghosts of the Greek underworld and invite the metaphoric speculation that their altered state represents the difficulty of the modern poet's reviving the heroic past, but neither of these meanings can be insisted upon. For all the obscurity of the events that comprise the narrative, to the extent that it exists, the poem succeeds in creating and projecting a mood and a unified effect. Despite its lack of developed meaning, the work is admirable, even though Yeats (whom Pound could not convert to free verse) could not be comfortable with it. The poem stands as testimony to the modern idea that meaning is only one of several formal dimensions of poetry and that any given work may, without detriment, be more or less fully developed in any one of these. To the idea, in other words, that poetic form is open and relative.

In his translations of this period, Pound shifted from the poetry of southern Europe to other, more productive sources. Although the Romance tradition of his early studies was to supply a continuing strain in *The Cantos*, the poetry of other cultures provided fresh suggestions and conventions to Pound as an innovative modern poet. In his version of the Anglo-Saxon poem "The Seafarer," the pagan speaker tells of a harsh, fated life on northern seas, cut off from the security and comfort of the life of the burghers ashore. Without faith in any providential order or "earth-weal eternal," impressed by the frailty and transience of the "doom-gripped body," he can only hope that he may leave some work, in word or deed, that will let his name live on " 'mid the English." In life, nothing remains for him but to "fare forth" and endure the rigors of the voyage, a "wretched outcast / Deprived of my kinsmen." The opening lines of the poem, which observes the traditional pattern and conventions of Anglo-Saxon alliterative verse, establish the sense of the speaker's dark view of life and resolution in confronting it:

> May I for my own self song's truth reckon,
> Journey's jargon, how I in harsh days
> Hardship endured oft.
> Bitter breast-cares have I abided,
> Known on my keel many a care's hold,
> And dire sea-surge . . . .

In several ways, the persona of the seafarer serves Pound better than that of the troubadour. To the modern poet in a period of disillusionment, the pagan sense of a fated life is more compelling than the romance or the careless cynicism of the Christian vagabond poet. The sense of alienation from the comforts and conventions of bourgeois society is especially suited to self-exiled or alienated writers. There is also the strong appeal of the hazardous Odyssean voyage, which writers like Pound in *The Cantos* and James Joyce in *Ulysses* see as the image of a search for sustaining values in the modern world. Metrically, the harshness and intensity of the repetitive alliteration of interrupting consonants like *j*, *b*, and *k* are better suited to the outlook and mood of the modern poet than the mellifluous musicality of troubadour verse. Pound was to make a limited but effective use of the metrical conventions of Anglo-Saxon poetry in both *Mauberley* and *The Cantos*.

In 1913, when the widow of Ernest Fenollosa asked Pound to be the literary executor for her husband's work, Pound was fortunate to find, unexpectedly and without effort, a treasure of fresh material which came to be a catalyst and shaping agent for his own poetry. The formal conventions of "The Seafarer" had proved useful, but they had required too rigid an adherence to the set metrical patterns and the prolixity of the Anglo-Saxon alliterative tradition. The more imagistic Chinese mode not only permitted but demanded a greater concentration and a greater freedom of form. It helped Pound develop "modern" techniques for the precise rendering of the "thing," whether subjective or objective, in verse remarkable for its clarity, economy, and freedom from the emotionalism and musicality of much Victorian poetry.

Fenollosa's essay "On the Chinese Written Character as a Medium for Poetry," which Pound edited and published in his own collection of critical essays, *Instigations* (1920), stressed the imagistic qualities of the Chinese ideograph. Fenollosa also argued that what impressed him as the active, transitive quality of the Chinese language needed to be combined with a sensuous imagism for the writing of good poetry in English as well as Chinese. Pound hailed Fenollosa as a true "forerunner" of modernism and based his own ideas about the ideogrammic method, as set forth in the first chapter of the *A B C of Reading* (1934), on Fenollosa's earlier work. More likely than not, it was Fenollosa who stimulated Pound's new emphasis on the dynamism of the poetic image as he moved from his earlier idea of Imagism to the position set forth in his essay "Vorticism," with its definition of the image as "a VORTEX, from which, and through which, and into which, ideas are constantly rushing." Looking back at this early theory from the vantage of twenty years, Pound comments, in the *A B C of Reading*: "The defect of earlier imagist propaganda was not in misstatement but in incomplete statement. The diluters took the handiest and easiest meaning, and thought only of the STATIONARY image. If you can't think of imagism or phanopoeia as including the moving image, you will have to make a really needless division of fixed image and praxis or action." The shift in emphasis from the stasis of the sensuously pure image to the dynamism of the Vortex is also in key with Pound's turning from the aestheticism of his early modern period to the sense of social engagement of the postwar *Cantos*.

All thirteen of the Chinese poems of Pound's *Cathay* (1915) are based on Fenollosa's translations, made with the assistance of Japanese scholars, of classic Chinese poems. Most are by Li Po, who wrote in the eighth century A.D. and whom Pound, working from Fenollosa's notes, identifies as "Rihaku," the Japanese form of the same name.

54

The precise, Imagist technique of these poems, in Pound's rendition, can be seen in "The River-Merchant's Wife: A Letter." The speaker is a young wife, married at fourteen, who expresses, largely through images, the loneliness and isolation she feels in separation from her husband, absent on a five-month business trip, and her eagerness to be reunited with him:

> You dragged your feet when you went out.
> By the gate now, the moss is grown, the different mosses,
> Too deep to clear them away!
> The leaves fall early this autumn, in wind.
> The paired butterflies are already yellow with August
> Over the grass in the West garden;
> They hurt me. I grow older.
> If you are coming down through the narrows of the
>   river Kiang,
> Please let me know beforehand,
> And I will come out to meet you
>   As far as Cho-fu-Sa.

The effect of an intense, repressed emotion is conveyed through carefully selected images and minimal statement—a method productive of the kind of poetry at which the Imagists were aiming: a precise, objective rendering.

In "Lament of the Frontier Guard," also by Rihaku, there is a persistent sense of loneliness, of exile, of hazardous struggle in an alien land. The speaker sees the desolation and sorrow wrought by "Barbarous kings" who have turned "gracious spring" to "blood-ravenous autumn" through "a turmoil of warsmen, spread over the middle kingdom," or China.

The much older Chinese poem, "Song of the Bowmen of Shu," was attributed in the first edition of *Cathay* to Kusugen, fourth century B.C.; in later editions to Bunno, "reputedly 1100 B.C."; and finally to Shih-ching. Pound placed it at the beginning of his collection, perhaps because of its age, perhaps also because it is so perfectly keyed to the temper of any time in which soldiers fighting on foreign soil are oppressed by battle weariness, doubts of survival, and longing for the security of home:

Here we are, picking the first fern-shoots
And saying: When shall we get back to our country?
Here we are because we have the Ken-in for our foemen,
We have no comfort because of these Mongols.
We grub the soft fern-shoots,
When anyone says "Return," the others are full of sorrow.

There is also the familiar yearning for a definite end to it all—
a date to look forward to:

We grub the old fern-stalks.
We say: Will we be let to go back in October?

Even in poems not concerned with war, a mood of loneliness
is common. A sense of stark isolation is established by the open-
ing lines of "Taking Leave of a Friend," in which the natural
setting dwarfs the human figure, making it seem insignificant
and alien:

Blue mountains to the north of the walls,
White river winding about them;
Here we must make separation
And go out through a thousand miles of dead grass.

Besides its suggestion of loneliness, the setting presented through
rigorously selected images has the abstract quality of a Chinese
painting. It also has the purity of the objective Imagists' ideal
of a faithful rendering of the "thing" through precise, evocative
imagery.

Other formal devices, which interact with the patterns of
images, are also important. In all of these poems, the dominant
technique of imagistic presentation is reinforced and intensified
by the skillful use of a varied, flexible, never-oppressive syntac-
tical parallelism.

In these "old" poems, which he succeeded in making new with
a dead man's help, Pound realized most fully the program which
he and the Imagists had developed for a new, modern poetry.
The poems of *Cathay* represent an ancient tradition and deal
with a vanished place and time, but there is nothing archaic or
quaint about them. In diction and technique, they represent an

achieved balance and harmony between the relics of an ancient Oriental culture and the sensibility of a modern Western poet in the time of the first great war of the twentieth century.

The theme of wartime disillusionment is carried over, in a contemporary context, in *Hugh Selwyn Mauberley* (1920), where it is combined with a general satire of English society and of the character of Mauberley as an inadequate aesthete-artist. Considered as a whole, the work invites the charge of incoherence, since it consists of eighteen individual poems which fall into two sequences. The first thirteen poems—of which the last, "Envoi (1919)," is of a kind that ordinarily marks the end of a work—are followed by five further poems under the general title "Mauberley/1920." In this second and in a sense appended group, some of the poems are numbered and some have titles: I, II, "The Age Demanded," IV, "Medallion." The situation suggests an indifference to, if not ignorance of, the simplest principles of outlining or logical organization—one aspect of the form sense that may help to explain some of the difficulties of Pound's other work, including *The Cantos*.

The second sequence, "Mauberley/1920," parallels the first in that it has its own introductory poem, echoing that of the first group, and its own envoy under the title "Medallion." It would seem only natural that a poet who wished to have a group of eighteen poems regarded as a whole or as two integrally related sequences would arrange to have so valedictory a title as "Envoi" appear at the end of the whole group rather than two thirds of the way through. Pound, however, placed his "Envoi" at the end of the first sequence, which *is* coherent, in a manner suggesting that what follows may be an afterthought, or a parallel treatment from an altered perspective, since the focus and the tone of the poems of the second sequence are markedly different from what precedes.

In the first sequence, the speaker, who can more easily be identified with Ezra Pound than with Hugh Selwyn Mauberley, is relatively objective and detached. Aware of the problem of self-identity, he is to a greater extent regardful of the London social and literary scene, which is almost impersonally subjected to satiric analysis as decadent and suppressive of the honest artist. The second sequence is, in contrast, subjective and even impressionistic. It is focused, also satirically, not upon the social environment but upon the character of the passive, ineffectual Mauberley as a kind of decadent artist. He is not merely an aesthete, since he creates a "medallion" art, but he is cut off from the main stream of social and intellectual life. Mauberley is not to be confused with Pound the man—though Pound was acutely conscious of his own problem of identity. He is more probably the representative of the too but not wholly pure aestheticism Pound imagined himself to be casting off as he left England and his apprenticeship behind for postwar Europe and the continuing work on *The Cantos.*

In contrast, the first sequence is not chiefly concerned with the title character at all, even though in the opening poem, "E. P. Ode pour l'élection de son sépulchre," the speaker somewhat satirically looks back at himself as a Mauberley-like poetaster who, "out of key with his time," had striven "to resuscitate the dead art / Of poetry; to maintain 'the sublime' / In the old sense. Wrong from the start—." But, except for the "Envoi (1919)," the remaining twelve poems of the first group are focused outward, with remarkable incisiveness, upon examples of social and literary decadence that are viewed with scorn and revulsion: upon the "tawdry cheapness" of taste in a mass society in which "The pianola 'replaces' / Sappho's barbitos"; upon the war with its hopeless daring and wastage, leading to disillusionment; upon the pathetic aesthetes of the 1890s, for whom Pound felt an affinity; upon the perversion of values in the "successful" professional writer, Mr. Nixon, who is contrasted with the figure of the artist who refuses to surrender his integrity, the "stylist," who, like Ford Madox Ford, was forced to take refuge upon the land as an unsuccessful farmer; upon the false patronage extended to the arts, from mixed and dubious motives, by the Lady Valentine in her London salon. The strain of rejection running through the poems culminates in the scornful presentation of this useless haven for the arts in the only center of English culture, where "The sale of half-hose has / Long since superseded the cultivation / Of Pierian roses." The incongruous Byronic-Browningesque rhyme dismisses hope for the arts in this society. Britannia of the cashbox has no sustenance for the Muses.

Yet the "Envoi" that follows these poems of rejection reaffirms the poet's commitment to his art. Speaking in his own voice, not Mauberley's, Pound charges his "dumb-born book" to tell his mistress, "her who sang me once that song of Lawes," that her beauty and her gift for song may be perpetuated in his poem. Through a traditional image of roses preserved in amber, Pound boasts the permanence of human beauty fixed in art:

> I would bid them [her graces] live
> As roses might, in magic amber laid,
> Red overwrought with orange and all made
> One substance and one colour
> Braving time.

Although he speaks with the confidence of an earlier poet like Edmund Waller, whose "Go, Lovely Rose" he echoes, his voice is not that of a seventeenth-century but of a modern poet writing in a modern idiom. At this point, however, at the end of the first sequence of poems, he modifies his diction and measure to harmonize with those of an earlier age, and through a traditional theme he expresses his faith (in the face of discouragement) in the power of his art. He does so in a way that demonstrates his skill in reconciling past and present in lines in which the cadences of modern speech blend with a prevailing iambic rhythm—most fully expressed in so regular a line as "When our two dusts with Waller's shall be laid." In this poem, Pound's carefully balanced verse carries the full weight of a modern poet's sense not of alienation, but of identification with a long tradition.

In the five poems that follow under the title of "Mauberley/ 1920," there is a shift from the assurance of the poet of the "Envoi" to the ironic self-contemplation of the aesthete-poet Mauberley. His inadequacies as an artist are treated in the first four poems of this second sequence. Three of these echo, internally or in their titles, phrases from the poems of the first, more objective sequence. The first poem of the second sequence picks up the phrase from "E. P. Ode pour l'élection de son sépulchre," "His true Penelope was Flaubert," and goes on to describe Mauberley's technique as that of an engraver working within self-determined limits:

> Firmness,
> Not the full smile,
> His art, but an art
> In profile . . . .

In keeping with the idea of a limitation of power in Mauberley, the phrase which occupies a full line in the earlier "Ode" becomes two verses of the more constricted stanza of the later poem:

"His true Penelope
Was Flaubert,"
And his tool
The engraver's.

The second poem describes Mauberley's urge to "convey the relation / Of eye-lid and cheek-bone / By verbal manifestation" and his aim, as an artist conscious of his limitations, to present a series "Of curious heads in medallion." In the third poem, it is recognized that Mauberley's sensuous and subjective preoccupations have insulated him from social reality and largely confined him to self-expression: "Lifting the faint susurrus / Of his subjective hosannah." But this isolation has also protected him from the sycophancy of the literary establishment and helped him to protect an integrity that Pound acknowledges in Mauberley (and in himself):

Non-esteem of self-styled "his betters"
Leading, as he well knew,
To his final
Exclusion from the world of letters.

In the fourth poem the final fate of the aesthete wrecked in the tides of modern life is rendered through the ironic identification of Mauberley with Homer's Elpenor, who fell to his death from Circe's roof and reappeared as a ghost to charge Odysseus to build him a barrow marked by the oar he had plied. But Mauberley's final admonition is more modest and self-deprecating:

Coracle of Pacific voyages,
The unforecasted beach;
Then on an oar
Read this:

"I was
And I no more exist;
Here drifted
An hedonist."

To an American ear the final phrase which couples the article
an with a voiced *h* has an appropriate effect of foppishness.

The final poem, "Medallion," which parallels the envoy of
the first sequence, is an example of Mauberley's art. In contrast
with the envoy's promise of immortality, it simply presents an
imagistic portrait of a singing woman, who may be the subject
of the earlier poem. In this respect, it is a more sensuously pure,
if more limited poem, conceived perhaps as a fulfillment of the
poet's earlier boast. Without comment, except for allusions to
Anadyomene in Reinach's *Apollo* and to "King Minos' hall,"
the poet provides a "verbal manifestation" of a cameolike por-
trait, a beautiful "head in medallion." It is linked to the earlier
"Envoi" through a reference to amber and through the colors
(reminiscent of the "red overwrought with orange") of the
"sleek head" with its "Honey-red" braids emerging from the
"gold-yellow frock" and the topaz eyes. But the head is not
presented in profile:

> The face-oval beneath the glaze,
> Bright in its suave bounding-line, as,
> Beneath half-watt rays,
> The eyes turn topaz.

Although the poem is an admirable imagistic presentation, the
phrase "Beneath half-watt rays" acknowledges the lack of full
power and intensity.

Despite the problems suggested by its separability into two
sequences and its shift of focus from the literary environment
to the sensibility of Mauberley, *Hugh Selwyn Mauberley* has
been generally admired as a "whole poem" for its precision,
coherence, and consistent irony. The disparate nature of the
second group of poems has either been ignored or explained
(most effectively by Hugh Kenner) as a "coda" in which "the
Mauberley persona comes to the fore; gathering up the motifs
of the earlier sections, the enigmatic stanzas mount from in-

tensity to intensity to chronicle the death of the Jamesian hero who might have been Pound."

The praise *Mauberley* has received may be deserved, but it is misdirected to the extent that it assumes a unity or consistency among the poems, especially as these fall into two sequences or parts. The first, with the ironic introduction of the Mauberley-like E. P. ("For three years, out of key with his time"), the incisive disillusioned analysis of environment, and the stubbornly affirmative "Envoi," does have a remarkable unity as a well-integrated and effective work. Brief though it is, it has much in common with *A Portrait of the Artist as a Young Man*, which had first appeared in the columns of *The Egoist* through Pound's influence in 1914 and 1915. In his *Portrait*, Joyce had also introduced an aesthete hero, subjected him and his uncongenial environment to ironic scrutiny, and ended with a leave-taking and dedication to the vocation of the artist.

But the second sequence is not an integral part of the whole. As an analysis of the sensibility of the Mauberley persona, a legitimate concern, it is out of scale in the larger work. It bulks disproportionately in relation to the first sequence of poems, which had already treated an impressive range of subjects with remarkable compression and intensity. The poems of the second sequence seem something of an indulgence. It is incongruous with the profession of an "art in profile" that so much space is lavished on a subject that could be treated more concisely—perhaps in one or two poems. The argument that such indulgence may be appropriate to the characterization of Mauberley as a sensuous aesthete hardly excuses Pound for what amounts to diffuseness of treatment. Furthermore, the poems of the second group give the impression of being an appendage or even "notes to" the first sequence because they are based on allusions to and amplifications of the motifs of the earlier poems.

One is tempted to wonder whether at some stage in the gestation of *Mauberley* Pound may have been experimenting with two ways of treating his subject—one from a relatively objective viewpoint; the other from a viewpoint representing Mauberley's subjective responses—and decided, perhaps unwisely, to issue both as a single work, distinguished only by the "Envoi (1919)" which closes the first sequence and the "Mauberley/1920" which introduces the second.

But to recognize certain weaknesses in form is not to damn *Mauberley*, which is in many ways a distinguished work. Although it is not fully coherent, one may as well recognize that perfect unity is, as Pound has noted of beauty, difficult—hard to come by for the modern artist, whose world view can not be so easily ordered as that of a Dante or even a Sophocles.

The first sequence does provide, in brief compass, a satiric anatomy of the poet's English environment at the time of the First World War. The poems are suffused with a passion of indignation at the waste and destruction of war and the sterility of a commercial society. Pound draws upon tradition and adapts the conventions of earlier literatures to his needs with economy and precision. A line from Pindar's second Olympic Ode ("What man, hero, or god [shall we praise]") is incorporated into the ironic last stanza of poem III ("The tea-rose tea-gown, etc."):

> O bright Apollo,
> τίν' ἄνδρα, τίν' ἤρωα, τίνα θεόν
> What god, man, or hero
> Shall I place a tin wreath upon!

With the English *tin* echoing the repeated τίν' of the Greek.

Poems IV ("These fought in any case") and V ("There died a myriad") are a memorable expression of postwar disillusionment. The Horatian dictum "Dulce et decorum est pro patria mori" is succinctly rejected in Pound's "Died some, pro patria, / non 'dulce' non 'et decor'. . . ." The Anglo-Saxon conventions of "The Seafarer" are deftly used to express indignation and regret at the loss of young blood:

> Charm, smiling at the good mouth,
> Quick eyes gone under earth's lid . . . .

The treatment of war is a far cry from the mindless braggadocio of the youthful "Sestina: Altaforte."[2]

The nostalgic treatment of the poets of the '90s in "Siena mi fe . . ." is appropriately touched with dark humor as Monsieur

---

[2] See above, p. 51.

Verog reminisces, in rhymed stanzas, about the tarnished glories of the past:

> For two hours he talked of Galliffet;
> Of Dowson; of the Rhymers' Club;
> Told me how Johnson (Lionel) died
> By falling from a high stool in a pub . . .
>
> But showed no trace of alcohol
> At the autopsy, privately performed—
> Tissue preserved—the pure mind
> Arose toward Newman as the whiskey warmed.

The satiric portrait of the Lady Valentine in XII ("Daphne with her thighs in bark") reveals the bankruptcy of the literary life of London's West End during the war years. But it is followed by the "Envoi," in which Pound harmonizes his voice with that of the seventeenth-century past in a full-voiced, lyrical affirmation of his poetic calling—and of his powers, which are abundantly demonstrated in *Hugh Selwyn Mauberley*.

Despite the lack of overall coherence, both sequences of the poem end not with fragments, like *The Waste Land*, but with clearly defined and well-integrated images that represent a settled viewpoint and established values. Like Eliot, Pound projects a picture of a decadent society. But unlike Eliot, who could find no adequate secular substitute for a lost religious faith, he maintains an unwavering belief in the power of natural beauty, in his vocation as an artist, and in the importance of art as a source of needed cultural values. Underlying the social criticism and the self-criticism of *Mauberley* there is a resolution—a strength of personality, of the ego—that was to sustain the poet through the voyages and hardships of *The Cantos*.

6. Ezra Pound: *The Cantos*

ADMIRED THOUGH *Mauberley* has been, the poem is slight in comparison with Pound's work as a whole. For better or worse, his reputation is staked largely on *The Cantos*, the long never-to-be-completed poem already under way when he wrote in *Mauberley* the coda to one phase of his career. With this task accomplished, Pound turned to the larger problem of assimilating the conventions and traditions of many literatures, Eastern as well as Western, in a major poem—of shaping a modern epic to take its place beside the great poems of earlier, more unified cultures.

Although Pound pointed to certain models, the formal organization of *The Cantos* has remained a persistent problem. Homeric and Dantean parallels are obvious and traceable, but many readers have complained of a general effect of discontinuity and incoherence. One has even remarked that, although the mode of expression in *The Cantos* is conversational, the conversation is about nothing. Another has seized upon a comparison once thrown off by Pound himself and described the work as a rag bag. Such judgments, which would dismiss rather than attempt to understand the poem, surely fail to do it justice. Despite Pound's stress on a few simplifying ideas, such as *usura*, the world of *The Cantos*, like the real world, may appear to be complex and confusing, without clearly established guidelines or standards of value. Yet it represents a largely consistent viewpoint, and it is formally organized according to principles that have become more understandable with the addition of successive groups of cantos.

Certain unifying devices persist from the beginning. The two most important and closely related are the quest theme and Pound's distinctive view of history. The image of the Odyssean voyage which Pound introduces in Canto 1 supplies the main strand of thematic continuity for a work which can best be understood as an epic (defined by Pound as "a poem including history") focused on the poet's quest for values in the modern world. As a voyager in the stream of history from the classical past to the present, Pound develops an unchronological, highly personal view of a process of deepening cultural decay from the classic age of Greece and Rome, with their high cultures; through the Middle Ages, which still preserved a semblance of cultural unity through the influence of the Catholic Church; through the Renaissance, which saw the rise of capitalism (the modern form of *usura*) and the breaking of the communal ties of feudalism; into the modern age with its disruptive forces of mass revolutions and world wars.

But collectively, *The Cantos* have a positive and optimistic as well as a negative emphasis. Pound does not only condemn the forces that have corroded social bonds. He also points to historical periods (the Confucian age in China; the Revolutionary period in America) and exceptional persons (princes, public servants, ethical teachers, incorruptible artists) as models of the values he is eager to promote. He is, in fact, attempting to provide specifications and a manifesto for a new culture deriving from the best and most enlightened values of a heritage that he has sifted and graded in an eclectic and highly individual fashion.

66

To the reader of *The Cantos*, the poet's voice often seems that of a dogmatic teacher or preacher, sure of his lesson but impatient with the density and resistance of his pupils. If the world would only listen and take heed, it would find a cure for its ills and a prescription for reforms that would usher in a cultural New Jerusalem. In his role as a self-anointed prophet, Pound is firmly in the Romantic tradition of numerous poets who, since the beginning of the nineteenth century, have attempted to formulate the gospel of a new order that might rise from the ruins of the old. In America, his two most important predecessors were Emerson, whom he could not acknowledge, and Whitman, whom he grudgingly recognized as a forerunner but whose verbosity he deplored. As he wrote in "A Pact" (1916):

> I make a pact with you, Walt Whitman—
> I have detested you long enough.
> I come to you as a grown child
> Who has had a pig-headed father;
> I am old enough now to make friends.
> It was you that broke the new wood,
> Now is a time for carving.
> We have one sap and one root—
> Let there be commerce between us.

Although unified by a controlling viewpoint which did not change in any essential way since he began his ambitious project, *The Cantos* do convey the inescapable impression of radical discontinuity and fragmentation. There are at least two principal reasons for this effect, which has succeeded in discouraging many readers. One is that Pound, although admittedly embarked upon an epic, or a "poem including history," refused to observe consistent historical sequence or logical progression in any of the successive groups of cantos. Another is that each of the successive groups, often issued as *decads*, or clusters of approximately ten poems, tends to reflect the shifting preoccupations of the poet and the vicissitudes and winds of opinion of the period in which it was composed. These groups, which appeared at intervals over the span of a half century, never reached a formal conclusion. Nor should they have. But in a number of ways *The Pisan Cantos* (1948), inspired by the poet's ordeal of imprisonment, stands out as the dramatic culmination of Pound's epic.

Although the first commercially published group, *A Draft of XXX Cantos*, did not appear until 1930, Pound had been working on the poem since the war years and had published a number of the cantos, either singly or in groups. Cantos numbered 1, 2, and 3, but differing considerably from later versions, appeared in the first American edition of *Lustra* (1917). In 1925, a limited edition of *A Draft of XVI Cantos* was issued by William Bird's Three Mountains Press in Paris.

This first substantial installment of sixteen cantos reveals Pound's conception of the pattern of his projected work. Spanning the centuries between the Homeric age and the First World War, the group begins with the descent of Odysseus into the underworld and continues through successive cantos that celebrate such heroes as Sordello, El Cid, and Sigismundo Malatesta, condemn the rise of usury and its attendant corruptions, point to the wisdom of Confucius as a saving norm, and descend again, this time to the hell of the modern usurers, loathsomely represented by the munitions mongers and profiteers of the First World War.

In Canto 1, which launches the poet upon his voyage, Pound follows the text of Andreas Divus' sixteenth-century translation of the *Odyssey* to relate, in the first person, the story of Odysseus' visit, at Circe's behest, to the land of the dead to hear from Tiresias the prospects of his returning home. Though his source is the Latin translation of a Greek epic, Pound makes effective use of the Anglo-Saxon alliterative verse conventions of "The Seafarer" as, in the person of Odysseus, he undertakes the fateful voyage:

> And then went down to the ship,
> Set keel to breakers, forth on the godly sea, and
> We set up mast and sail on that swart ship,
> Bore sheep aboard her, and our bodies also
> Heavy with weeping, and winds from sternward
> Bore us out onward with bellying canvas . . . .

The visit to the underworld, in which Odysseus encounters the ghosts of the dead, including those of his mother and his comrade Elpenor, who had died in a drunken fall from Circe's roof, metaphorically suggests the poet's preparation for his search for values by an imaginative return to the dead past and by a necessary withdrawal or introspection for the purpose of contemplation and self-examination. The closing apostrophe to Aphrodite of the golden crown, spoken in the modern poet's voice, as he drops the manner of Divus' Odysseus, is an acknowledgment of the female principle of beauty and generative power as a necessary complement to the active male principle embodied in Odysseus, the intellectual quester.

To offset any suggestion that the individual poem, or even the larger work, may be thought of as a self-contained and self-sufficient entity, Pound begins his opening canto with the conjunctive "And," in keeping with the traditional idea of the epic as beginning *in medias res* and, more significantly, with the modern poet's conception of history as a continuing process and of his own work as a part of this larger continuum. The effect is reinforced by the uncompleted "So that:" with which Canto 1 does not so much conclude as lead into the ongoing imaginative voyage of the succeeding cantos.

Canto 2 opens with a violent shift to the nineteenth century:

> Hang it all, Robert Browning,
> there can be but the one "Sordello."
> But Sordello, and my Sordello?

The allusion to Sordello as either the hero of Browning's most obscure poem or the actual figure of the medieval Provençal poet of that name is a link not only with Browning, one of the favorite poets of Pound's youth, but also with Dante, who introduces Sordello in the tenth canto of the *Inferno*.

Sea imagery then brings another shift to the story of Alcœtes and Dionysus, or Bacchus, which Pound adapts from the version in Book III of Ovid's *Metamorphoses*. In Pound's treatment, the god's magical transformation of the ship upon which he was being shanghaied into a forest setting with ivy, grapevines, and potent beasts like lynxes, panthers, and leopards is a demonstration of the creative power of Dionysian passion as it is expressed through metamorphosis—a necessary resource not only for the

69

god of legend but for the poet. The canto ends with a demonstration of the poet's metamorphic power in an imagistic presentation of a Mediterranean seascape in which the sensuous beauty of immediate perception and the evocative appeal of classic myth are interfused:

> Olive grey in the near,
>> far, smoke grey of the rock-slide,
> Salmon-pink wings of the fish-hawk
>> cast grey shadows in water,
> The tower like a one-eyed great goose
>> cranes up out of the olive-grove,

> And we have heard the fauns chiding Proteus
>> in the smell of hay under the olive-trees,
> And the frogs singing against the fauns
>> in the half-light.
> And . . .

The effect of the uncompleted statement parallels that of the ending of the first canto.

After the introduction of El Cid, another hero of romance, the following cantos, which range over the ages from the remote past to the poet's present, point to the Renaissance as the blossom time of the black flower of *usura*. In Cantos 8–11, Sigismundo Malatesta is idealized as a model of the Renaissance prince who tried to build his ideal city (a recurrent image in *The Cantos*) in the face of opposition from the Church and "the Medici bank." These cantos begin with an allusion to the closing lines of *The Waste Land*, which Pound had recently helped Eliot prepare for publication: "These fragments you have shelved (shored)." Like Eliot, Pound is structuring his work upon fragments of the past in an effort to encourage a revival of values in the present.

But Pound's viewpoint is more secular and humanistic than Eliot's, as can be seen in his introduction of Confucius (Kung) in Canto 13 as an exemplar of the virtues of moderation, benevolence, and self-discipline:

70

And Kung said, and wrote on the bo leaves:
            If a man have not order within him
He can not spread order about him;
And if a man have not order within him
His family will not act with due order;
            And if the prince have not order within him
He can not put order in his dominions.
And Kung gave the words "order"
and "brotherly deference"
And said nothing of the "life after death."
And he said
            "Anyone can run to excesses,
It is easy to shoot past the mark,
It is hard to stand firm in the middle."

In Cantos 14–15, the enlightenment offered by Kung gives way to the hell of the usurers, described in graphic, obscene detail. Among these are the "betrayers of language":

            And those who had lied for hire;
            the perverts, the perverters of language,
                        the perverts, who have set money-lust
            Before the pleasures of the senses . . . .

The concluding canto of the first group of sixteen brings the poet out of hell, bathing in a lake of acid to free himself of the "hell ticks," and then presents a sudden vision of an "oasis" as he passes into the quiet air of a "new sky" and sees, as an inspiration from the past, "the heroes, / Sigismundo, and Malatesta Novello, / and founders, gazing at the mounts of their cities." Although the vision of the ideal city gives way to the violence of war and revolution before the canto ends, it persists throughout *The Cantos* as an image of a renovated culture.

Besides revealing Pound's original conception of the pattern of his poem, this first group of cantos also suggests, more fully than any later version, the Dantean hell-purgatory-heaven structure that Pound early claimed as one of his models—although he typically emphasizes flux and avoids the systematic progression of levels of the *Commedia*.

By the time the first sixteen cantos were reprinted in *A Draft of XXX Cantos* (1930), the world was suffering from an international depression generally regarded as the final convulsion of the capitalistic system. *Eleven New Cantos: XXXI–XLI* (1934) reveals the economic preoccupation Pound shared with his contemporaries in this period of crisis. These cantos, in which he turns back to the period of the American Revolution and the early Republic for guidelines, are largely given over to portraits, drawn from correspondence and biographies, of Thomas Jefferson and John Adams as disinterested public servants and leaders dedicated to the common good and implacably opposed to usurious private banking interests.

In Pound's view, the republican virtues of these leaders were fostered during the extension of the Jeffersonian era through the administrations of Madison, Monroe, and Van Buren (to Pound the last great, and ignored, champion of the public good against the bankers). The election of 1840, won by money Whigs masquerading as frontiersmen, brought in the vice of *luxuria*. It marked the beginning of the rise of the plutocracy that was to enslave the Republic in the course of the nineteenth century.

Although focused primarily on the early national period, the eleven cantos, like those preceding, range over many centuries as Pound quotes from and alludes to other sources and events in history and literature. Two cantos depart from the prevailing economic and political concerns of the group. Canto 36 is largely given over to Pound's rendering, in archaic language, of Guido Cavalcanti's "Donna mi prega." Canto 39, which one critic has described as a window through which one can see the underlying Odyssean symbolism of the *Cantos*, evokes the sensual abandon of Circe's house and acknowledges Odysseus' healthy acceptance of her invitation to love. The celebration of physical passion as a creative force ("His rod hath made god in my belly . . . I have eaten the flame") looks back to the invocation of Aphrodite in Canto 1 and stands in contrast to the sterile lust of the usurers. Canto 41, the last of the group, ends with a reference to the munitions makers as hucksters of death, a recurrent theme in Pound's poetry during these years:

> Copper from England thru Sweden . . . Mr Hatfield
> Patented his new shell in eight countries.

72

Another operator of the same breed is portrayed in Canto 38:

> and he, Metevsky said to the one side . . .
> he said: the other boys got more munitions . . .

> Don't buy until you can get ours.
> And he went over the border
>   and he said to the other side:
> The *other* side has more munitions. Don't buy
>   until you can get ours.

The Fifth Decad of Cantos (1937) is also dominated by Pound's economic interests, now focused on the Guild Socialism of A. R. Orage, editor of the *New Statesman,* and on the Social Credit theory of Major C. H. Douglas. Pound absorbed elements of the radical theory of both these men into his own developing "Jeffersonian-Confucian" viewpoint. In these cantos, he groups Orage and Douglas with Mussolini (whom he had earlier likened to Jefferson and Adams) as "constructive" men who seek to defend the commonwealth from the predations of usurers. Beyond the disruption of equitable distribution caused by capitalism, there is the root sin, to which Pound keeps coming back, of profits which come from the possession of money rather than productive labor. Pound sees the system as one under which banking interests can create out of nothing (*ex nihilo*) and manipulate the medium for which others must labor at a disadvantage:

> Hath benefit of interest on all
> the moneys which it, the bank, creates out of nothing.

Pound's argument is most effectively set forth in Canto 45, which stands out in gemlike clarity amidst the splintered history of most of the cantos as it details the human costs of *usura,* branded a sin against nature:

> With *Usura*
> With usura hath no man a house of good stone
> each block cut smooth and well fitting
> that design might cover their face . . . .

73

Beyond the sacrifice of craft to profit, there is the corruption of the economy as products are adulterated, of art as values are corroded, and "the line grows thick" with *usura* as the Baroque emerges from the decadence of the Renaissance. Beyond the thwarting of productivity and creativity, there is an interference with biological fertility as:

> Usura slayeth the child in the womb
> It stayeth the young man's courting
> It hath brought palsey to bed, lyeth
> between the young bride and her bridegroom
>   CONTRA NATURAM
> They have brought whores for Eleusis
> Corpses are set to banquet
> at behest of usura.

In this brief but fully realized poem, the destructive force of *usura* is demonstrated more dramatically and effectively than it could be in Pound's prose tracts or in the tractlike passages of the other cantos of this period.

In Canto 47, he turns back again to Circe's cave to celebrate natural passion and fertility in a setting free of the influence of money:

> The light has entered the cave. Io! Io!
> The light has gone down into the cave,
> Splendour on splendour!
> By prong have I entered these hills:
> That the grass grow from my body . . . .

Cantos LII–LXXI (1940), the largest separately published group, appeared in a volume of 167 pages with a table of contents that shows it to consist of two differing but thematically related "decads." The "Chinese" cantos (52–61) present in a highly selective and compressed fashion a survey of more than four millennia of Chinese history in which dynasty follows dynasty with a staccato rapidity not unlike that of the interminable "begats" of the Old Testament chronicles. Confronted with a kaleidoscopic overview of a vast and unfamiliar subject, the reader is not likely to achieve any sense of the pattern of Chinese history, although he can recognize that Pound is singling out for praise rulers who exemplify the Confucian virtues and who try to conserve and renew the common resources of the nation. In the Adams cantos (62–71), Pound is more successful in his effort to create poetry out of the materials of history. Even with the fragmentation of detail that had by this time become characteristic of his work, Pound's portrait of John Adams manages to convey a coherent sense of the personality and viewpoint of the man he admired as the "clearest head in Congress" and an unselfish public servant who hated the "swindling banks" that had "ruin'd our medium. . . ."

In the Chinese cantos, which reveal the hazards of Pound's ideogrammic method of presenting what he thought of as "piths and gists" rather than sustained argument, the reader who makes his way through may be able to extract certain nuggets of wisdom basic to Pound's avowed Confucianism: He will find that Pound considers "the true base of credit" to be "the abundance of nature / with the whole folk behind it," in keeping with the Confucian ideal of adjustment of human culture to the natural process; that he approves of the principle of *ching-ming*, that is, to call *things* by their right *names*; and that he believes in the necessity of renewal in art as in nature. In Canto 53, he praises the emperor Tching Tang, who wrote "MAKE IT NEW" on his bathtub and who, during a period of drought and scarcity in 1766 B.C., opened a copper mine, "made discs with square holes in their middles / and gave these to the people / wherewith they might buy grain." Tching did not go to the bankers of his day, whose interest demands would have raised an insurmountable artificial barrier between the people and the fulfillment of their needs. Quite properly, he assumed the power of the government to originate money and thus create the resources for the welfare of the people.

In the Adams cantos, Pound makes use of some secondary but more often primary sources in the form of Adams's letters to his wife, Abigail, and to political associates, especially Jefferson. Perhaps because of his immersion in these chronologically ordered sources, Pound follows Adams's career in a more systematic and orderly fashion than usual: from Adams's early involvement in the Revolutionary movement in Boston and long period of service as an American representative in France,

Holland, and England, through the years of his presidency and his retirement, culminating in the historic correspondence with his old ally and rival, Thomas Jefferson, until the time of their common rendezvous with death on the fiftieth anniversary of the Declaration of Independence.

Pound admires Adams for his unselfish devotion to public service: "I don't receive a shilling a month, wrote Mr Adams to Abigail / in seventeen 74." He also approves Adams's humanitarian concern for the welfare of seamen, interest in the conservation of fisheries and other natural resources, promotion of friendly relations abroad, and avoidance during his presidency of Indian troubles and of war with France. Pound is especially sympathetic with Adams's distrust and impotent hatred of the banking interests and makes use of a marginal bar to accentuate Adams's judgment of banks of discount:

> Every bank of discount is downright corruption
> taxing the public for private individuals' gain.
> and if I say this in my will
> the American people wd/ pronounce I died crazy.

The link with the Chinese cantos is made explicit by Pound's repeated use of the *ching-ming* term and ideograph to endorse Adams's habit of clear perception and plain speaking. At the end of Canto 70, Adams's statement "I am for balance" is followed by one of Pound's favorite ideographs, the sign 中 "to stand firm in the middle." In this way, the American leader of the early Republic is identified with the Confucian emperors admired by Pound, with the difference that the historical context and the character of the American are more familiar to the reader and more fully specified by the poet. There are also important differences, not acknowledged by Pound, between the traditional monarchist views of the Chinese rulers and the progressive republican outlook of the (conservative) American revolutionary.

In the groups of cantos that followed the first sixteen, Pound turned to history, under the pressure of events, and wrote poems in which the Odyssean quest, with its classical context, persisted only as a largely submerged theme while he attempted to find answers to the economic dilemma of his time. His impulse to explore the roots of his native culture was one he shared with many other American writers during the 1930s, a period of intense cultural assessment and revaluation.

With the appearance of *The Pisan Cantos* (1948), another shift occurred as Pound, writing as a prison poet, was forced to take account of his own predicament and adjust to it. As a political prisoner, he was in large measure a victim of history rather than, as formerly, a confident historical theorist. But he was also a man alone, under duress, faced with the problem of survival, not only in physical but in moral and psychological terms. Although the mythic and historical preoccupations of the earlier parts were not left behind entirely, in these eleven cantos (74–84) Pound found it necessary to confront, directly and personally, the problem of the values upon which his life depended. In doing so, he considered more fully and directly than in any of his earlier work his relations with his fellow men and nature and his vocation as an artist.

Besides being the most personal of all Pound's poems, the Pisan cantos are the only ones in which there is a definite sense of the poet's immediate environment as it impinges upon him inescapably. The place is the American army's prison camp ("Disciplinary Training Center") near Pisa, where Pound was confined from May to November 1945 (for three weeks in a steel cage) before being flown to Washington, indicted for treason, and remanded to St. Elizabeth's Hospital. Living in the midst of murderers, rapists, thieves—the army's most hardened offenders—Pound looks out in these poems upon the ruins of not only Mussolini's Fascist order in Italy, which he had supported, but the "broken ant-hill" of Europe. Nostalgically but unsentimentally, he mourns the loss of better days and gone companions. Resisting the crushing pressures of prison life, he struggles to sustain himself through his contacts with nature, his memories of the past, and his commitment to art. Though his reforming pedagogic spirit has not died, it is in abeyance. There is a continuation of the theme of *usura* as the prime root of social evil, but without the strident exhortations of some of the earlier cantos. What preaching there is introduces a new note of humility: "Pull down thy vanity. . . ."

Occasionally, however, there are eruptions of prejudice, including unfeeling allusions to the Nazi treatment of the Jews.

There are also some condescendingly humorous references to "niggers" and "shades," as in "I like a certain number of shades in my landscape." Intrusions of this kind disfigure the poetry and offend the reader. They are greatly outweighed, however, by passages in which Pound is at the height of his powers as a master of imagistic lyric verse.

Sometimes, in fact, the reader must be impressed by the poetry and the sensibility it represents, even when he cannot share Pound's sympathies. The first canto opens with the image of Mussolini and his mistress hung by the heels in Milan after having been killed by partisans. Characterizing the Duce as a "twice crucified Christ," Pound identifies the lost leader with Malatesta as an architect of a visionary city:

> To build the city of Dioce whose terraces are
> the colour of stars.
> The suave eyes, quiet, not scornful,
> rain also is of the process.
> What you depart from is not the way
> and olive tree blown white in the wind
> washed in the Kiang and Han
> what whiteness will you add to this whiteness,
> what candor?

The dream is that of Pound, not Mussolini (upon whom it is projected), and the compelling power of the lines derives from the intensity of the poet's aspiration, not the discredited leader's. The vision of a renewed order, based on the poet's Jeffersonian and Confucian ideals, seems defeated, but it is one that Pound will not let go:

> I surrender neither the empire nor the temples
> plural
> nor the constitution nor yet the city of Dioce

The idealism of Pound's secular dream is admirable, even though he mistakenly identifies his objective with the program of a shoddy Fascist regime.

The identification with Odysseus with which Pound had begun *The Cantos* continues, but with a greater emphasis on the adversities of the hero as "noman" and "a man on whom the sun has gone down." Pound identifies his own ordeal in the cage made from steel airfield landing mats with Odysseus' wreck before being cast up on the shore where Nausicaa found him:

> hast'ou swum in a sea of air strip
>> through an aeon of nothingness,
> when the raft broke and the waters went over me . . . .

More significantly, Pound appears in these cantos in his own person, self-designated as "Old Ez"—itself something of a persona, as his old friend William Carlos Williams observed. He describes his experiences and thoughts as a prisoner, looks back at his past life, and sums up his present outlook. He who had been "hard as youth sixty years" is forced to recognize the toll of age and deprivation. He speaks of fatigue "deep as the grave" and notes, in an unprecedentedly personal way, "the loneliness of death came upon me / (at 3 P.M., for an instant)." The second last of the Pisan cantos ends with the impatient plea, "Oh let an old man rest." Yet there is a dignity and basic disinterestedness in Pound's acceptance of his situation:

>> Old Ez folded his blankets
> Neither Eos nor Hesperus has suffered wrong at my hands

There is always the oppressive reality of the prison into which he has been thrust, "with Barabbas and 2 thieves beside me." Looking about, he reflects, "so lay men in Circe's swine-sty." But these men are his companions, and as a reject himself, a defiant outsider like Villon, Pound shares their hatred and contempt for the grand offenders who wield power in a corrupt society:

> and the guards op/ of the . . .
>> was lower than that of the prisoners
> "all them g.d. m.f. generals c.s. all of 'em fascists"

Though his closest ties lie elsewhere, Pound recognizes that humanity and charity are "to be found among those who have not observed regulations." It was a fellow prisoner, a Negro, who had made him a writing desk from a packing case. The Confucian (as well as Christian and democratic) virtue of "filial, fraternal affection" which Pound praises as the "root of humaneness / the root of the process" is to be found among what society regards as its dregs as well as in higher places.

But this recognition is not enough to ease the desolation of an artist, no longer young, cut off from everything that had made up his life and cast into degrading confinement. Thrown drastically on his own resources, he finds support in his contact with nature and in memories of old times and old companions. The night sky with its constellations seen through the smoke hole of his tent is a link with the primitive world of the epic heroes. It is nature not through Homer—à la Pope—but nature encountered as closely and immediately as a cultured Homeric Greek (not an unlettered primitive) would see it. There is a new immediacy in Pound's observation of "the smell of mint under the tent flaps / especially after the rain," the white-chested martins on the barbed wire of the fence, the neat house of clay built under the tent roof by "Brother Wasp." "When the mind swings by a grass-blade," he comments, "an ant's forefoot shall save you."

He acknowledges a bond with the birds he fed and with the lizard which, he says, "upheld me." There is a sensitivity to the beauties of nature, especially in its freest and most accessible forms, the clouds, which Pound observes repeatedly, with the judgment that "The Pisan clouds are undoubtedly various / and splendid as any I have seen." And finally, in the last of these cantos, the affirmation:

> Under white clouds, cielo di Pisa
> out of all this beauty something must come . . . .

More important, since Pound is essentially a humanist, he finds solace in memories of old friends and companions, many now dead and commemorated as "lordly men . . . to earth o'ergiven," in a line recalled from his early translation of "The Seafarer." Among these men, dead and living, remembered as forerunners or leaders of the modern revolution, are W. B. Yeats, sometimes recalled humorously as Uncle William; Henri Gaudier-Brzeska, an early London friend and promising sculptor, lost in the First World War; James Joyce, "Jim the comedian singing"; Ford Madox Ford, formerly Hueffer, known familiarly as Fordie; William Carlos Williams, a close friend since student days at the University of Pennsylvania; Wyndham Lewis, painter-novelist and fellow Vorticist whose portrait of Pound hangs in the Tate Gallery; T. E. Hulme, coleader of the Imagist movement, like Gaudier-Brzeska, killed in the war; E. E. Cummings, "kumrad" because of the interest in Communism that had led him to make a disillusioning trip to Russia; Henry James, not a friend, but glimpsed and remembered as a link with the past; and that old friend and former ally, T. S. Eliot, often referred to as the Possum, sometimes as tse-tse.

In confinement, Pound characteristically finds his greatest stay in his commitment to beauty and his sense of identity as an artist. He quotes and later repeats Aubrey Beardsley's observation that "beauty is difficult." He remembers the Philistine neglect of the first edition of Fitzgerald's *The Rubaiyat of Omar Khayyam*, which lay unnoticed, in London, "till Rossetti found it remaindered at about two pence." He regrets his neglect of an opportunity to meet Swinburne ("my only miss"), not just for Swinburne's sake but because Swinburne had seen Landor plain. He thinks of Whitman, ignored and rejected in his own time—"exotic, still suspect / four miles from Camden"—and quotes two verses of the mockingbird's song of frustration and grief in "Out of the Cradle Endlessly Rocking": "O troubled reflection / O Throat, O throbbing heart." He thinks of himself, rejected and looking out at a ruined world, but still the artist: "As a lone ant from a broken ant-hill / from the wreckage of Europe, ego scriptor." And he invokes the image of "the rose in the steel dust" as a symbol of the beauty abstracted and ordered through art, just as steel filings are ordered by the power of the magnet.

This commitment to poetry and confidence in its power are typical of Pound, who had earlier voiced the same sentiment in the face of the disillusion of the First World War in the "Envoi" of *Hugh Selwyn Mauberley*. But in *The Pisan Cantos*, the belief in art is combined with a belief in the human capacity for endurance and love. What is most striking about these poems is a persistence of confidence in the midst of conditions that had brought Pound to the brink of disintegration during his ordeal in the cage. The affirmation is based on the bedrock of human amity and love. It is what remains as an unquenchable inner

81

resource when a cultured, humane man is stripped of his accustomed associations and his place in the world. "Nothing matters," Pound repeats, "but the quality of the affections." He develops the theme in a traditional lyric (reminiscent of the earlier "Envoi") which begins:

> What thou lovest well remains,
> the rest is dross
> What thou lov'st well shall not be reft from thee
> What thou lov'st well is thy true heritage

The subsequent admonition to be humble before the green world ("Pull down thy vanity") leads into a contrasting statement of humanistic pride in having tried as a man to realize his ideals in action:

> But to have done instead of not doing
> this is not vanity
> To have, with decency, knocked
> That a Blunt should open
> To have gathered from the air a live tradition
> or from a fine old eye the unconquered flame
> This is not vanity.
> Here error is all in the not done,
> all in the diffidence that faltered . . .

Although *The Cantos* from the beginning represented a humanistic quest for values in the modern world, the Pisan cantos differ from all that preceded in their focus on an irreducible personal integrity as the necessary foundation of the poet's values and attitudes—subject to human error though these might be.

In addition to Pound's established technique of fragmented rather than sequential presentation (an old subject of criticism), the shifts in his viewpoint and his preoccupations during the three decades covered by the first eighty-four cantos inevitably detract from the unity of the poem as a whole. But these changes, sometimes very abrupt, as in the new direction assumed by the *Eleven New Cantos* (1934), are perhaps more appropriate to a modern epic than a classical unity of subject and tone would be. For *The Cantos* is obviously a poem written "in process" by a poet aware of the problems of historical novelty and change and of the difficulties of maintaining a steady course as a voyager in the stream of twentieth-century culture. In view of the misfortunes that befell him, it is remarkable that this Odyssean wanderer did not go under utterly in the course of his voyage.

Although *The Pisan Cantos* might well have provided a fitting conclusion to Pound's modern odyssey, they were not the end of the poet, or his expression, since he survived imprisonment. There were three further volumes of cantos, but all seem something of a decline from the power displayed in *The Pisan Cantos*. In *Section: Rock-Drill 85–95 de los Cantares* (1956) and *Thrones 96–109 de los Cantares* (1959)—both written during his confinement in St. Elizabeth's Hospital in Washington (1946–58)—Pound reverted to his earlier polemical concerns. Surrounded by disciples, including political crackpots and racist demagogues as well as illusioned younger poets, Pound assumed again the role of an economic and social prophet and attempted to disseminate his ideas through pamphlets and a huge correspondence that reached all quarters of the globe. Both *Rock-Drill* and *Thrones* are loaded with allusions (unintelligible to most readers) to Pound's current reading and economic concerns. They also contain lyric passages of undiminished power celebrating love and natural beauty and candor or clarity of expression. While acknowledging his shortcomings and failures, Pound insists, as in *The Pisan Cantos*, that he will not surrender his *paradiso*, or dream of an ideal order (the "city of light").

The same qualities mark the poems of Pound's last collection, *Drafts and Fragments of Cantos CX–CXVII* (1969), in which the limpid sensuous beauty of the seascape at the end of Canto 2 infuses passages like the following from Canto 110:

> And in thy mind beauty, O Artemis,
>   as of mountain lakes in the dawn,
> Foam and silk are thy fingers,
>   Kuanon,
> and the long suavity of her moving,
>   willow and olive reflected,
> Brook-water idles,
>   topaz against pallor of under-leaf
> The lake waves Canaletto'd
>   under blue paler than heaven . . . .

In the draft of Canto 116, Pound sees the advance of human knowledge and of his own understanding as "a little light / in great darkness." He admits his "failures and wrecks" and his inability to give unity to his vision (imaged often as a crystal ball): "I cannot make it cohere." ("Crystal," "Clarity," and "Light" recur frequently as associated images in the later cantos.) He continues to affirm the principle of disinterested love celebrated in *The Pisan Cantos*: "Charity I have had sometimes, / I cannot make it flow thru." The confession characteristically suggests a concern for the structural incoherence of *The Cantos* rather than for a personal inadequacy.

Pound's testimony points up the central formal problem of *The Cantos*: a radical discontinuity which may well be in accord with Pound's theory of the ideogram and his presentation of meaning in the form of "gists and piths" but which works against the possibility of a fully satisfying grasp of the pattern of the work as a whole. One can recognize the continuing interaction of past and present and the alternation of episodes representing "descents" to hell, of one sort or another, and visionary experiences of ideal beauty, love, and social harmony which Pound associates with the idea of a necessary *paradiso*. In both Homer and Dante, these devices function within a larger progressive pattern of events, a kind of mythos that is not present, in the same way, in *The Cantos*.

There are other models for the structure of events within *The Cantos*. In the immediate post-World War I years, when his poem was already under way, Pound discovered an analogue to his own work in the frescoes of Francesco del Cossa in the Palazzo Schifanoia in Ferrara. The frescoes are painted in three parallel strips or bands which extend around the inside walls of the hall of the palazzo. In the words of Hayden Carruth, who consulted with Pound about the relevance of the frescoes: "The top strip, based on Petrarch's *Trionfi*, comprises abstract scenes, allegories of the virtues, which Pound calls 'studies in values'; they correspond to the themes in the *Cantos* which represent 'the permanent, what is there'—the sea, myth, feeling embodied in art, etc. The middle strip of the frescoes is devoted to figures representing the signs of the zodiac, *i.e.*, the turning of the stars or cosmology. They correspond, Pound feels, to the recurrent elements of the *Cantos*, the recurrent images of history—voyages, discoveries, political rivalries, love stories. . . . The third and lowest strip of the Ferrara frescoes consists of scenes from the actual life of Borso d'Este (1413–1471), Duke of Ferrara, who also is a conspicuous figure in several of the Renaissance sections of the *Cantos*. These scenes, Pound says, correspond to the wealth of contemporary detail in the poem, reported as Pound himself has seen it; that is, to 'what is trivial, the casual.' The permanent, the recurrent, the ephemeral—these are the aspects of historical, cultural, and moral value in the *Cantos*; they govern not only the choice of objective substance but the thematic placement, usually in associative contrasts, of the incidents, types, and examples in the poem."

No doubt the best justification for the fact that Pound intermingles events from these three thematic levels—that of the personal present, history, and the ideal or myth—is that *The Cantos*, to an even greater extent than *Mauberley*, is a poem written in process, and one that comprehends a range of experience of discrete cultures, which understandably baffles the efforts of a modern poet toward unification or synthesis. Yet the fact remains that other modern writers, like James Joyce, have managed to impose an aesthetic unity upon materials of comparable complexity and that evidence of systematic organization is lacking in all of Pound's longer works.

Nevertheless, for all its confusion and complications, Pound's modern epic is unified by the central motive of the quest as an intellectual and aesthetic voyage of discovery—a journey through time, embracing both the poet's actual world and his heritage, and directed toward illumination or enlightenment for himself and his society. In the late draft of Canto 116, he speaks modestly of "The Vision of the Madonna / above the cigar butts" and of his impulse to affirm the "gold thread in the pattern" and to provide "A little light, like a rushlight / to lead back to splendour."

It is typical of the chastened mood of Pound's final years that the one brief draft of a canto (still uncollected) that he seems to have planned as a possible last word and conclusion to his work should express a like humility:

> I have tried to write Paradise
>
> Do not move.
>   Let the wind speak.
>   that is paradise.

Let the Gods forgive what I
have made
Let those I love try to forgive
what I have made.

It is only natural that the reader who confronts a lifework
of such magnitude and complexity should look for evidence of
some fulfillment of the poet's quest and consider what cantos
or groups of cantos may represent the reward of his effort. Some
have found Pound's fullest illumination in the celebrations of
light in the late cantos of *Rock-Drill* and *Thrones*. It seems to
me, however, that for most readers the Pisan cantos, with their
sharply defined world and their theme of existential self-revela-
tion, must stand as the climax and culmination of Pound's efforts
to achieve a modern epic.

It is significant that these cantos, in contrast to those that
precede, violate the modernist requirements of objectivity
and dramatic detachment which Pound, like Eliot, had
long supported. Yet his dropping of the mask, his speaking forth
in his own person of his deprivations and his rewards, re-
sulted in a poetry of greater emotional depth and intensity,
perhaps of greater authenticity, than most of his earlier more
pure and technically consistent work. Besides a current of deep
feeling new in his poetry and a lyricism reminiscent of his early
verse, there is a sense of the writer as a human presence behind
the moving words. In the essay "Vorticism" (1914), Pound
referred to his assumption of a sequence of masks or *personae*
as a search for selfhood and "sincere self-expression" in the con-
fusion of modern life. It might be argued that the long quest
ends successfully in the incongruous setting of the military
stockade at Pisa as the prison poet attempts to define *himself*
and his relation to his immediate world. For all their effect of
fragmentation, these poems are informed by Pound's indomitable
will to endure as a man and to persist in his work in the face
of great odds.

7. E. E. Cummings

BEST KNOWN for his eccentric typography and verse arrangements, Edward Estlin Cummings assumed the role of an irrepressible rebel against convention. He was actually one of the most traditional of modern American poets. Unlike most of his generation, who thought of themselves as anti-Romantics if not "classicists," Cummings gladly acknowledged the inspiration of the Romantic poets and embraced their ideas and attitudes, with certain variations of his own.

The autobiographical *i: six nonlectures* (1953) describes his happy childhood in Cambridge, Massachusetts, his early reading, his love of nature, his education at Harvard, his introduction to New York City, and his experiences in the First World War. Among the poems of love and nature he chose for reading with the "nonlectures," the first in order and importance is Wordsworth's "Ode: Intimations of Immortality from Recollections of Early Childhood," which had been a favorite of his mother's. Also included, in addition to selections from Shakespeare, Dante, and the classics, are Keats's "Ode on a Grecian Urn," the closing stanzas of Shelley's *Prometheus Unbound*, and the chorus "When the hounds of spring are on winter's traces" from Swinburne's *Atalanta in Calydon*.

Typically Romantic is the account of his childhood initiation into the mysteries of nature in Norton's Woods:

> Here as a very little child, I first encountered the mystery who is Nature; here my enormous smallness entered Her illimitable being; and here someone actually infinite or impossibly alive—someone who might almost (but not quite) have been myself—wonderingly wandered the mortally immortal complexities of Her beyond imagining imagination . . . . The wonder of my first meeting with Herself is with me now; and also with me is the coming (obedient to Her each resurrection) of a roguish and resistless More Than Someone: Whom my deepest selves unfailingly recognized, though His disguise protected him from all the world.

Cummings committed himself early to the heart and the life of instinct and to the belief that the creative imagination of the poet is radically different from the mechanistic reason of the scientist. He shared with Emerson, Thoreau, and Whitman a confidence in the divine self-sufficiency of the individual; and, unlike almost all of his contemporaries, he refused to accept any idea of the diminution of the self as a condition of life in the modern world. Like the Romantics, he believed that reality is subconsciously ideal or "spiritual" rather than rationally or objectively real and that this deeper reality manifests itself spontaneously through organic symbols and symbolic forms.

The modern revolution gave the organic principle a new impetus. Leaders like Ezra Pound endorsed the Romantic theory, even though they thought themselves opposed to Romanticism, when they called for verse composed in the sequence of the musical phrase rather than in the rhythm of the metronome. By the 1920s, Dadaism and Surrealism, with their emphasis on spontaneity and their rejection of conventional reality, had captured the imagination of many poets and artists of the *avant-garde*.

88

Cummings's first book of poems, *Tulips and Chimneys* (1923), established the attitudes and conventions that were to distinguish all his work. He wished to reject formal typography and syntax (the logic of language) in celebrating the life of feeling and passion of which spring was the "omnipotent goddess." He preferred the lower-case "i," which designates the natural unsophisticated self, to the "I" which represents the rational censorious ego; he assumed that it was the natural self that spoke through the poems of e. e. cummings.

Yet Cummings did not actually dispense with syntax, an essential principle of poetic as of linguistic structure. What he did was to distort and modify conventional syntax for his own ends, with the effect of establishing what his readers came to accept and to understand as a distinctively Cummingsesque species of syntax, admirably suited to his viewpoint and needs.

In metrics too, Cummings was not a complete revolutionary. In addition to many original poems in free forms, there are many others in conventional, often sing-song rhymed quatrains or in more or less strict sonnet patterns. Whatever their metrical pattern, most of his poems are Romantic celebrations of love and nature. There are others, however, quite different in tone, in which he speaks as a skillful satirist against any and all efforts to curb the freedom of the individual or ignore the reality of his vision.

Cummings's distinctive typography and verse arrangements quickly became a hallmark of his work. These mechanical conventions, the most commonly imitated features of his poetry, are usually functional, although the function may sometimes be obscure and the devices self-defeating.

The avoidance of capitalization at the beginning of sentences and the scrambling of punctuation represent an effort to break down the syntactical (logical) integrity of the sentence. The capitalization of letters within words is often intended to serve as a guide to emphasis and a key to meaning, as in this opening stanza of a brief mood poem:

> mOOn Over tOwns mOOn
> whisper
> less creature huge grO
> pingness

It is appropriate that the moon be magnified as the luminary of the subliminal dream world, the "real" world of the Romantic and Surrealist alike. The capitalization of the *O* in "tOwns" suggests a common property in and a link between the natural and human worlds. The large double *OO*'s of the "mOOn" may also suggest the eyelike gaze of a presiding spirit in nature.

It has been objected that such devices of capitalization are mere tricks of the eye that have no functional relationship to the poem as it is read and remembered. But these and other visual arrangements of the verses upon the page do condition the reader's response to and memory of the poem. They also can be recognized as a contribution to the Objectivist effort to establish the reality of the poem as a visual arrangement, an arti*fact*, rather than as simply a verbal sequence in the mind of the reader or rememberer.[1]

Cummings often breaks words to continue them in the next line or lines. Sometimes he fragments them so that their separate sounds occupy the position of lines or verses on the page. Often he develops the movement and conformation of the lines in a way that conveys a sense of the nature of the subject. In the poem beginning "O sweet spontaneous / earth," the sentence units are broken and the verses arranged to reinforce the suggestion of the sexual rhythms of the earth, personified and celebrated for its powers of renewal. The method is especially effective in the poem's closing lines:

> (but
>
> true
>
> to the incomparable
> couch of death thy
> rhythmic
> lover
>
> thou answerest
>
> them only with
>
> spring)

[1] See below, pp. 120–22 and 208.

Cummings's metrical arrangements are in accord with the organic theory of form which stems from Coleridge, Emerson, and Whitman. But beyond the functionalism prescribed by the Romantics, Cummings was interested in peculiarly modern ideas of form suggested by the painting of Picasso (whom he greatly admired) and the Cubists, among others. A number of his poems reveal an effort to resist the sequential and necessarily temporal nature of language and to achieve through word patterns some of the effects of simultaneousness of painting and the spatial arts. A poem describing the world transformed by fog combines the presentation of a scene with an interpolated, fragmented indication of time. It begins with a vertically arranged pattern of constricted verses:

un
der fog
's
touch

slo

The marginally extruded *slo* (the first fragment of the word *slowliest*) interrupts the presentation of a transformed world in which "people / be / come / un" as their forms are enveloped by the fog, which also turns "whichs" (echoing *witches*) into "whos"—or gives things the appearance of living creatures. The effect, as in the moon poem, is to undercut conventional reality and establish through metamorphosis, in nature as in art, a dream world. The attenuation achieved through the breaking and extending of words is appropriate to the gradual progress of the transformation. The interpolated "slo . . . wli . . . est," however, cannot be read sequentially as a part of a poetic continuum. The eye must turn back to reconstruct the word and to recognize its relation to the process of metamorphosis with which the whole poem is concerned. By thus combining temporal and spatial elements, the reader achieves a multidimensional conception of the poem comparable to the multidimensional effects of a Cubist painting.

Through his method, Cummings achieves a peculiar, yet typical, combination of the effect of precise observation and description of nature and, by virtue of his subject, that of an interfused sense of the dreamlike unreality (or superreality) of the scene.

One of Cummings's love poems introduces a vision of pigeons seen for an instant in the narrow sky above a city street:

l oo k-

pigeons fly ingand

whee(:are,SpRiN,kLiNg an in-stant with sunLight
then)l-
ing all go BlacK wh-eel-ing

The parenthetical insertion of shifting light imagery within the word *wheeling* is designed to fuse in time the perception of the movement of the birds and the simultaneous perception of brilliant changing colors (represented by the sprinkling of capital letters) that flash for only an instant in a flight that moves from sunlight into a shade in which the birds all go "BlacK." The spacing of the repeated "wh-eel-ing" suggests the tempo and the arcing movement of the solid flight of the flock. It is quite possible that the twinned *o*'s of the initial "l oo k," like those of the "mOOn" poem, are intended to suggest eyes in the act of seeing.

In one of Cummings's later poems, the word *loneliness* is similarly broken, though in a vertical arrangement, for the parenthetical observation "(a / le / af / fa / ll / s)." The vertical attenuation is in keeping with the path of the falling leaf, and the arrangement of the word fragments serves as an object of static contemplation rather than, as in the previous poem, a graphic approximation of vital movement. In both poems, the effort to represent organically and precisely a perception of a natural phenomenon confirms the fact of the coexistence, in much of Cummings's work, of an impulse toward the exact rendering of the visible world and an attempt to communicate, surrealistically, a sense of the more mysterious, unseen instinctual world.

Some of Cummings's verse reveals a fondness for overingenious and mechanical contrivance that was to become habitual.

In poem 9 of *No Thanks* (1935), the letter *o* is placed marginally at the left of the first line of the first stanza:

```
o pr
  gress verily thou art m
  mentous superc
  lossal hyperpr
  digious etc i kn
  w . . .
```

Confronting such a text, the reader is necessarily more preoccupied with the mechanics of reading than with the poet's rather obvious theme of the emptiness of technological progress. The arrangement seems to hold more interest as a visual puzzle than as a complex of various aspects of form. In this respect it more closely resembles the work of the later concretist poets,[2] who were influenced by Cummings, than it does most poetry in the modern organic tradition.

Sometimes the mere reading of a tortuously dismembered text requires such effort that the reader may feel pushed beyond the point of diminishing returns:

```
SNOW

cru
   is
     ingw Hi
sperf
     ul
lydesc


BYS FLUTTERFULLY IF

(endbegi ndesginb ecend)tang . . .
```

The appearance of Cummings's poems upon the page often obscures the fact that many are extremely conventional in their metrical patterns. Behind the disguise of fragmented words and

---

[2] See below, pp. 203–5.

dislocated lines, and sometimes without disguise, are many poems in regular rhymed iambic and tetrameter verses. Unlike most of his contemporaries, Cummings was fond of the sonnet, which he often used for the expression of typically Romantic attitudes. One such begins:

> this is the garden: colours come and go,
> frail azures fluttering from night's outer wing
> strong silent greens serenely lingering,
> absolute lights like baths of golden snow.
> This is the garden: pursed lips do blow
> upon cool flutes within wide gloom, and sing
> (of harps celestial to the quivering string)
> invisible faces hauntingly and slow.

The meter and rhyme scheme of the octave (abbaabba) and the following sestet (cdeecd) are those of the conventional Italian or Petrarchan sonnet. The central image of the garden suggests a retreat beyond the world of time, a dream world that can be identified with the subconscious. The sensuous qualities of this realm (its color and music), its fixity, and the presence of a "silver-fingered fountain" (the culminating image of the sestet) all suggest that the garden may, in the manner of Romantic and Symbolist poetry, represent the relatively stable world of art as distinguished from the flux of the temporal world. The vagueness of the imagery ("frail azures" and "strong silent greens") and the mellifluousness (often a swooningly smooth mellifluousness) of phrasing (as in "greens serenely lingering") are appropriate to the dream world setting. In its argument, metrical form, and personification of time and death (in the sestet), the poem is extremely conventional. It is also not among the best of Cummings's sonnets.

In other poems, the same kinds of conventions often exist, but less obviously, and sometimes even deceptively. One "disguised" sonnet begins:

> structure,miraculous challenge,devout am
> upward deep most invincible unthing
> —stern sexual timelessness,outtowering
> this noisy impotence of not and same . . . .

94

Despite the strangeness of the abstract imagery and the appearance of fragmentation and irregularity, the pattern of the traditional sonnet is only slightly roughed up. The rhyme scheme of the complete poem (abba cdcd efg egf) is a modest variation of the Petrarchan form. For all its appearance of idiosyncrasy and freedom, the sonnet is traditional in form and argument. The octave apostrophizes the "devout am" and "stern sexual timelessness" as attributes of the eternal life force. The eighth and ninth lines provide a transition to the sestet, which shifts the focus to "humanity," a small "hoping" (not hopping) insect which through its cycle of birth and death ("moult beyond difficult moult") achieves an "amazing doom" through identification with the life force. The argument is not novel. Historically, it is closest to Romantic pantheism, but beyond this it is reminiscent of Christian and more primitive forms of the rebirth archetype.

Many of Cummings's best-known poems are written in the ballad stanza, or variations thereof, or in tetrameter quatrains made up of couplets in exact or slant rhymes, as in "anyone lived in a pretty how town" and "my father moved . . .":

> my father moved through dooms of love
> through sames of am through haves of give,
> singing each morning out of each night
> my father moved through depths of height

This and other poems have a singsong regularity that might be defended on the ground of appropriateness to Cummings's cyclical and pantheistic viewpoint. Yet they are rhythmically less interesting and satisfying than the best of Cummings's free verse poems. There are fortunately enough of the latter to stand as a solid contribution to the revolutionary tradition and an inspiration to younger poets.

Cummings's language and imagery set him apart from most of his contemporaries. In a period in which objective presentation and the impersonal method were in vogue, Cummings preferred to speak directly, subjectively, and discursively, as in this first stanza of a typical short poem:

> since feeling is first
> who pays any attention
> to the syntax of things
> will never wholly kiss you . . . .

Syntax stands for reason, an enemy to spontaneous feelings. But Cummings himself is developing a logical argument. Despite the use of the archaic "who" for "he who," the stanza is a syntactically impeccable sentence. (It is also a classic example of the poetry of statement, an ill-favored mode among modern poets committed to the theory of the image.)

Cummings's diction and imagery have drawn a good deal of negative criticism for their failure to meet standards of precision and sensuous concreteness. A familiar example is R. P. Blackmur's early essay, "Notes on E. E. Cummings' Language" (1930). Blackmur complains of a "vagueness of image and a constant recurrence of words" which tend to be abstract and typical rather than concrete and specific. They include, among others, *thrilling, flowers, serious, absolute, sweet, unspeaking, utter, gradual, ultimate, final, serene, frail, grave, tremendous, fragile, groping, dim, tremulous, keen, ecstatic.* Of all these, *flower* stands out as a key word, pregnant with mystic suggestiveness but indeterminate in its reference. Cummings's association of this word with an abstract idea and his tendency to treat the poem as a private dream rather than as an expression objectified by established language conventions rob his work of "communicable precision" in Blackmur's opinion.

But undue emphasis on this one test of poetic language may be unreliable, especially for Cummings. A "vagueness of image" and generalized diction seem especially suited to his anti-intellectuality and his preference for the world of dream, with its protean imagery, over the more stable world of waking reality.

Moreover, Cummings's repeated words are not meaningless in their contexts. One ignored by Blackmur is *spring*, the "omnipotent goddess." Introduced as a personification in the first poem of his first book (where it is identified with the earth and the earth goddess), it recurs almost obsessively in his subsequent work. For Cummings, spring, in all its manifestations, is the life force in nature, existing in man as the libido. His devotion to this power is constant, although his tone may vary from the playful familiarity of "spring slattern of seasons you / have dirty legs and a muddy / petticoat. . . ." More seriously regarded, spring is the mysterious reality which underlies and determines all the shifting forms of the phenomenal world:

Spring is like a perhaps hand
(which comes carefully
out of Nowhere) arranging
a window, into which people look (while
people stare
arranging and changing placing
carefully there a strange
thing and a known thing here) and

changing everything carefully . . . .

One does not have to share Cummings's outlook to recognize that he is adapting to his needs the familiar language of nature mysticism. Although antecedents of his nature poems can be found in Wordsworth and Emerson, the closest parallels are with Whitman's *Leaves of Grass*. Both Whitman and Cummings view human love as a manifestation of a more than human power, and both express their pantheism in sensuous and often sensual terms. In an early poem, "when god lets my body be," Cummings describes a process of transformation in which, after what is regarded as death, trees will sprout from his eyes and a rose issue from his lips. The poem ends:

My strong fingers beneath the snow

Into strenuous birds shall go
my love walking in the grass

their wings will touch with her face
and all the while shall my heart be

With the bulge and nuzzle of the sea

Although the regularity of the couplet form, only thinly disguised by the spacing of the poem, makes for awkwardness in wording, the argument is something like that of Whitman in section 5 of "Song of Myself" ("I mind how once we lay . . ."), which brings the realization, through a sensuous mystical experience, that "a kelson of the creation is love." There is a further likeness, despite the greater delicacy and even prettiness of

97

Cummings's imagery, between the two poets' use of nature and the sea. Cummings's "bulge and nuzzle of the sea" is in spirit much like Whitman's sensual sea imagery. His conclusion is also reminiscent of Whitman's pungent farewell at the end of "Song of Myself":

> I bequeath myself to the dirt to grow from the grass I love;
> If you want me again look for me under your boot-soles.

Although Cummings's language and imagery are not meaningless, there is a weakness in his ideas. His poems of love and nature tend toward monotony because his viewpoint is rigid and unqualified. His poems of praise too often lack intellectual fiber and awareness of complexities and contradictions. Cummings celebrates spring as a symbol of a controlling force behind each life and at the same time insists upon the freedom of the individual. The inconsistency is not novel, especially among American writers, but it points to a problem that forebears like Emerson and Whitman recognized.

But Cummings is not only a rhapsodist. As a social observer and satirist he speaks in quite another voice. The viewpoint is much the same, but in his satirical poems emotion is subordinated to wit (though often a wit suffused with strong feeling), and the poet's hostile attention is sharply focused upon such targets as middle-class conventionality, commercialism and materialism, social and political regimentation, and that crowning inhumanity, war.

One of Cummings's best-known early poems is in the form of a modified Italian sonnet (abcd dcba efg gfe) which begins:

> the Cambridge ladies who live in furnished souls
> are unbeautiful and have comfortable minds
> (also, with the church's protestant blessings
> daughters, unscented shapeless spirited)
> they believe in Christ and Longfellow, both dead,
> are invariably interested in so many things . . . .

In contrast to the generalized language of many of Cummings's love poems, that of his satirical verse tends to be concrete and precise. The allusions and images work as novel devices to

98

expose various facets of the familiar theme of the pettiness and sterility of the New England genteel tradition. The reference to Christ as dead is not so much a denial of Jesus, whom Cummings admires, as a condemnation (like that of Emerson and the Transcendentalists) of the institutional stultification of Christianity.

The phoniness of modern civilization ("illusion" in the Romantic vocabulary) is a frequent theme. Among specific targets of Cummings's satire is commercialism and the resulting standardization of the life of people who live by sentimental clichés, applauding, as Cummings observes in "Humanity i love you," all "songs containing the words country home and / mother when sung at the old howard."[3] The theme is extended in "Poem, or Beauty Hurts Mr. Vinal," which cites the trademarks and slogans (current in the 1920s) in which the citizens of the Republic, like Arthur Miller's Willy Loman, put their trust:

> . . . my country, 'tis of
>
> you, land of the Cluett
> Shirt Boston Garter and Spearmint
> Girl With The Wrigley Eyes . . .
> . . . of you i
> sing:land of Abraham Lincoln and Lydia E. Pinkham,
> land above all of Just Add Hot Water and Serve—
> from every B. V. D.
>
> let freedom ring . . . .

In "a salesman is an it that stinks Excuse," the huckster is treated as a thing rather than a man because he represents a system in which men lie for their livelihood, in which deceit is essential to success. But the salesman is not just a clerk or commercial traveler. He is also, in Cummings's poems, the successful evangelist, selling the good news; the successful editor, selling scandal, but not telling the truth when it touches money interests; the successful politician ("an arse upon / which everyone has sat except a man"), selling the public.

[3] The "Old Howard" was a Boston burlesque house much frequented by Harvard students and visiting sailors.

The literary world is permeated by the same tendencies. In a single quatrain, Cummings neatly dusts off a minor poet and major anthologist (Louis Untermeyer) for pushing his own work through his collections and thus selling "the many on the few / not excluding mr u." The poem on Mr. Vinal (already cited) ridicules the standardized fare of the little magazines ("radically defunct periodicals"), introducing the poet of the school of T. S. Eliot, whom Cummings elsewhere calls "Tears" Eliot, crouched on the "sternly allotted sandpile" (the waste land) in the agony of expression.

Ever since the disillusioning experience of a visit to Russia described in *Eimi* (1933), Cummings had been hostile to the idea of the welfare state and of progress based on science. Economic security means the surrender of the individual to the state. Progress is a disease in which the victim (man) plays, through science and technology, "with the bigness of his littleness." He contrasts the dead world of science ("a world of made") with the vitality of the organic world ("a world of born"). The view is in key with his habitual opposition of feeling and thought:

> (While you and i have lips and voices which
> are for kissing and to sing with
> who cares if some oneeyed son of a bitch
> invents an instrument to measure Spring with?

Amusing though these lines may be, they flaunt a crude anti-intellectualism which is one of the less attractive strains in Cummings's Romanticism.

Cummings's poems, like Emerson's lecture-essays, are aimed at an elite of beautiful souls capable of sharing the writer's transcendental view. His outlook also incorporates some of the upper middle-class Protestant New Englander's ingrained social attitudes. Members of a lower stratum are treated with condescension and distaste in a number of poems written in a "tough guy" language:

> buncha hardboil guys from duh A.C. fulla
> hooch kiddin eachudder bout duh clap an
> talkin big how dey could kill
> sixereight cops . . . .

Cummings's prejudice extends to the "kike," whom he describes as "invented . . . out of a jew a few / dead dollars and some twisted laws."

War is a subject that Cummings attacked in various moods. A member of the war generation, with the special experience of incarceration in a French military prison—lyrically described in his first book, *The Enormous Room* (1922)—Cummings early became disenchanted with organized slaughter. Among lighter poems on the subject, "my sweet old etcetera aunt lucy" playfully contrasts home-front illusions about the First World War with the reality of life in the trenches. A grimmer poem, in which the soldier-subject is himself fatally illusioned, is that beginning "plato told / him:he couldn't / believe it(jesus / told him;he / wouldn't believe / it). . . ." The closing lines reveal the lesson learned too late:

> . . . we told him
> (he didn't believe it,no
>
> sir)it took
> a nipponized bit of
> the old sixth
>
> avenue
> el;in the top of his head:to tell
>
> him

In a completely serious and indignant vein, "i sing of Olaf glad and big" details the ways in which an idealistic and uncompromising conscientious objector, committed to love and creativity, is repressed and finally destroyed by the military system.

Like twentieth-century novelists from Dos Passos to Joseph Heller, Cummings saw the military organization as a microcosm of the modern industrial state, which he hated and feared. Its pressures upon the individual provided him with a persistent theme.

Poems of the Second World War and the postwar years reveal the same commitment to freedom and protest against its violation. Objecting to the sacrifice of morality to political expediency, Cummings heaps scorn, in "Thanksgiving (1956)," upon both the United Nations and the United States for standing aside indifferently and letting Hungary's gallant bid for freedom from a "slave's unlife" be quelled by Russian force.

Most of Cummings's satire looks back to the Romantic tradition in its defense of individual freedom and criticism of social conformity and corruption. It is also part of a literature of social criticism and protest that began in America with the Romantics and continued to flourish in the fiction of the late nineteenth and early twentieth centuries. As a distinguished verse satirist, Cummings made a unique contribution to this tradition of protest and dissent.

8. Marianne Moore

THE POEMS of Marianne Moore, one of the most original members of the individualistic generation of the moderns, are distinguished by intelligence, humor, and needle-point precision. Although Miss Moore was devoted to the principle of organic form, her poems differ from those of her fellow free verse writers in their observance of a strict measure or count of syllables. The line lengths of any one of her stanzas may vary, but the syllabic pattern of the stanza as a whole corresponds closely with that of others in the same poem. Though seemingly eccentric and arbitrary, her arrangements are usually appropriate to their subjects.

The principle of syllabic verse is of course far from new. Stemming from classical Latin verse, this type of measure was favored by nineteenth-century English poets, including Walter Landor. In the twentieth century, Marianne Moore was certainly the most distinguished and consistent syllabic poet among the writers of the years between the wars. More recently, syllabic verse has proved attractive to many poets involved in the resurgence of free verse during the post-World War II years, because it provides a restrictive discipline that encourages condensation and intensity, while at the same time the method permits a good deal of natural freedom. In a recent interview, Donald Justice has commented on his interest in syllabic verse as a resource for the modern poet:

> Syllabics are a guide, a clue, a help, an aid to the writer in establishing for himself the sense of form he's working with in the poem. But I don't think they are of much use to the reader. . . . They don't seem to do anything for the ear of the reader. But they seem to have had something to do with shaping the idea, or allowing it to shape itself for the writer. I look on syllabics as a writer's form instead of a reader's form.

The concern for the shaping principle of a given poem, as an organic expression of the writer's perception and thought, is a distinguishing feature of the work of Marianne Moore.

Miss Moore's interest in detailed patterns might well suggest a rationalistic belief that the world is susceptible to easy ordering. But the impulse toward order in her poems exists side by side and in tension with a full awareness of irrationality, disorder, and violence as inescapable conditions of life. The mind, she believed, must recognize the intransigence of experience as it pursues, carefully and flexibly, the task of informing its world with meaning. By exploiting imaginatively the very limitations of life and of the metrical patterns she devised, Marianne Moore created poems of unusual freshness and distinction.

Her idea of organic form is concisely expressed in "To a Snail," a twelve-line poem that begins, "If 'compression is the first grace of style,' / you have it." Admired for its "contractility," "absence of feet," and concealed "principles," the snail is a compendium of modest virtues that distinguish it not simply as a creature adapted to its natural environment but as a symbol of aesthetic and specifically poetic form. A concluding reference to "the curious phenomenon of your long occipital horn" suggests the sensory apparatus of the poet, who must also maintain intimate contact with his environment, avoiding undue intellectual abstraction—even though his single horn, like that of the mythical unicorn, is a talisman of the "magical" power of meta-morphosis. But this snail is not symbol-ridden. It retains its individuality. By respecting its identity while relating it to her own, Miss Moore performed the feat of composing at once an imagistic poem and a brief aesthetic of organic poetry without the overt didacticism of Archibald MacLeish's "Ars Poetica": "A poem should be palpable and mute / As a globed fruit . . . . A poem should not mean / But be."

The treatment is in keeping with Marianne Moore's disposition toward all creatures, whether of land, air, or sea. The range of her interests can be seen in the wide array of her subjects— many exotic and the result of reading rather than immediate observation—about which she wrote. They include, among others, the jerboa, pelican, buffalo, monkey, ostrich, snake, octopus, skunk, elephant, chameleon, jellyfish, giraffe, crow. To all she paid the uncommon courtesy of close attention, viewing them with respect and, more often than not, with a lively interest in their aesthetic implications. In its root sense, aesthetics is concerned with the act of perception (*aesthanesthai*, "to perceive"). Miss Moore spoke of her poems as "observations," a word she took as the title for her second collection of verse (1924).

The ostrich is the subject of "He 'Digesteth Harde Yron,' " a poem admired by Wallace Stevens, who wrote an essay about it. Characteristically precise is the description of the bird as one "whose comic duckling head on its / great neck revolves with compass-needle nervousness / when he stands guard." Contrasting the ostrich with the extinct roc and moa, Marianne Moore attributes its survival to solicitude for its young, defensive rather than offensive strength, and wariness, especially of men. It is contrasted with human beings, who use disguise and stratagem, the techniques of the confidence man, to hunt it:

. . . How
could he, prized for plumes and eggs and young,
used even as a riding-beast, respect men
hiding actor-like in ostrich skins, with the right hand
making the neck move as if alive
and from the bag the left hand

strewing grain, that ostriches
might be decoyed and killed!

105

In its lack of greed and guile the ostrich is a reproach to its hunters. Miss Moore's treatment, although focused on the characteristics of the bird as bird, involves moral implications in her admiration of what should be human virtues.

"The Pangolin" is a tribute to the exotic armor-scaled toothless Asian anteater. Although it preys on insects, its strengths, like those of the ostrich, are mainly defensive. Even more than the ostrich, the pangolin is adapted to its environment in its physical structure and behavior. It has a machinelike equilibrium and efficiency that Miss Moore recognizes as grace. In beast as well as man, this virtue involves poise and functionalism:

> . . . Pangolins, made
> for moving quietly also, are models of exactness,
> on four legs; on hind feet plantigrade,
> with certain postures of a man.

The comparison leads to a contrast and an implied qualification of the praise of the animal. It can achieve grace more easily than man, who must struggle under such burdens as the responsibility of choice and the awareness of limitations. Man is more prone to mistakes, writing "error with four r's." But he possesses the saving grace, beyond the reach of beast, of a "sense of humor," essential to self-recognition and growth:

> . . . Among animals, one has a sense of humor.
> Humor saves a few steps, it saves years. Unignorant,
> modest and unemotional, and all emotion,
> he has everlasting vigor,
> power to grow . . . .

This power, however, is limited and circumscribed by fear. Despite his proneness to pride and vanity, man lives under its shadow because of his awareness of limits and contingencies:

> Not afraid of anything is he,
> and then goes cowering forth, tread paced to meet
> an obstacle
> at every step . . . .

Yet his fear is wondrously balanced by a persistent hope and expectancy, the source of a kind of courage that makes it possible for him to say to the "alternating blaze":

> "Again the sun!
> anew each day; and new and new,
> that comes into and steadies my soul."

Metrically, the poem is suited to its subject. The irregular stanzas, consistently repeated with lines progressively indented so that the left margin of each stanza scallops inward, are like the overlapping armor plates of the animal. The compactness and regularity of the following verses suggest the compactness and self-contained nature of the pangolin, which assumes a position of defensive withdrawal as he

> rolls himself into a ball that has
> power to defy all effort to unroll it;
> strongly intailed, neat
> head for core, on neck not breaking off,
> with curled-in feet.

The incurled posture of the soft creature within its shell is reinforced by the sound pattern of the lines, in which numerous long vowels are enclosed by such hard and abrupt consonants as *c*'s, *k*'s, and *t*'s.

The virtues celebrated in Miss Moore's ample bestiary often have aesthetic implications. "The Paper Nautilus" describes a female marine cephalopod (genus Argonauta) distinguished by a delicate papery shell. The poet praises this "devilfish's" solicitude for its unhatched eggs. The opening lines, which contrast the selfless motives of the nautilus with those of commercially inspired writers, express concern for the proper motives of the artist:

> For authorities whose hopes
> are shaped by mercenaries?
> Writers entrapped by
> teatime fame and by
> commuters' comforts? Not for these
> the paper nautilus
> constructs her thin glass shell.

The patterning of the shell produced by the freeing of the eggs ("wasp-nest flaws / of white on white") and the "close- / laid Ionic chiton-folds / like the lines in the mane of / a Parthenon horse" suggest the formal design of an artifact. The concluding acknowledgment of love as "the only fortress / strong enough to trust to," a tribute to the instructive maternal care of the sea creature, also implies that care and solicitude for a poem or other work are essential to the artist.

Miss Moore's comparisons are often humorous. In "The Wood-Weasel," the skunk, though outlawed for his offensive odor, is admired as an "inky thing / adaptively whited with glistening / goat fur." The natural foe of aggressors, he "smothers anything that stings." Yet he is a playful creature. The poet identifies herself with him ("Only / wood-weasels shall associate with me") on the strength of the traits they possess in common.

Despite her natural sympathies, Marianne Moore was neither sentimental nor romantic in her view of nature. In several poems the sea figures as an image, not of eternity nor the reality of spirit, but of the rapacity and indifference of nature. In "A Grave," the sea has nothing to offer but a "well excavated" place of burial:

> and the ocean under the pulsation of lighthouses and noise of
> bell buoys,
> advances as usual, looking as if it were not that ocean in which
> dropped things are bound to sink—
> in which if they turn and twist, it is neither with volition nor
> consciousness.

The sea also provides an image for the unusually discursive title poem of the volume *What Are Years* (1941), in which awareness of mortality is a paradoxical source of a peculiar strength:

> . . . He
> sees deep and is glad, who
> accedes to mortality
> and in his imprisonment rises
> upon himself as

        the sea in a chasm, struggling to be
        free and unable to be,
            in its surrendering
            finds its continuing.

In the third and last stanza, the image of the sea as uncon-
scious physical energy (the life force in man) is replaced by
that of a caged bird whose singing is a symbol of human will
and aspiration:

                . . . The very bird,
            grown taller as he sings, steels
        his form straight up. Though he is captive,
        his mighty singing
        says, satisfaction is a lowly
        thing, how pure a thing is joy.
            This is mortality,
            this is eternity.

Marianne Moore thus found in existential limitations a source
of a strength to affirm values in the face of loss. Metrically, the
limitations are represented by the verse patterns she devised.
Their appropriateness can be seen in the contrast between the
relatively regular, limited lines of the stanzas of "What Are
Years?" within the confines of which the straitened poet sings,
and the long flowing lines of "The Grave," in which the all-
enveloping sea is the abyss that finally claims all human goods.

Miss Moore prized the discipline of working and living within
limits, of making do with minimal means. Just as she admired
the snail for the economy of its form, she praised the reindeer
of "Rigorists," living in a cold climate on "scant *reino* / or
pasture," as models of adaptability and beauty.

Partly because of her economy and restraint, the imagery of
her verse gives the impression of a satisfying integrity and inde-
pendence. Even when it supplies a clearly discernible pattern
of metaphoric meaning, the structure of imagery is not sym-
bologically burdened or exploited for ulterior ends. Sometimes,
in fact, her poems do not show fully developed patterns of
metaphor, and the reader is left with unsolved if not insoluble
problems of interpretation.

"The Steeple Jack," with its New England seacoast town set on the edge of the ocean waste, presents an attractive ordered scene, with an abundance of detail reminiscent of the engravings of Dürer:

> Dürer would have seen a reason for living
> in a town like this, with eight stranded whales
> to look at; with the sweet sea air coming into your house
> on a fine day, from water etched
> with waves as formal as the scales
> on a fish.

This order, human and natural (with gulls soaring around the town clock and the lighthouse), stands in contrast to the eruption of uncontrollable disorder as the

> whirlwind fife-and-drum of the storm bends the salt
> marsh grass, disturbs stars in the sky and the
> star on the steeple; it is a privilege to see so
> much confusion.

In her first published version, Miss Moore broke off the stanza at this point, departing from the precise six-line pattern established by the first stanza and introducing a note of metrical disorder in keeping with her subject. In a later, revised version of the poem (1961), the stanza was regularized and followed by an insertion of five new stanzas devoted largely to a celebration of the exotic profusion of nature in even a New England setting. In both versions, the poet took account of an energy that defies human control and dwarfs human efforts to impose order and form upon nature.

In the last five stanzas of the poem, the scene shifts back to the center of the town, which has "a schoolhouse, a post-office in a / store, fish-houses, hen-houses, a three-masted / schooner on / the stocks," and focuses upon a human figure precariously suspended from the church spire and certified by a sidewalk sign as "C. J. Poole, Steeple Jack." The poem concludes with a further observation:

It could not be dangerous to be living
      in a town like this, of simple people,
who have a steeple-jack placing danger signs by the church
while he is gilding the solid-
      pointed star, which on a steeple
stands for hope.

Although the opening presents an ordered scene, the storm
introduces a principle of disorder which makes for a continuing
tension or conflict. The conclusion seems to acknowledge a nec-
essary human impulse toward order and value, tenuous and
inadequate though these must be. The church star, an emblem
of faith in an earlier day, is an insufficient symbol for the poet,
who recognizes the complexities and hazards of the world and
the puniness of human efforts to order it. Yet these efforts are
necessary if a human community is to exist. Miss Moore, who
achieves a kind of order in her own highly individualized fashion,
is aware of her kinship to the steeple jack.

The observation that "It could not be dangerous to be living /
in a town like this" raises a question. As Marianne Moore knew
well, it *is* dangerous to live in any town. One must conclude that
her tone is ironic—although its negative force is tempered by
admiration for the courage and persistence of human efforts to
achieve a necessary and necessarily fragile order in any place,
under any circumstances.

Miss Moore's interest in imagistic order and abstract design
resulted in some poems in which patterns of metaphoric mean-
ing, although obviously present, are neither fully developed nor
fully ascertainable.

In "The Fish," the opening verses, which require the title as
their subject, are imagistic and presentational:

THE FISH

wade
through black jade.
      Of the crow-blue mussel shells, one keeps
      adjusting the ash heaps;
            opening and shutting itself like

an
injured fan.

The repetition of the short, irregular stanzas is appropriate to the movement of the fish as they expand and contract their gills and move their fins to maintain equilibrium. (The stanzas are even somewhat fin-shaped.) The water as a medium which both transmits and distorts light rays transforms the scene, however, and the bodies of the fishes as identifiable shapes give way to a submarine landscape in which the forms represent the poet's perceptions—in which the abstract and phenomenal qualities of the scene are intensified:

> . . . The water drives a wedge
> of iron through the iron edge
> of the cliff; whereupon the stars,
>
> pink
> rice-grains, ink-
> bespattered jellyfish, crabs like green
> lilies, and submarine
> toadstools, slide each on the other.

The focus has shifted from the fish to an aquatic world of constant change and flux in which starlike and plantlike creatures and flora appear in a shifting scene of merging forms. The reader may begin to wonder whether this watery realm of changing forms—in which likenesses are established by the poet—may be intended to suggest the spontaneous transforming power of the human imagination, with "shafts of the sun" (introduced earlier as features of an abstract scene) serving as a symbol of poetic perception.

Such symbolic interpretation can be further supported by the image of the cliff introduced in the passage just quoted and in the last three stanzas, in which the subject announced by the title is seemingly forgotten:

> All
> external
> marks of abuse are present on this
> defiant edifice—
> all the physical features of

ac-
cident—lack
    of cornice, dynamite grooves, burns, and
    hatchet strokes, these things stand
        out on it; the chasm side is

dead.
Repeated
    evidence has proved that it can live
    on what can not revive
        its youth. The sea grows old in it.

Whatever the full range of suggestion may be, the fact that the cliff bears "dynamite grooves, burns, and hatchet strokes" marks it as an artifact and probably as a symbol of art. One might therefore infer that the contrast between the sea and the cliff suggests contrast and tension between the realm of living nature, which embraces human experience and the poetic imagination, and the realm of art as a product of the human imagination—a natural medium shaped by the human will which outlasts the life that produces it.

One might say these things and be consistent with the implications of other of Miss Moore's poems, but one could not assert them dogmatically. They are suggested rather than firmly established by the image patterns and statements of a poem that remains basically imagistic, abstract, and resistive to a fully developed, consistent symbolic interpretation.

The reader of such poems is sometimes inclined to wish for a surer presentation by the poet, and for himself a surer grasp of patterns of symbolic meaning. But there is in Miss Moore's work a conscious aversion to overt symbolism which she shared to a greater or lesser extent with such contemporaries as Ezra Pound and William Carlos Williams. Excessive symbolism, like hyperrationality (of which it is an unacknowledged manifestation) was distasteful to this poet, who satirized the rationalistic classifying mind in "To a Steam Roller":

The illustration
is nothing to you without the application.
    You lack half wit. You crush all the particles down
        into close conformity, and then walk back and forth on them.

113

Sparkling chips of rock
are crushed down to the level of the parent block.

If "sparkling chips" are taken to mean the particularities of experience, and of the imagery of a poem, the implication is that they would be flattened and impoverished by subordination to a system of symbolism. The argument is rational, like that of most satire, but it is directed against rigid rationality of the kind William Carlos Williams also ridiculed when he characterized the "slowly hardening brain of an academician" as having "the crystalline pattern of new ice on a country pool." It is this strain of skeptical rationalism that helps to account for Miss Moore's tendency toward satire and her affinity for Montaigne, Voltaire, and La Fontaine, whose *Fables* she lovingly versified.

Reason and the mind are important, but the mind must be flexible and aware of its limitations in the face of complexity and disorder. The very profusion of apparent disorder, as in the myriad forms of nature that overwhelm the human observer, is a pledge of the richness of experience and the infinite possibilities of imaginative perception.

"The Mind Is an Enchanting Thing" is the title of a poem which continues, looking back to its title for its subject,

> is an enchanted thing
>   like the glaze on a
> katydid-wing
>   subdivided by sun
>   till the nettings are legion.
> Like Gieseking playing Scarlatti . . . .

The mind is not to be confined by the lockstep of logic. It feels its way "as though blind," walking "with its eyes on the ground." It is bound to the treasured past through memory. It is conscientious and self-admonishing, tearing away "the temptation, the / mist the heart wears, / from its eyes." It is, finally, *not* rigid and *not* repressive: it is "not a Herod's oath that cannot change."

It is mind understood as the disciplined effort of the intellect and sensibility to achieve a tentative order that is perhaps the most distinctive principle of Marianne Moore's poetry, the expression of a unique, sensitive intelligence, enchanted by the abundance of experience, enchanting as it orders this experience through measured verse (*in + cantare*). A characteristic and abiding concern for responsible thought lies behind her reference in one of her later poems to poetry as a realm "where intellect is habitual."

This devotion to mind reveals a tie to the Enlightenment that she acknowledged in "Light Is Speech" and that sets her off from an uninhibited poet of the libido like E. E. Cummings, an inheritor of the Romantic animus against the intellect as a divisive and destructive enemy of the heart. Miss Moore did not believe in the Romantic head-heart dichotomy. To her, the mind was not unfeeling. Nor was it divorced from passion.

She was attracted to subjects that dramatize the virtues of a mixture of thought and feeling, civilization and wildness, humane order and passion. In "The Buffalo," she contemplates the wild American bison and the docile Vermont ox (which has been castrated) and then expresses her preference for the "mettlesome" buffalo of India, which combines the virtues of civilization and savagery. In another poem, she observes that in Leonardo da Vinci's painting of St. Jerome and his lion, the two "somehow became twinned," so that the saint partakes of the qualities of the lion and the beast those of the man. Of the saint, Miss Moore comments and asks: "Pacific yet passionate—? for if not both, how / could he be great?"

Passion is linked with humane qualities which depend upon but can not entirely sublime away its primal potency. Libidinal energies animate the creatures of this poetic world. Marianne Moore acknowledged the force of passion in many forms, but Eros unmasked rarely appears in her work. When it does, the effect can be startling, as in "Love in America?":

> Whatever it is, it's a passion—
> a benign dementia that should be
> engulfing America, fed in a way
>   the opposite of the way
> in which the Minotaur was fed.
> It's a Midas of tenderness;
>   from the heart;
> nothing else . . . .

115

Since "The Minotaur demanded a virgin to devour once a year," as a note reminds us, the endorsement of sexual as well as humane love is unmistakable, even though it is expressed with deliberate indirectness. The brief poem ends:

> Whatever it is, let it be without
> affectation.
>
> Yes, yes, yes, *yes.*

The reiterated *yes*'s of this ardent conclusion, reminiscent of Molly Bloom's valediction in Joyce's *Ulysses*, are a departure from Marianne Moore's usual restraint. But their insistent affirmation is implicit in all her work.

The praise of human love is less common a subject, however, than the celebration of a wildness and disorder that Miss Moore obviously relished for its excitement, its threat of violence, and its challenge to the ordering mind and imagination. To come to terms with disorder as the unforeseeable and thus apparently random events of life requires a special poise or "propriety," a word that Miss Moore used as the title of a poem. Propriety is a property of nature as well as man. In nature, it involves a functional, organic adaptation:

> The fish-spine
> on firs, on
> somber trees
> by the sea's
> walls of wave-worn rock—have it . . . .

In human expression, in art, it means a sense of fitness and proportion—of a resistance combined with acquiescence, as in Bach's "cheerful firmness":

> Come, come. It's
> mixed with wits:
> it's not a graceful sadness. It's
> resistance with bent head, like foxtail
> millet's. Brahms and Bach,
> no; Bach and Brahms. To thank Bach

for his song
first, is wrong.
　　Pardon me;
　　both are the
unintentional pansy-face
uncursed by self-inspection; blackened
because born that way.

Aspiration, disciplined effort, unself-conscious courage, and
individual achievement are qualities Marianne Moore found in
a wide range of subjects. Despite a fastidiousness which some-
times has aristocratic overtones, as when she approvingly quoted
her father on "superior people," she discovered and praised the
virtues she admired, without regard to class or circumstance, in
animals, from skunks to lions; baseball players, especially her
beloved Brooklyn Dodgers; steeple jacks; jockeys; and artists, in-
cluding musicians classical and jazz. In "Tom Fool at Jamaica,"
which celebrates a jockey's feeling for a special horse, the move-
ment of the horse and the beat of its dancing hooves are a
"rhapsody." The same poem remembers another champion and
master of rhythm, Fats Waller, "with the feather touch, giraffe
eyes, and that hand alighting in / Ain't Misbehavin'!"
Loyal also to her American Revolutionary heritage, Marianne
Moore is outstanding among poets of her generation in her com-
mitment to the virtues of individual freedom, independence, and
reasonableness. She remains a consistent though quiet spokes-
man for humane morality and rationality in a period in which
critics have tended to deny the moralistic and didactic role of
the poet and the importance of reason in human affairs and art
alike. Their arguments are controverted by Miss Moore's poetry,
which is the expression not of a rigid, hyperlogical mind, but
of a flexible, inquiring intelligence, conscious of its limitations
but conscious also of its power to find form and value, not
abstractedly, but in the warp and sensuous woof of life as it is
seen, felt, and understood by an unusually perceptive poet-
observer.

9. William Carlos Williams: The Early Poems

A CLOSE CONTEMPORARY and lifelong friend of Ezra Pound, William Carlos Williams worked at his craft for many years before winning his place as a modern poet of the first rank. Conscious of standing in the shadow of leaders like Pound, whom he admired, and Eliot, whose *Waste Land* seemed to him a disastrous influence, Williams acknowledged that his place in literary history would probably be that of a poet of limited achievement. But history has a way of confounding prophecy and even modest prediction. The shift in sensibility in the years following the Second World War brought Williams full if belated recognition and a high place, equal to Pound's and greater than Eliot's, in the eyes of the younger poets of the Third Generation.

Born in 1883 in Rutherford, New Jersey, to an English father and a Puerto Rican mother, Williams was educated at Manhattan's Horace Mann High School and the Medical College of the

University of Pennsylvania, where he met Ezra Pound, two years his junior but already dedicated to the life of a poet. After an internship in New York and study abroad at Leipzig, in pediatrics, Williams returned to Rutherford in 1910 to begin his career as physician and poet. Although he devoted full time to his medical practice, Williams still managed to publish as much enduring work as many of his contemporaries who devoted all their energies to poetry.

Unlike Pound, who chose exile from the "half savage country" of his birth, Williams felt always a deep attachment to his home locality and a pride in his Americanism—a pride intensified by youthful resentment of the Englishness of his father. Pound called him a two-hundred-per-cent American. His patriotism was combined with a temperamental equalitarianism, a feeling for the common life, and a passionate openness to experience. These qualities help to explain the affinity he felt for Whitman and the effort he made in *Paterson* and other poems to endow his local experience with universal significance. Resisting Pound's repeated urgings to come to Europe and "bite off a chunk of it," Williams clung tenaciously to the red clay soil and unlovely industrial sprawl of his native New Jersey, finding the subject of his poems in what Emerson had approvingly called "the near, the low, the common"—taking the speech of America, as he once said, from the mouths of Polish mothers, but purging and refining it to an unostentatious elegance.

His first book, *Poems* (1909), privately printed in Rutherford, appeared under an epigraph adopted from "Ode on a Grecian Urn," by John Keats, one of his early favorite poets: "Happy melodist forever piping songs forever new." The poems of this first collection are largely conventional and often, like Pound's in the same period, somewhat archaic in manner and diction. But Williams responded quickly to the new ideas about poetry of the Imagists and Vorticists, maintaining through a long transatlantic correspondence a lively dialogue with Pound. A marked change appeared in his second volume, *The Tempers* (1913), which includes, besides love songs from the Spanish (reflecting a continuing interest in translation from that language), successful poems in a modern manner like "To Mark Anthony in Heaven" and "Portrait of a Lady." In *Al Que Quiere: A Book of Poems* (1917), Williams revealed full mastery of the free verse forms that he was to work in for the rest of his long career.

The term Williams preferred to *Imagism* and sought to establish through critical essays and his editorial association with the little magazine *Contact* (especially during its first run in 1920–23) is *Objectivism*. His Objectivism has sometimes been mistaken as a purely objective Imagism: an effort to copy or imitate (*re*present) physical objects in nature. But to Williams, the primary object was the poem itself, the thing of words which the poet creates or "invents" in a manner determined by the nature of his perception. His chief commitment, accordingly, is to the reality and integrity of the poetic object rather than to the physical reality of its "subject," even though this physical reality is important to him both in itself and as a stimulus or inspiration to his work. The forms created by the poet enhance and enlarge the common life of the writer and his readers. As Williams remarked in a prose passage from *Spring and All* (1923), "in great works of the imagination A CREATIVE FORCE IS SHOWN AT WORK MAKING OBJECTS WHICH ALONE COMPLETE SCIENCE AND ALLOW INTELLIGENCE TO SURVIVE," and, further, "works of art . . . must be real, not 'realism' but reality itself—."

The view may be illustrated by one of the most familiar of all Williams's short poems, "The Red Wheelbarrow," also from *Spring and All*:

> so much depends
> upon
>
> a red wheel
> barrow
>
> glazed with rain
> water
>
> beside the white
> chickens.

The poem has often been cited as an example of objective Imagism, an effort to devise a verbal representation of a thing

120

in nature. The sensuous values of the rain-glazed barrow and the chickens are important, but it is also clear that what is presented is not so much a scene from nature, with all its profusion of detail, but a telling metrical composition of rigorously selected images in a symmetrical pattern. The entire poem consists of sixteen words measured into four two-line stanzas of three and one words each.

The discursive opening, "so much depends," points to the question of the significance of the images. If one thinks of them as *representing* nature on the level of physical commodity, in Emerson's terms, he is made to reflect that human civilization depends upon the interrelated forces of the machine (the wheelbarrow lever), the natural force of fertility (rain), and animal life (the chicken as a source of food and a symbol of human fertility). To Williams, who is not an Emersonian Transcendentalist, these basic physical values are not to be despised.

But the traditional wooden barrow has also been transformed and enhanced by the red paint and the rain water that glazes its surface; and the selective arrangement of which it is a part has value beyond the physical values of the represented natural objects. In Williams's Objectivist view, the "so much" that depends must primarily refer to to the aesthetic value of the poem as an arrangement in words that he has contrived, although the economic values of the presented objects cannot be excluded. Nor would Williams, a lover of the sensual life, wish to do so. As he acknowledges in the quotation from *Spring and All*, "Much may be represented actually."

This view is one Williams shares with many modern poets and critics. Even the Imagists' presented "thing," as required by their tenets, can if properly understood (and not confused with a physical *Dinglichkeit*) be identified with Williams's poetic object. The effect of this distinctively modern theory is to place a value on the poetic image as a unique reality rather than as a representation or symbol of a pre-existing reality. Like Marianne Moore and more than Pound, Williams was actively antisymbolic in much of his early poetry. (His later tendency toward symbolism grew during the writing of *Paterson*.) He wished to renew language by placing words and images in fresh contexts that would cleanse them of conventionalized symbolic associations and free them to reveal new meanings and relationships.

121

He wished, in other words, to present the image as image, with meanings suggested only by its immediate context, and to avoid both symbolism and discursive statement.

There has long been a tendency, recently renewed, to take Williams largely on his own terms, as an "Objectivist," and to view him as principally an imagistic poet in his earlier, pre-*Paterson* poems. This line of interpretation is a healthy one because it counteracts the prevailing impulse to focus on the symbolic meaning of poems at the expense of other aspects of poetic form. But Williams, characteristically, was not a consistent practitioner of his Objectivist theory. He was fully aware of the inescapability of the metaphoric and symbolic values of poetry and acknowledged them in his own work. The brief poem "A Sort of a Song" comments on the importance of metaphor as a device to "reconcile the people and the stones"—his own symbolic way of asserting the interrelationship of human values and experience, or idea and image, in poetry.

From the time of the earliest poems there is also a persistent tendency toward the poetry of statement. The much anthologized "Tract," from *Al Que Quiere*, is a discursive and frankly didactic poem in which the speaker attempts to teach the proper way "to perform a funeral": Objecting to the usual funeral, with its standardized conventions which have the effect of insulating mourners from the meaning of death, Williams would substitute for the polished black hearse a "rough dray" to be dragged over the ground, with no decoration other than the possibility of gilt paint applied to the wheels for the occasion. In place of the usual wreaths or hothouse flowers, the speaker recommends "Some common memento . . . / something he prized and is known by: / his old clothes—a few books perhaps— / God knows what!" He would have the driver pulled down from his perch to "walk at the side / and inconspicuously too!" His final admonition is to the mourners:

> Walk behind—as they do in France,
> seventh class, or if you ride
> Hell take curtains! Go with some show
> of inconvenience; sit openly—
> to the weather as to grief.

Or do you think you can shut grief in?
What—from us? We who have perhaps
nothing to lose? Share with us
share with us—it will be money
in your pockets.
                    Go now
I think you are ready.

At first glance, the poem seems the baldest kind of poetry of statement, as the speaker attempts to reform his neighbors' ideas about the proper conduct of a familiar rite by setting forth specific precepts. But the impulse toward reformation reveals a preoccupation with the idea of form that goes beyond the ostensible subject. The fact that the funeral is a common ritual is a reminder that any such group activity is inevitably symbolic and, in Williams's view, a kind of art—in this case, a bad kind. In this perspective, the particular example is generalized, and the speaker's injunctions apply not simply to one rite but to the whole range of symbolic activity in which members of a community may be involved. Metaphorically, the "tract" becomes a statement of an aesthetic as the poet asserts his commitment to certain principles of form which he urges upon his unenlightened townspeople. These are, not surprisingly, the familiar tenets of an organic theory in which rigid predetermined conventions are rejected in favor of forms which are free and functional and adapted to the circumstances from which they arise. The separate assertions of what had seemed a poetry of statement are finally revealed to be integral parts of a more comprehensive, dramatically unified symbolic act.

In some poems, Williams's more typical penchant for imagistic presentation coexists with a tendency toward symbolism. In "The Yachts" (1935), there is an interesting and unusual shift from an imagistic to a symbolic mode halfway through the poem. The occasion is a yacht race in a bay protected from the "too-heavy blows / of an ungoverned ocean." During the preparations for the race, the viewer is impressed by the physical beauty of the graceful craft, "Mothlike in mists, scintillant in the minute / brilliance of cloudless days, with broad bellying sails." Although the appeal is primarily imagistic, there is metaphoric suggestion

123

in the observation that the yachts, surrounded by more clumsy "sycophant" craft, "appear youthful, rare / as the light of a happy eye, live with the grace / of all that in the mind is feckless, free and / naturally to be desired."

But as the race begins, after a delaying lull, the scene changes ominously. The waves of the roughening water now seem to be human bodies overridden and cut down by the sharp bows of the yachts: "It is a sea of faces about them in agony, in despair / until the horror of the race dawns staggering the mind." The original imagistic appeal of the spectacle of the pleasure boats is broken and displaced by the revelation of deeper meaning. The race is finally shown to be a symbol of human struggle, in which the mass of men are cut down and destroyed.

There remains a question as to the nature of the struggle: whether it is to be understood simply as a common battle for survival in nature, in Darwinist terms, or whether it may have more specific social implications. Despite their intrinsic beauty and glamor, the yachts inevitably suggest a privileged life. As the fruits of surplus wealth acquired within a protected socioeconomic preserve (like an enclosed bay), the leisure and beauty of the life they represent can exist only at the expense of an exploited class. For all its seductive appeal, supported by long custom and tradition, the spectacle of the yacht race in a poem of the Depression period must be a reminder of social inequality and injustice.

The movement of the poem from imagistic charm to symbolic horror is in accord with the shift in the poet's perception from a preoccupation with sensuous phenomena to an awareness of human meaning and value—the necessary movement, in short, from image to metaphor, without which the poetic presentation of such an event would remain an innocuous imagistic diversion.

The range of Williams's uses of imagery, from a relatively pure Objectivist presentation to a definite symbolism, can be seen in three poems (all first collected in *Selected Poems* [1934]) concerned with trees. In "Young Sycamore," which has been singled out as an example of Williams's Objectivist technique, the speaker begins, "I must tell you," and proceeds to detail, imagistically, in the order in which his eye takes it in, the form of the young tree, which rises,

>   bodily

>   into the air with
>   one undulant
>   thrust half its height—
>   and then

>   dividing and waning
>   sending out
>   young branches on
>   all sides—

In keeping with Williams's Objectivism, his effort in this poem seems to be to perfect a verbal object (representative of a perceived object) with an integrity of its own, free of irrelevant or obtrusive symbolic or metaphoric associations.

Yet as the poem closes, the "it," the tree, is seen to thin until nothing is left,

>   but two

>   eccentric knotted
>   twigs
>   bending forward
>   hornlike at the top

and the reader is left with the question of whether the hornlike twigs are simply perceived objects or whether they may have associations that link the tree with the animal world and/or with a primitive animistic but distinctively human view of nature. Coming as it does at the end of the poem as the culminating event in a process of continuous perception, the image is not only open to such speculation but invites it. To block it in the interest of Objectivist purity would be a too interested and limiting response.

"The Trees" is a different kind of poem. The trees, which here "thrash and scream . . . , damning the race of men," who "haven't even sense enough to stay out in the rain," are not treated as distinctive entities to be particularized but as symbols of instinctive libidinal energy ("Loose desire!") too repressed

125

by civilized men. Moreover, the treatment makes it clear that the trees are meant to represent values incorporated in mythologies which can no longer command belief:

> There were never satyrs
> never maenads
> never eagle-headed gods—
> These were men
> from whose hands sprung
> love
> bursting the wood—
>
> Trees their companions
> —a cold wind winterlong
> in the hollows of our flesh
> icy with pleasure—
>
> no part of us untouched

The primitive passional values are still vitally important and in need of expression, but not through traditional mythological symbols. Instead, the modern poet must make use of images from nature and experience in fresh ways to reaffirm the values of spontaneity, fertility, and renewal.

In contrast to "Young Sycamore" and "The Trees," "The Botticellian Trees" reveals a suggestive but not fully resolved interaction of imagistic and symbolic values. In the course of this lovely poem, which opens,

> The alphabet of
> the trees
>
> is fading in the
> song of the leaves

a contrast is drawn, and a tension developed, between the structure of the trees as they appear in winter ("The strict simple / principles of / straight branches") and the texture with which they are enhanced in spring and summer as they are "modified / by pinched-out / ifs of color, devout / conditions / the smiles

of love—" until in full foliage the "stript sentences" of the
branches

> move as a woman's
> limbs under cloth
>
> and praise from secrecy
> quick with desire
>
> love's ascendancy
> in summer—

In summer, the poem concludes, "the song / sings itself / above
the muffled words—."

The imagistic tension has metaphoric implications in several
contexts, none of which is fully developed. Most simply and
easily, perhaps, one might be tempted to interpret the branch-
foliage contrast as a Romantic conflict between head and heart,
with the "logic" of the branches finally overpowered by "love's
ascendancy." But in this poem, the "principles" of the branches
are not rejected. The branches have an austere beauty, and they
are recognized to be necessary and integral supporting parts of
the tree as a whole. It might even be argued that they are more
important than the foliage (though there is an interdependence
of the two) because they are essential to the continuity of the
tree's existence through the seasons of the years.

What is perhaps more important is that the idea of expression
through a "song" dependent upon an "alphabet" or language
is sustained throughout the poem. The basic language, however,
the medium, does not become song (or poetry) until it is infused
with sensuous thought and feeling, the "devout conditions" of
art as well as love—until word and feeling, that is, are brought
together in a metrical harmony which Williams has called the
"marriage of language and metric," comparable to the organic
unity of the full-leafed tree in summer.

The title of the poem, "The Botticellian Trees," may be a
help in following this line somewhat further. It suggests the pos-
sibility, for one thing, that Williams may simply have been
trying to develop an Objectivist poem as a verbal equivalent of

the properties of the distinctive trees he saw in the paintings of Botticelli—trees rendered with a striking combination of painstakingly defined structure and feathery foliage. But the metaphoric implications already noted discourage so limited a view. If the poem is to be thought of in relation to painting, it seems much more likely that Williams was responding to a conception of art that he found in Botticelli's trees. It is that poetry, like painting or any art, involves two reciprocal and interdependent tendencies—one toward abstract design or a purely formal relationship of elements or images, the other toward metaphor and symbol as forms and images meet human necessity by evoking, through association, peculiarly human feeling and value. Both are essential to artistic expression and perception. If they were to be separated, the one tendency would lead to a sterile formalism, the other to a rigid and stultifying symbolism. It is typical of Williams's disposition that, although he acknowledges both tendencies in art, and in his own poetry, this poem ends with praise of the persistent human heart as the "song" that sings itself "above the muffled words."

Concern for human feeling and value is strong in Williams's poetry from the beginning. Like Whitman, he identifies himself with the common life and regards himself as its recorder and critic. The cultural interests of *Paterson* do not represent a sudden shift of interest or only a late development in his work (although these interests certainly deepened in his later years). Side by side with his technical preoccupation with the form and direction of modern poetry is a steadfast commitment to the role of social poet. As early as "The Wanderer: A Rococo Study" (1914), Williams presents himself as spokesman for the life of the modern metropolis as, with the "great towers of Manhattan before me," he confronts the question, "How shall I be a mirror to this modernity?" Accepting baptism in the "Passaic, that filthy river," a recurrent symbol of the corruption of the common life, he nevertheless identifies his own life with it.

In a number of poems, including the early "Tract," Williams assumes the role of a poet conscious of his social duty even though it may be ignored by his fellow citizens. In "Gulls," he tells his townspeople that it would be more profitable for him to live "in the great world," where his talents would be recognized, and urges them to listen because they "will not soon have another singer." He begins another poem, "Apology," by asking "Why do I write today?" and proceeds to answer himself:

> The beauty of
> the terrible faces
> of our nonentities
> stirs me to it:
>
> colored women
> day workers—
> old and experienced—
> returning home at dusk
> in cast off clothing
> faces like
> old Florentine oak.

More importantly, there is in the early verse the same impulse not only to present but to criticize his society and its values that finds its fullest expression in *Paterson* and other poems of Williams's later years. It appears in *Spring and All* (1923), the collection of poems and prose observations that included, as number XXI, "The Red Wheelbarrow." In XXVI, "At the Ball Game," Williams takes account, in a peculiarly modern way, of the capriciousness of the crowd of spectators, which is capable of both disinterested pleasure in the game, as a shared aesthetic experience, and destructive prejudice and aggression. The point is driven home by the insistent repetitive parallelism of the verses:

> It is alive, venomous
>
> it smiles grimly
> its words cut—
>
> The flashy female with her
> mother, gets it—
>
> The Jew gets it straight—it
> is deadly, terrifying—

It is the Inquisition, the
Revolution

It is beauty itself
that lives

day by day in them
idly—

Here is a foretaste of the more fully developed ambivalent treat-
ment of the "great beast," the crowd in the park in Book 2 of
Paterson.

But the closest of these poems to the cultural concerns of
Paterson is XVIII, "To Elsie," which begins, "The pure products
of America / go crazy—." The products are most specifically
the inbred and culturally deprived hill people of Kentucky and
particularly northern New Jersey, with "its isolate lakes and /
valleys, its deaf-mutes, thieves . . . / devil-may-care men who
have taken / to railroading / out of sheer lust of adventure—"

and young slatterns, bathed
in filth
from Monday to Saturday

to be tricked out that night
with gauds
from imaginations which have no

peasant traditions to give them
character

One such is Elsie, a girl reared by the state and sent out to work
in "some doctor's family" (the poet's) in the suburbs. The poem
moves toward the realization that Elsie's plight is general, that
she, as Williams acknowledges, expresses

. . . with broken

brain the truth about us—
her great
ungainly hips and flopping breasts

         addressed to cheap
         jewelry
         and rich young men with fine eyes

The materialism and lack of adequate cultural values are seen
as the failure not only of Elsie but of the poet and his society,
which are alike uncontrolled and directionless:

         and we degraded prisoners
         destined
         to hunger until we eat filth

         while the imagination strains
         after deer
         going by fields of goldenrod in

         the stifling heat of September
         Somehow
         it seems to destroy us

         It is only in isolate flecks that
         something
         is given off

         No one
         to witness
         and adjust, no one to drive the car

The effect of unevenness achieved by the abrupt alternation of
long and short lines in Williams's envelope stanzas is appropriate
to the erratic nature of the society.

   The "isolate flecks," like the "radiant gist" of Book 4 of
Paterson, represent the imagination and its needed creative func-
tion, in both the arts and sciences, as a resource for the discovery
of values that may bring meaning and fulfillment to empty lives.

   Williams's growing social consciousness and his lifelong in-
terest in the problem of poetic form converge in *Paterson* and
other poems of the 1940s and 1950s.

10. William Carlos Williams:
Paterson and the Later Poems

DURING THE DECADE of the Second World War, Williams concentrated his efforts on his ambitious, long-projected poem *Paterson*, which appeared in four successive books in 1946, 1948, 1949, and 1951. In 1958, seven years after the poem as conceived in four parts had been completed, *Paterson Five* was published. As early as 1952, Williams had written to Robert Lowell, "Maybe there'll be a 5th book of *Paterson* embodying everything I've learned of 'the line' to date." The comment reveals Williams's interest in the problem of poetics as a central theme of the poem. The extension of the ostensibly complete work is entirely in keeping with his idea of poetic form as tentative and relative, subject to varying interpretations in relation to the changing experience of the writer and reader.

Despite his sensitivity to the variability and even unpredictability of form and meaning, Williams was confronted, in his effort to write an epic or culture poem comparable to *The Waste Land* or *The Cantos*, with the problem of developing a relatively stable pattern of symbolism in his treatment of setting, character, and incident (or "plot"). The setting is Paterson, New Jersey, in its historical and contemporary aspects, both as an American industrial city at the falls of the Passaic River, which provided power for its early industries, and as the city of man, seen in its mean and trivial actualities and its ideal possibilities. In this setting, the "hero"—often manifested only as a pervasive central consciousness, sometimes as other characters, including Dr. Paterson—is the writer himself, who as a poet and physician must try to establish his identity in relation to his society and to express this relationship in an effective form. This effort supplies a central theme of the entire poem—a theme that may be defined as the poet-hero's quest for form.

The river that flows through the first four books of *Paterson* is literally the Passaic. Metaphorically, it has many meanings: it suggests, most basically, the irresistible life force, the stream of energy that animates the poet and the human and natural world of which he is a part. It is the stream of time, with its continuing flow of experience as it is reflected in the stream of the poet's consciousness. It is also the stream of language, which rolls "heavy with numbers." The "numbers," which represent the rhythms of the spoken language more than the traditional meters of poetry, point to a problem of form upon which Williams had commented, "we are trying . . . to seek (what we believe is there) a new measure or a new way of measuring that will be commensurate with the social, economic world in which we are living as contrasted with the past. It is in many ways a different world from the past calling for a different measure." In his preface to *Paterson*, the poet warns himself to "beware lest he turn to no more than the writing of stale poems," following the stereotypes of the past.

While out of the river,

> . . . rolling up out of chaos,
> a nine months' wonder, the city
> the man, an identity—it can't be
> otherwise—an
> interpenetration, both ways . . . .

133

The search for form and the quest for identity are the same. Neither the city, the poet, nor the poem is a self-sufficient entity. All are interdependent parts of a cultural complex, and the definition of any one involves the others. The poet as a man like any other may walk through the streets of an industrial city, but both the city and he as an individual achieve definition through the language of the poem, which is an abstraction or selection from the language the poet has heard and read.

The discovery of identity requires the poet's understanding of his immediate local environment and his historical roots, including experience of language. For Williams, with his vivid perception and empathic responses, the question of *individual* identity often gets lost sight of:

> Why even speak of "I," he dreams, which
> interests me almost not at all?

This tendency to identify and merge helps to explain the shifts in viewpoint and in the personae of the protean poet-hero. The shifts complicate the poem, but they are not wholly capricious, though they may seem to be, for they reflect the poet's sensitivity to the problem of identity and of communication.

In Book 1, "The Delineaments of the Giants," which deals with the early history of Paterson in an effort to define the "elemental character of the place," the city is linked with the as-yet-undiscovered identity of the poet. The river, which "comes pouring in above the city," is the stream of history and of life, as well as the stream of language from which the poet must derive his speech:

> (What common language to unravel?
> .   .   combed into straight lines
> from that rafter of a rock's
> lip.)

The failure of the language of the past, which is also a failure of the society, is dramatized through the stories of Mrs. Sarah Cumming, "consort" of the Reverend Hopper Cumming, who died in a plunge into the falls during a sight-seeing excursion in 1812, and the daredevil Sam Patch, who began his career at

Paterson and ended it in a fatal leap at the falls of the Genesee River at Rochester in 1826. In these episodes, Williams uses prose to represent the language and character of the earlier time. The sentimentalized newspaper account of Mrs. Cumming's death ignores the reality of suicide and reflects a hypocritical and stifling gentility. "A false language," the poet remarks.

As for Patch, the account of his reckless career and his final leap reveals the crowd's hunger for sensation and violence, empty marvels, but more particularly the substitution of unthinking action for meaningful speech. For both Mrs. Cumming and Patch, society was an inhibiting force, and the final, desperate recourse of the individual blocked in his impulse toward expression is an act of self-destruction. In death, both Mrs. Cumming and Sam Patch are "silent, uncommunicative." The recurring word *communicate*, reinforced by such negative forms as *uncommunicative* and *incommunicado*, implies the relationship of communication and community and points to a lack of shared values in Paterson or any American city from its beginnings, and the consequent waste and frustration of individual lives.

Another instance of the warping influence of society in the early history of the place is a "monster." Like the falls, the hydrocephalic dwarf Peter is a celebrated and exploited local "attraction." The dwarf's name is a link between the city and the poet. The pattern of human life represented by Peter, Mrs. Cumming, and Patch is seen as "monstrous" and expressed, naturally enough, in a deformed and corrupted language. In an appended note to Book 1, Williams quotes from J. A. Symonds's *Studies of the Greek Poets* (1873) a passage describing the sprung verse of Hipponax as appropriate because of "the harmony which subsists between crabbed verses and the distorted subjects with which they dealt—the vices and perversions of humanity. . . ."

The quotation is in accord with Williams's own rejection of traditional metrics in favor of a new measure, appropriate to his time, which he called the "relativistic or variable foot." Like the Imagists' "musical phrase," Williams's much-discussed term can best be understood as the expression of a preference for a unit of free rhythmical expression determined by the poet's perception and the nature of his subject over the fixed, metronomic foot of traditional metrics. Throughout *Paterson* (and all of Williams's work), the search for appropriate form involves the related problems of diction and measure or what he sometimes also referred to as "musical pace."

Book 2, "Sunday in the Park," presents the "modern replicas" of the life of the past. The park, "female to the city," brings the poet into contact with the immediate physical world, the sensual life that he must transform. Here the Sunday crowd, the "great beast" (as Alexander Hamilton had called the people), takes its pleasure, pursues its desires among the "churring loves" of nature and within the sound of the voice of the evangelist Klaus Ehrens, who vainly tries to bring them into the truth through the language of traditional religion, which Williams regards as outworn and simply another block to expression. He elsewhere comments that the Church "is likely to be an insuperable barrier today if the major function of the artist—to lift to the imagination and give new currency to the sensual world at our feet —is envisaged."

Self-designated as Faitoute, the poet-hero strolls through the park, troubled by the problem of creating a poem commensurate with his world when "the language is worn out." In his thoughts, he rejects both the crowd, the "beast," which he identifies with unthinking sensuality, and the conventional religious clichés of society. The denial of purely physical love and reproduction as an end in itself is painful for Williams, who prizes the sensual life in which the poem must *begin*. As he thinks of the voluptuous woman who is both his Muse, offering the inspiration of the physical, and the Circe who would enfold him and hold him in the web of flesh, the image that began in the flesh becomes transformed in imagination:

> Her belly   .   her belly is like a white cloud   .   a
> white cloud at evening   .   before the shuddering night!

In the poetic process, metaphor involves an idealization of the physical, whereas the purely physical life is imaginatively unproductive: "Stones invent nothing, only a man invents." The river, as a symbol of the sensual life, is a "terrifying plunge, inviting marriage—and a wreath of fur." The wreath of fur, a token of the surrender of human to animal life, contrasts power-

136

fully with the conventional wreath of laurel, a dead image, useless to the modern poet except as the implicit base of his striking trope.

In Book 3, "The Library," the poet turns in his search from his immediate world to the literature (broadly interpreted) of the past. Confused by the roar of experience in the park, the poet is attracted by the "cool of books," which will "sometimes lead the mind to libraries of a hot afternoon." Turning over old newspapers, he is struck by the failure of their language to convey the meaning of events:

> . . . —a child burned in a field,
> no language. Tried, aflame, to crawl under
> a fence to go home. So be it. Two others,
> boy and girl, clasped in each others' arms
> (clasped also by the water) So be it. Drowned
> wordless in the canal . . . .

The violence and the blockage of expression reinforce the examples of Mrs. Cumming and Sam Patch in Book 1.

Seclusion in the library, no longer a welcome retreat, breeds revulsion. The sound of books, the pressure of the past, becomes a roar in the ears, nearly as overpowering as the impact of immediate experience. In contrast to the roar of the "wadded library" is the Beautiful Thing, often personified as a woman, to which the poet-hero's mind drifts. This phrase, recurring almost like a refrain, applies to the immediate physical world, which the poet knows through his senses and out of which he makes poetry, by invention, in an appropriate language. The Beautiful Thing, which harks back to the woman of Book 2, is the muse and inspiration of Williams as a poet of the visible world.

The roar of the library, like the roar of the falls, merges with the roar of "cyclone, fire, and flood," all actual events in the history of the city. Metaphorically, these events are also associated with the creative process. Fire symbolizes poetic artifice for Williams in much the same way that it does for W. B. Yeats in "Sailing to Byzantium" and other poems. The creation of the poem, a new object, from the commonplace of life is suggested by the image of an old bottle, warped and transformed by the Paterson fire:

> An old bottle, mauled by the fire
> gets a new glaze, the glass warped
> to a new distinction, reclaiming the
> undefined.

The creative fire is a waterfall reversed, "shooting upward" to assert a new reality rather than subsiding into the anonymity of nature. The flame "surpasses heat," and the glass is splotched with rainbows of "cold fire" that attest the transmutation and distancing of experience in the poetic process. The fire destroys the literature of the past, just as the poet must reject its language to forge his own out of the living speech of the present. This is the revolutionary violence of art. The "vulgarity of beauty" of the Beautiful Thing surpasses the perfections of the art of the past. It is a manifestation of immediate life challenging expression in contemporary terms. In this process the Beautiful Thing becomes

> —intertwined with the fire. An identity
> surmounting the world, its core—

The Paterson flood recalls both the Biblical flood and the almost overwhelming flood of language in which the poet feels immersed. He describes his situation in terms of the subsidence of an actual flood: the world is slimed with a "fertile(?)mud" which is also a "pustular scum" breathing forth a revolting stench that "fouls the mind."

Attempting to re-order a world burdened by a false and dead language, the poet muses on the persistent problem of form:

> How to begin to find a shape—to begin to begin again,
> turning the inside out : to find one phrase that will
> lie married beside another for delight   ?
> —seems beyond attainment

Yet, standing by the river, he cannot ignore the task of finding "a speech." Under the compulsion to make a "replica" of the falls, a poem commensurate with his present reality, he can find his meaning only in the sliding water at the brink, where he must, as he observed in beginning, "comb out the language," inadequate though his vocabulary and measure may seem, to give expression to whatever "episodes," or incomplete truths, he may have attained.

Book 4, "The Run to the Sea," is "reminiscent of episodes—all that any one man may achieve in a lifetime," as Williams observes in his Author's Note to *Paterson*. The three main subjects of the first two parts of Book 4 are, first, love—of various kinds, each with its own frustrations—in the figure of a triangle involving a New York poetess (a Lesbian), a young nurse (the female Paterson and a Beautiful Thing), and Dr. Paterson, the poet-physician; second, science, through the lecture on atomic fission to which Dr. Paterson takes his son as an introduction to the knowledge of his time; and third, money as the cause of the concentration of capital and social corruption. These three subjects all relate to the theme of divorce or alienation (the "sign of knowledge in our time") introduced in Book 1. They are also closely related to the problem of language and expression.

Madame Curie's discovery of radium is cited in the discussion of science:

> A dissonance
> in the valence of Uranium
> led to the discovery
>
> Dissonance
> (if you are interested)
> leads to discovery

The radioactive energy released by the breaking down of uranium represents poetic as well as scientific knowledge or truth. It is only through the breakdown of the old forms that the poet can hope to discover truth for his time. There is a curative power in the energy released by the emergence of new forms ("a dissonance . . . may cure the cancer"). So too there is a restorative power in the poet's reworking of an exhausted language in an effort to give expression to a new culture. The same principle of renewal through the transformation of a decaying order applies to love and economics within a society.

The third and last part of Book 4 returns to an explicit concern for language. As the spent river winds slowly toward the sea and as the poet contemplates the waning of his life, he comments on the need for leisure and detachment: "Virtue . . . is a complex reward in all languages, achieved slowly." A brief prose paragraph continues:

> Kill the explicit sentence, don't you think? and expand our meaning—by verbal sequences. Sentences, but not grammatical sentences: dead-falls set by schoolmen. Do you think there is any virtue in that? better than sleep? to revive us?

Williams does not of course actually reject the sentence. For him, as for his fellow free verse poets, the abandonment of traditional metrics actually gave an added importance to syntax (not necessarily "grammatical") as a formal device.

As the river approaches the sea, of death, of unconscious nature into which the individual life merges, Williams asserts that the sea is *not* our home. The fourth book ends with an image of renewal but not of rebirth in a religious or mystical sense. A figure is seen far out, swimming. First taken to be a duck or a dog, it proves to be a man swimming toward the shore. On the beach, a large black dog, yawning and stretching, gets up to meet him as he emerges from the water. After resting he gets up, slips into faded overalls, a shirt with rolled-up sleeves, and a hat:

> Climbing the
> bank, after a few tries, he picked
> some beach plums from a low bush and
> sampled one of them, spitting the seed out,
> then headed inland, followed by the dog

Williams comments on this episode: "In the end the man rises from the sea where the river appears to have lost its identity and accompanied by his faithful bitch, obviously a Chesapeake Bay retriever, turns inland toward Camden where Walt Whitman, much traduced, lived the latter years of his life and died. He always said that his poems, which had broken the dominance of the iambic pentameter in English prosody, had only begun his theme. I agree. It is up to us, in the new dialect, to continue it by a new construction upon the syllables."

The sea of Book 4 is not a symbol of rebirth and unity in the traditional sense of immortality for the poet and a perfectly realized form for his work. It is rather the sea of nature, the sea of the mass of indifferent men, as Williams himself called it. The figure emerging from the water (the Odyssean wanderer or the Whitmanesque poet of the open road) suggests both the new generation of poets and the aging poet of *Paterson*, completing his poem as one phase of his career and rededicating himself to his continuing quest for a form which is never to be perfectly realized.

There were many changes in Williams's outlook during the seven-year interval between the publication of Book 4 and the appearance of *Paterson Five*, which he characterized as a "breakthrough." While the new book reveals a substantial continuity of image and theme and metrical form, there are significant differences in Williams's attitudes and in the treatment of certain themes carried over from the earlier books.

Although he still refers to himself as Paterson, the poet is less bound by his locality and his immediate present. A sense of freedom from time and place is proclaimed in the opening lines, in which the winglike contour of the verses is suited to the sense:

> In old age
> 	the mind
> 			casts off
> 		rebelliously
> 	an eagle
> from its crag

In this new-found freedom, the poet-hero tends to identify himself with man, or Western man, rather than with the citizens of Paterson, New Jersey, past and present. The references to the city are few. The falls, which sounded through the first four books, is not heard. The only river specifically mentioned is the

141

Ohio, with its falls at Louisville, below which Audubon, the artist-observer with whom the aging poet identifies himself, left his stranded boat to walk overland to his Henderson, Kentucky, home across three states of the still-primitive continent.

There is also a greater preoccupation with the past, not as an inhibiting influence but as a source of tradition in art that has sustained and guided the poet. The art museum, unlike the library of Book 3, is not rejected. On the contrary, its permanence and authenticity are affirmed:

> —the museum become real
> > *The Cloisters*—
> > > on its rock
> > casting its shadow—
> > > "la réalité! la réalité! . . ."

There is also a new sense that the struggle for recognition has finally been won. Paterson is more confident of his position, although he does not consider it a terminus, and derives comfort from the thought that the world of art, of which he is a citizen, has through the years

SURVIVED!

Reconciled with the past, he looks forward to the future, with which his own work is a link, and to the opportunity of helping younger poets in their efforts. There is a continuation of correspondence with a younger poet originally introduced in Book 4 as A. P. (Allen Paterson), with the difference that the younger man is now more clearly identified, and dissociated from the older Paterson, as A. G. (Allen Ginsberg).

Metrically, there is a predominance of the staggered breath-spaced scheme introduced in Book 2 in the passage beginning:

> The descent beckons
> > as the ascent beckoned
> > > Memory is a kind
> of accomplishment
> > a sort of renewal . . .

In Book 5, this flexible form is beautifully adapted to the poet's needs. There is not the same emphasis on the failure of communication and expression that marked the first four books.

Although the term is not used, the poet-hero's concern for the Beautiful Thing persists, most obviously in the figure of a woman in slacks who walks through his town. He is attracted, he desires, from a distance of time as well as space, but there is no possibility of his establishing a relationship comparable even to the abortive romance with the nurse Phyllis of Book 4. In this way, the theme of thwarted love is continued, as are the themes of violence (war), and the corruption of the economic system (the latter supported by the inclusion of an unsigned letter from Ezra Pound).

These concerns are less urgent, however. The frustration and dissatisfaction of the younger Paterson are now relieved by the assurance that art can provide a release for blocked desire. The greatest frustration is, of course, death, or the sense of death, "the hole in which we are all buried." But the poet now points to an escape hatch at the bottom of the hole, through the imagination, "which cannot be fathomed."

The tension between the sensual life and that of the imagination continues, but the demands of the libido are less urgent in advancing age. The "dog" of the poet's thoughts

> has shrunk
> to no more than "a passionate letter"
> to a woman, a woman he had neglected
> to put to bed in the past

Writing now provides a more satisfying outlet for desire.

Art also affords a sense of community to relieve the alienation of earlier years. The twelfth-century tapestries preserved in the New York museum, the Cloisters (the group dealing with the hunting of the unicorn is foremost in Williams's mind), are the creation of many hands following a common plan, working together:

> together as the cartoon has plotted it
> for them. All together . . . .

143

So too the tradition with which Williams identifies himself represents an endeavor shared over many years. Besides Peter Brueghel the elder, the roster includes Gertrude Stein, Paul Klee, Picasso, Juan Gris—all participants in the development of modern abstract art, all artists concerned with movement and sensuous detail. Henri de Toulouse-Lautrec, to whose memory Book 5 is dedicated, is the artist of the whorehouse, the poet of the sensual life prized by Williams as the basis of all art.

The most important and suggestive new image is that of the unicorn, taken from the tapestries Williams admired at the Cloisters. Although it is unlike most of Williams's earlier imagery because of its origin in traditional myth and legend, it does relate back to the earlier parts of *Paterson*, especially to the beast life of Book 2. With its animal shape and magical qualities, this creature represents a fusion of the physical and the imaginative life. It also synthesizes past and present, for in its range of suggestion are merged the European past (the wounded beast of the tapestries), the primitive American past (the horned beast seen in the moonlight by Audubon on his long walk), and the poet-hero's present situation, as the sense of the waning potency of age is evoked by the image of the "milk white one horned beast" penned in by a low wooden fence. As a wounded victim (like the crippled painter Toulouse-Lautrec) and a survivor of violent struggle, the unicorn is identified with the artist. In the tapestry, the beast surviving the hunt wears a "jeweled collar," while the hound he has gored lies nearby. The beast Williams imagines Audubon to have seen lies wounded in a field,

> its neck
> circled by a crown!
> from a regal tapestry of stars!

The crown testifies not so much to Audubon's claim to royalty (the Dauphin legend) as to his achievement as an artist (essentially more noble) whose expression derives from the sensual life with its conflict and suffering.

The implications are reinforced by Williams's description of the imagination escaping the trap of death, bearing

> . . . a collar round his neck
> hid in the bristling hair.

144

The beast's collar stands in striking contrast to the wreath of fur (in Book 2) which invited a sinking into the anonymity of the physical life—an impulse rejected. The jeweled collar of Book 5 is the image of the individual expression of the artist that distinguishes him from the beast. It is the badge of his identity and of his membership in a select community.

Through his measured expression, the poet achieves the only truth and reality he can ever know. Represented by the figure of a dance, this truth is dynamic and relative rather than static and absolute. The poet-hero of *Paterson* concludes, or rather interrupts himself, on this note:

> We know nothing and can know nothing
> > but
> the dance, to dance to a measure   19½
> contrapuntally,
> > Satyrically, the tragic foot.

Echoing the old confusion between satire and satyr, *satyrically* links the values of sensuality and art, as in the ancient drama with its chorus of satyrs. Counterpoint as a necessary feature of form implies not only the use of complementary and contrasting rhythmical patterns but also the tension between the physical and the imaginative life as expressed by comparable and contrasting images like the wreath of fur and the jeweled collar.

The measure of the dance represents the poet's knowledge of reality, a knowledge which is relative and incomplete. The dance of art sustains the imagination " 'unless the scent of a rose / startle us anew' " as the claims of the immediate sensual life intervene. The dance, at any given time and place, is a form which is tentative, straining toward completion, subject to interruption and change. In short, a dynamic organic form.

In either four or five books, *Paterson* is a complex and difficult poem. Yet it is honest and uncompromising. There is no suggestion of the possibility of a wholeness representative of a systematized world view in a world in which wholeness is intellectually indefensible. In this respect, *Paterson* is more truly modern and representative of its science-minded, skeptical age than myth-oriented poems like *The Waste Land* of Eliot and

The Bridge of Hart Crane, which depend for their basic organization upon the pattern of the rebirth archetype.

Together with this skepticism and distrust of wholeness as an unattainable goal, there is a growing confidence in many of Williams's later poems in the power of the poetic imagination and in his own vocation as a poet. This new assurance is boldly asserted in "The Host," first collected in *The Desert Music* (1954). Based upon a trip to the Southwest and Mexico, the poem describes a meal in a railroad restaurant. Besides the speaker, there are, at separate tables, representatives of several religious groups: a Negro evangelist, two young Irish nuns, and a white-haired Anglican cleric. The poet-observer, who is much interested in his surroundings, and in interpreting the scene, is struck by the absence of any spirit of communion or shared imaginative awareness of the meaning of the common experience of eating together. Yet none is apparent, not even the orthodox meaning which the church people might be expected to derive from their rituals and creeds. The poem ends:

> No one was there
> > save only for
> > > the food. Which I alone,
> being a poet,
> > could have given them.
> > > But I
> had only my eyes
> > with which to speak.

To Williams, the food he might supply is poetry, the only "host" capable of providing imaginative communion in a world fragmented by competing viewpoints and conflicting orthodoxies. Here, as in Book 2 of *Paterson*, the forms of organized religions are considered impediments to imaginative awareness. Though relieved by a quiet humor, the presumptuousness of Williams's claim is startling. But it represents the conviction of his later years that the poetic imagination is the fullest source of truth and that a commitment to it is akin to "Deep Religious Faith," the title of another late poem.

An extremely personal and moving expression of this belief appears in the Coda of "Asphodel, That Greeny Flower," a love poem addressed to the poet's wife, Floss. In the shadow of approaching death, Williams celebrates the "light" of imagination and love, which "for all time shall outspeed / the thunder crack."

In other pieces brought together in *Collected Later Poems* (1963), Williams develops original patterns of fresh imagery to express his sense of the power and necessary freedom of the poetic imagination.

In "Burning the Christmas Greens," the violent flame that leaps in the grate as the discarded evergreen branches go up in a roar is a symbol, like the fire in *Paterson*, of the transforming power of art. The green boughs are quickly changed into "an infant landscape of shimmering / ash and flame" which provides the sense of distancing and renewal associated with aesthetic response:

> . . . and we, in
> that instant, lost,
>
> breathless to be witnesses,
> as if we stood
> ourselves refreshed among
> the shining fauna of that fire.

"The Pink Church," first published in 1949, is Williams's most explicit symbolic expression of his view of art as a cultural institution. Although he has been reported as saying that it is a "Christian poem" and that the "Pink Church stands for the Christian Church," the work belies his words. The "saints" of the pink church include "Poe, Whitman, Baudelaire." The truth it reveals is contrasted with the teachings of philosophy:

> O Dewey! (John)
>   O James! (William)
>   O Whitehead!
>   teach well!
> —above and beyond
>   your teaching stands
> the Pink Church:
>   the nipples of
> a woman who never
>   bore a
>   child . . .

As an artifact, the madonna of the church is not of the world of generation. As a representative of art, she is technically sterile, even though art must draw its sustenance, in Williams's view, from the sensual life.

The central image of the poem, the pink jade stone of which the church is made, embraces the qualities of art and physical life as they are fused in the light of the imagination:

> Sing!
> transparent to the light
>   through which the light
> shines, through the stone,
>   until
> the stone-light glows,
>   pink jade
> —that is the light and is
>   a stone
> and is a church—if the image
>   hold . . .

Light as a symbol of the poetic imagination is supported by an established tradition with religious origins (in the light of grace). The association of pinkness with "a dawn in Galilee" in the opening line of the poem suggests a religious revelation, but elsewhere pinkness is identified with the flesh: "perfect as the pink / and rounded breasts of a virgin!" The stone through which the light shines is the medium of art, whether it be translucent jade or paint or words. The use of a stone which transmits light is especially appropriate to poetry, in which imagery in the form of a linguistic representation of the physical world is charged with human meaning and value in the metaphoric process. In a slightly earlier poem, "A Sort of a Song," collected in *The Wedge* (1944), Williams characterizes the function of poetry as the reconciliation, "through metaphor," of "the people and the stones."[1]

In one of Wallace Stevens's late poems, "Prologues to What Is Possible," in much the same way stones are associated with poetic imagery as the poet imagines himself being borne forward over the water in a boat:

[1] See above, p. 122.

The boat was built of stones that had lost their weight
    and being no longer heavy
Had left in them only a brilliance of unaccustomed origin . . . .

"The Pink Church" closes with the poet's admonition to "all you liveried bastards"—those limited by conventions and orthodoxies—to listen to his celebration of free form as a kind of redemption, even though the message cannot be heard by those whose "stupid ears" are "plugged by wads of newspulp":

Joy! Joy!
   —out of Elysium!

—chanted loud as a chorus from
    the Agonistes—

Milton, the unrhymer,
      singing among
          the rest . . .

    like a Communist.

Although Williams had spoken of a connection between the message of Jesus and primitive communism when he characterized "The Pink Church" as a Christian poem, the likening of Milton to a Communist is more probably an allusion to his status as a nonconformist and revolutionary in both politics and poetry. This kind of reading is supported by Williams's reference to the chorus of *Samson Agonistes*, the irregular verse of which Milton justified in his introduction to the work.

Williams's insistence upon the freedom of the mind and hatred of conventional restraints are most powerfully expressed in "The Clouds" (1948), a four-part poem in which the central image is the march of the ever-changing clouds across the sky. As natural phenomena, the stuff on which the mind and imagination feed, they symbolize the shifting flux of experience in which man must find human significance if he is to be more than a turtle in a swamp. They also represent the "unshorn" minds of free spirits like Villon, Erasmus, and Shakespeare, who "wrote so that / no school man or churchman could sanction him without / revealing his own imbecility. . . ." These minds, like the skeptical Socrates, "Plato's better self," accepted the fact of man's mortality and devoted themselves to the life of the mind and imagination—a life to which Williams gives precedence: "The intellect leads, leads still! Beyond the clouds."

In a brief and lively "Scherzo" (part three of the poem), Williams remembers coming as a tourist upon a priest in St. Andrew's in Amalfi, "riding / the clouds of his belief," as he performed a Mass "jiggling upon his buttocks to the litany":

I was amazed and stared in such manner

that he, caught half off the earth
in his ecstasy—though without losing a beat—
turned and grinned at me from his cloud.

To Williams, who recognizes the ritual to be an act of the imagination, the priest's cloud is not enough. In its regularity and neat order, reassuring though these may be to believers, it stands in contrast to "the disordered heavens, ragged, ripped by winds," which the poet who accepts a naturalistic outlook must confront in his search for form and meaning. The "soul" is the precious burden of the life of the imagination which each individual has a share in carrying forward, humanistically, from generation to generation: "It is that which is the brotherhood: the old life, treasured."

In all his work, Williams has carried forward a revolutionary heritage that has lately been welcomed by younger poets responsive to his example and influence. While steadfastly supporting the principle of free organic form, he has also helped to refresh and renew the language of poetry by freeing it from stereotyped associations. In his feeling for people, his passionate equalitarianism, he has been more attractive to the younger generation of poets than the more aristocratic Ezra Pound and T. S. Eliot. His writing reveals an openness to experience of all kinds and a refusal to accept doctrinaire theories and solutions. While insisting upon the authenticity of his own vision, he has at the same time insisted upon the relativity of all knowledge and the inadequacy of dogma. To this extent at least, despite his distance from the confident rationalism of the Enlightenment (which he also distrusted), his work as a whole supports the Jeffersonian principle of "eternal hostility to every form of tyranny over the mind of man."

11. The Conservative Counterrevolution: The New Criticism and the Middle Generation Poets

THE FULL FORCE of William Carlos Williams's influence on younger poets was delayed by the conservative trend in criticism and poetry that gained strength with the rise of the New Criticism in the late 1930s. The modern movement had from the beginning combined two contrasting strains, or parties, with Pound, Williams, and Marianne Moore in the vanguard of the more radical group. The conservative line led through T. S. Eliot and the Southern Fugitive poets[1] to the New Criticism and the verse produced by the Middle Generation of poets.

New Critics like John Crowe Ransom, Cleanth Brooks, and Allen Tate supported Eliot's classicism and his advocacy of the metaphysical conceit. They supplemented the impersonal theory of "Tradition and the Individual Talent"[2] with their own

[1] See above, p. 38.
[2] See above, pp. 36–37.

ideas of poetic structure—all based in differing ways on the notion of tension as a fundamental, self-containing principle of organization.

In spite of the professed anti-Romanticism they shared with Eliot, the New Critics were deeply in debt to Samuel Taylor Coleridge, although most of them gained access to his ideas indirectly, through I. A. Richards's *Principles of Literary Criticism* (1925) and *Coleridge on Imagination* (1935).

For twentieth-century poets and critics, Coleridge came to be recognized as the most important of earlier theorists, largely because of the appeal of his idea of poetry (and all art) as a creation of the human mind, and thus a psychic product, rather than as an imitation of a pre-existing reality. Coleridge identified the poetic faculty as the "esemplastic" imagination, a spontaneous synthesizing power which he distinguished from the analytic and mechanical fancy. At the end of Chapter 14 of *Biographia Literaria* (1817), the imagination is described as a fusing and unifying power which, "first put into action by the will and understanding, and retained under their irremissive, though gentle and unnoticed controul (*Laxis effentur habenis* ['is carried along with loose reins']) reveals itself in the balance or reconcilation of opposite or discordant qualities: of sameness, with difference; of the general, with the concrete; the idea, with the image; the individual, with the representative; the sense of novelty and freshness, with old and familiar objects; a more than usual state of emotion, with more than usual order; judgement ever awake and steady self-possession, with enthusiasm and feeling profound or vehement; and while it blends and harmonizes the natural and the artificial, still subordinates art to nature: the manner to the matter; and our admiration of the poet to our sympathy with the poetry."

To Coleridge, the imagination was a magical power, "a repetition in the finite mind of the eternal act of creation in the infinite I AM." Although most modern critics could not accept his supernaturalism, they took his principle of "the balance or reconciliation of opposites" and made it the keystone of their own theories of poetic form.

Coleridge also anticipated modern theory in his view of the artist as a creator of forms of consciousness rather than as an imitator of pre-existing metrical forms. As he observed in his essay "On Poesy or Art" (1818), if the artist were to confine himself to the "painful copying" of nature, he would "produce masks only, not forms breathing life." He must instead "out of his own mind create forms according to the severe laws of the intellect, in order to generate in himself that co-ordination of freedom and law, that involution of obedience in the prescript, and of the prescript in the impulse to obey, which assimilates him to nature, and enables him to understand her."

A hundred years later, I. A. Richards approached literary theory in the spirit of science, but at the same time drew heavily upon Coleridge's Romantic ideas. In *Principles of Literary Criticism* (1925), Richards announced his aim of bringing the methods of the laboratory to literary study and placing criticism upon an experimental basis. In pursuing this effort, he found a key to a "Psychological Theory of Value" (the title of his seventh chapter) in the problem of organizing impulses and attitudes in a manner least wasteful of human possibilities. As a cultural activity, art is especially valuable because it is able to organize many conflicting impulses and attitudes efficiently. While basing this view on Coleridge's principle of the "balance or reconciliation of opposite or discordant qualities," Richards substituted *irony* (like wit, a rational intellectual quality) for Coleridge's transcendentalist *imagination*. By focusing on irony as a basic organizing principle and a gauge of poetic value, Richards provided modern critics and poets with one of their most often invoked standards.

Despite his professedly scientific approach, Richards cites literary figures, especially the Romantics, far more often than psychologists. In his concluding pages, he remarks that the "Revelation Doctrines [of Coleridge], when we come to know what they are really about, come nearer, we shall see, to supplying an explanation of the value of the arts than any of the other traditional accounts."

Ten years later, in *Coleridge on Imagination* (1935), Richards gave even fuller support to Coleridge's theory. Largely abandoning his earlier attitude of scientific objectivity, he quotes and endorses Coleridge by describing poetry as the "myth-making faculty which most brings 'the whole soul of man into activity' (*B.L.*, II, 12)." In taking this position, Richards supplied a basis for the argument supported by many myth critics for the

154

mythopoeic origin of all knowledge and the integrative function of poetic myth. It is this assumption that underlies the claims of Ransom and other New Critics that poetry is superior to science because it supplies a "whole" or more "complete" knowledge than the skeletal abstractions of science. The idea is that myth is superior to science, history, or philosophy because it is less abstract.

The New Critics' theories of poetic structure can most simply be described as a poetics of tension. For Allen Tate, in his essay "Tension in Poetry" (1938), tension supplies the "meaning" of poetry through the full body of all the "extension or intension," or denotation and connotation, that can be found in it. For John Crowe Ransom, the tension arises in large part from the interplay of the poem's *structure* of general meaning and its decorative *texture* as the imagery, metrics, sound patterns, and so forth supply dramatic parallels or contrasts with the sense of the lines. Ransom speaks of the extralogical texture as providing a "curious increment of riches" that no paraphrase or rational summary can contain or exhaust. In the essays of *The Well Wrought Urn; Studies in the Structure of Poetry* (1947), Cleanth Brooks thinks of *paradox* and *irony* as the source of essential tension as the words and images of a poem are charged with contrasting meanings and values through their textual associations.

Tensional theory of this kind strongly influenced poetry and criticism written from the late 1930s into the 1950s. The interrelationship of the two can be most clearly seen in the work of the New Critics who were also poets. In "Narcissus as Narcissus" (1938), Allen Tate explicates his own poem "Ode to the Confederate Dead" (1928), describing its structure as the "objective frame for the tension between the two themes, 'active faith' which has decayed, and the 'fragmentary cosmos' which surrounds us."

The New Critics also carried forward the revival of the metaphysical tradition to which Eliot had contributed. In an essay entitled "Poetry: A Note on Ontology" (1938), Ransom distinguishes three types of poetry: physical poetry, which attempts to present things in their thinginess (*Dinglichkeit*); Platonic poetry, the poetry of ideas; and, finest of the three, metaphysical poetry, which combines idea and image through the medium of

155

sensuous metaphor and which has the added virtues of wit and complexity. In keeping with this preference, Ransom's own carefully crafted poems, written in traditional forms, are marked by metaphysical irony and wit and an aversion to sentiment so extreme that it seems almost an inversion of sentimentality.

The poets most deeply influenced by the metaphysical vogue of Eliot and by the later New Criticism were the members of the Middle Generation, which included, among others, Richard Eberhart, Randall Jarrell, Robert Lowell, Howard Nemerov, Theodore Roethke, Delmore Schwartz, Karl Shapiro, and Richard Wilbur. Born in the first and second decades of the century, in the midst of the modern revolution, they grew up in the shadow of the moderns, especially that of T. S. Eliot. As beneficiaries of the revolution, they incorporated many of the conventions of their elders, especially their use of irony and metaphysical imagery. Most reacted against the radical experimentalism of Pound, Williams, Cummings, and Marianne Moore. They worked instead, often with distinction, within the metrically regular forms approved by Ransom and most of the New Critics. Unlike Pound, Eliot, and Williams, they did not attempt the epic or ambitious culture poem. Eschewing broad social problems (except for those connected with their experience of World War II), they concerned themselves for the most part with the treatment of personal feelings and experiences, often from a first-person viewpoint. Their subjectivism marked the beginning of a postwar reaction against the impersonal theory of Eliot.

The range of interests and technique among these poets can be seen in the work of Robert Lowell, Karl Shapiro, Theodore Roethke, and Richard Eberhart. The career of Robert Lowell reveals the combined influence of Eliot and the New Criticism. Born in 1917, the year of Eliot's first book of poems, *Prufrock and Other Observations*, Lowell entered Harvard but transferred to Kenyon College, to which Ransom had moved from Vanderbilt University. Like T. S. Eliot, Allen Tate, and other of the conservative moderns, Lowell underwent a religious conversion and became a Roman Catholic in 1940, the year of his graduation. The poems of his early years (1944–51) reveal his inner conflicts through strongly metaphysical imagery reflecting, like Eliot's, an intense interest in mystical experience and religious history. He also shares with Eliot a sense of the decadence of New England culture and a Puritan preoccupation with death and the problem of personal salvation. These qualities strongly mark such early poems as "Colloquy in Black Rock" and "The Drunken Fisherman." In both, Lowell develops themes and images reminiscent of Eliot's *Waste Land* story of the Fisher King, within the metrically regular forms favored by Ransom and the New Critics. The last stanzas of the two poems are indicative:

> Christ walks on the black water. In Black Mud
> Darts the kingfisher. On Corpus Christi, heart,
> Over the drum-beat of St. Stephen's choir
> I hear him, *Stupor Mundi*, and the mud
> Flies from his hunching wings and beak—my heart.
> The blue kingfisher dives on you in fire.

> Is there no way to cast my hook
> Out of this dynamited brook?
> The Fisher's sons must cast about
> When shallow waters peter out.
> I will catch Christ with a greased worm,
> And when the Prince of Darkness stalks
> My bloodstream to its Stygian term . . .
> On water the Man-Fisher walks.

More recent poems, beginning with those of *Life Studies* (1959), reveal a shift away from his early models. In keeping with the trend of the times, the poems are in metrically freer forms. The habitual self-questioning and self-analysis, which have given Lowell a place among modern "confessional" poets, are carried on, but in an autobiographical rather than religious context. Some of the pieces, like the long prose narrative of Section II, "91 Revere Street," explore the writer's introverted childhood and painful family relationships. They are suffused with a sense of alienation and sickness. In "Waking in the Blue" and "Memories of West Street and Lepke," the images of the "house for the 'mentally ill' " in which Lowell was a patient and the West Street Jail in New York, in which he served time as a conscientious objector, are, like Thoreau's and Dickens's prisons, symbols of a more widespread moral and spiritual malaise.

An oppressive sense of general corruption (a link with Eliot) is perhaps the most distinctive quality of all Lowell's poetry. The irregularly metered and loosely rhymed "Skunk Hour" has as its setting a Maine coastal village which shares the decadence of the larger world through its hermit heiress, summer millionaire, and fairy interior decorator. The poet (not merely "the speaker") drives on a dark night to a hillside road to spy on "love-cars." Realizing that his "mind's not right," he remarks, "I myself am hell; / nobody's here." Returning to his house in the village, he finds only skunks patrolling Main Street, searching for a "bite to eat." The final image is of a mother skunk swilling at a garbage pail as she forages for her young:

> She jabs her wedge-head in a cup
> of sour cream, drops her ostrich tail,
> and will not scare.

The skunk is healthily performing a natural function, but Lowell is less interested in it as a creature to be respected for its own sake (in the manner of Marianne Moore) than as a symbol of the decay of the society on which it scavenges and, more directly, of his own unhealthiness and perversion.

The final poem of *Life Studies*, "Colonel Shaw and the Massachusetts 44th," looks back to the Civil War black regiment commanded by Colonel Robert Shaw, whose service and death in battle were commemorated by Saint-Gaudens in a bronze bas-relief memorial placed near the statehouse in Boston. As observed by Lowell on the occasion of this poem, both the memorial and the statehouse were shaking with vibrations from excavation for an underground garage. The memorial is a reminder of the never-to-be realized democratic idealism of the earlier Republic, now gravely undermined by the building of the modern industrial state.

As Lowell observes in his last stanza, the automobile, a servile, predatory machine, has displaced the aquarium which he frequented as a child in Boston and which represents to him the alien but seductive "dark downward and vegetating kingdom / of the fish and reptile":

The Aquarium is gone. Everywhere,
giant finned cars nose forward like fish;
a savage servility
slides by on grease.

In its metrical irregularity, the poem reveals a shift away from
Lowell's earlier practice and the influences of his youth, but the
theme, which involves a tension between a heroic past and a
degraded present, is firmly in the tradition of Eliot and the New
Critics. Lowell renamed this poem and used it as the title piece
of his next collection, *For the Union Dead* (1964). One is
reminded of Tate's earlier "Ode to the Confederate Dead," no
doubt intentionally, and also of Tate's explanation of its struc-
ture. His definition of a tension between " 'active faith' which
has decayed and the 'fragmentary cosmos' which surrounds us"
applies just as well to Lowell's poem, with the difference that
Lowell is concerned as Tate was not with the brutalizing effect
of the machine on modern life. By romantically idealizing the
American past as a foil to the present, both Tate and Lowell
ignore the corruption and brutality of the Civil War period.

The work of Lowell's close contemporary Karl Shapiro re-
veals a strong ambivalence toward T. S. Eliot, admired as the
model of a major modern poet but disliked for his conservative
and aristocratic ideas. In his early verse book of poetics, *Essay
on Rime* (1945), Shapiro brands Eliot an "intellectual" rather
than poet and yet acknowledges his enormous influence:

But in the interim
Between his deep and masterly despair
And the overt fulfillment of his faith
His word was our poetic law.

Shapiro's own early poems reveal a worldly disillusionment and
a satiric bent reminiscent of the verse of Eliot's preconversion
years. In form they tend, like Lowell's, toward a regularity which
may be attributed not only to the influence of the New Critics
but also to the prestige of W. H. Auden as a rising younger poet
of the 1930s, during Shapiro's formative years.

Some sections of Shapiro's "Recapitulations," a sequence of
autobiographical poems, have echoes of Eliot. In its syntax,

159

rhythm, and ironic tone, one on the soldier poet's wedding (XVI) sounds very much like "Sweeney among the Nightingales" and "Burbank with a Baedeker; Bleistein with a Cigar." Despite the difference in subject, the first two of Shapiro's eight stanzas can show the likenesses:

> The atheist bride is dressed in blue,
> The heretic groom in olive-drab,
> The rabbi, of more somber hue,
> Arrives upon the scene by cab.
>
> A brief injunction to the pair
> With no talk of the demiurge
> Gives them the gist of the affair;
> They sign the contract and emerge.

Although Shapiro came to reject the intellect, many of his most successful early poems are distinguished by a rationalistic ironic skepticism. They often are satiric and socially critical, like "Drugstore," in which "every nook and cranny of the flesh / Is spoken to by packages with wiles," and "University," in the Southern setting of which "to hurt the Negro and avoid the Jew / Is the curriculum."

For Shapiro and other poets of his generation, World War II, in which he served in the Pacific theater, provided the most important occasion for the treatment of social themes. "Elegy for a Dead Soldier" describes the military funeral service for a young American GI, one of many of the obscure victims of the war. Shapiro comments on the richness of his heritage as an American, even though he was not committed to the war, and insists upon his importance as an irreplaceable individual:

> However others calculate the cost,
> To us the final aggregate is *one*,
> One with a name, one transferred to the blest;
> And though another stoops and takes the gun,
> We cannot add the second to the first.

The appended epitaph poses the problem of moral responsibility for a more humane world:

Underneath this wooden cross there lies
A Christian killed in battle. You who read,
Remember that this stranger died in pain;
And passing here, if you can lift your eyes
Upon a peace kept by a human creed,
Know that one soldier has not died in vain.

The questions of whether the war dead can be thought of as
dying for a "cause" and whether peace might be secured through
any socially supported system of values are introduced without
judgment.

In "The Conscientious Objector," the soldier-poet praises one
who, like Robert Lowell, suffered imprisonment for his pacifist
ideals. Contrasting the lot of the objector and the soldier,
Shapiro concludes:

You suffered not so physically but knew
Maltreatment, hunger, ennui of the mind.
Well might the soldier kissing the hot beach
Erupting in his face damn all your kind.
Yet you who saved neither yourselves nor us
Are equally with those who shed the blood
The heroes of our cause. Your conscience is
What we come back to in the armistice

The implied lack of commitment which the poet shares with the
soldier-subject of his elegy is typical of many of his generation
influenced by the disillusionment and paralysis of belief and
action that Eliot dramatized in his earlier poems.

Over the years since the war, Shapiro has come to repudiate
the "intellectualism" and disillusionment of Eliot and the mod-
erns in favor of a poetry of Whitmanesque cosmic vision. Like
Lowell, he has shifted to the freer metrical forms favored by the
younger generation of poets. In *The Bourgeois Poet* (1958), he
has gone so far as to write prose poems in which the conven-
tions of rhyme and meter are ignored, although his use of para-
graphing and parallelism is reminiscent of Whitman's free verse
form. In one of these prose poems, "Why poetry small and
cramped," Shapiro suggests the motives that underlie his rebel-

161

lion against metrics, including a hostility like William Carlos Williams's against the confines of the sonnet and of any conventional rhyming:

> Why poetry small and cramped, why poetry starved and mean,
>   thin-lipped and sunken-cheeked? Why these pams,
>   these narrow-shouldered negatives? (The best we can
>   say is that they're seed catalogs.) And why those star-
>   ing eyes, so carefully fixed on the photographic plate?
>   Why no lips at all but in their stead the practiced line
>   of anger and the clamped jaw? Why always the dark-
>   ening halo, so seemingly satanic? (The best we can
>   say is that they are trying to mirror our lives. Do they
>   know our lives? Can they read past the symbols of our
>   trade?) Why so much attention to the printed page,
>   why the cosmetology of font and rule, meters laid on
>   like fingernail enamel? Why these lisping indentations,
>   Spanish question marks upside down? Why the at-
>   tractive packaging of stanza? Those cartons so pretty,
>   shall I open them up? Why the un-American-activity
>   of the sonnet? Why must grown people listen to
>   rhyme? How much longer the polite applause, the
>   tickle in the throat? . . .

Despite the denunciatory fervor of these lines, Shapiro has more recently experienced a lapse, or perhaps reconversion, in the sonnets of *White-Haired Lover* (1968).

Theodore Roethke and Richard Eberhart share some of the characteristics of Lowell and Shapiro. Born in 1908, Roethke grew up in Saginaw, Michigan, the son of a florist. The imagery of rank vegetable growth in many of his early poems reflects childhood experience in his father's greenhouse which may have encouraged a tendency toward nature mysticism unusual in poets of his generation. Among the moderns, Yeats rather than Eliot contributed to his growth as a poet. Roethke responded sympathetically to the musicality and the unsurrendered passional drive of Yeats's verse.

In the first part of his "Four for Sir John Davies" (1953), Roethke explains:

162

I take this cadence from a man named Yeats:
I take it, and I give it back again:
For other tunes and other wanton beats
Have tossed my heart and fiddled through my brain.
Yes, I was dancing-mad, and how
That came to be the bears and Yeats would know.

In theme and rhythm, this verse is closest to Yeats's poems of *The Tower* (1928). The central image in "Four for Sir John Davies" of a dance of love attuned to an imperfectly perceived cosmic dance is like the chestnut tree and dance image of Yeats's "Among School Children":

O chestnut tree, great rooted blossomer,
Are you the leaf, the blossom or the bole?
O body swayed to music, O brightening glance,
How can we know the dancer from the dance?

But in cadence and rhythm, Roethke is closest perhaps to "Sailing to Byzantium," as Yeats's last stanza shows:

Once out of nature I shall never take
My bodily form from any natural thing,
But such a form as Grecian goldsmiths make
Of hammered gold and gold enamelling
To keep a drowsy Emperor awake;
Or set upon a golden bough to sing
To lords and ladies of Byzantium
Of what is past, or passing, or to come.

In "The Vigil," the fourth part of Roethke's poem, the dance of love is given religious implications through an allusion to Dante's vision of Beatrice; it ends with an obscure but affirmative identification of sexual and spiritual ecstasy:

The world is for the living. Who are they?
We dared the dark to reach the white and warm.
She was the wind when wind was in my way;
Alive at noon, I perished in her form.
Who rise from flesh to spirit know the fall:
The word outleaps the world, and light is all.

The word has a poetic as well as religious significance, and the "form" the poet dies in possessing suggests both his muse or inspiration and his work.

"In a Dark Time" (1964) also reveals a mystical inclination in its likening of self-discovery to the discovery and revelation of God. The illumination is not easily won, however. In a Yeatsian way, Roethke recognizes madness as "nobility of soul / At odds with circumstance," and admits to the knowledge of "pure despair" in his own striving:

> Dark, dark my light, and darker my desire.
> My soul, like some heat-maddened summer fly,
> Keeps buzzing at the sill. Which I is *I*?
> A fallen man, I climb out of my fear.
> The mind enters itself, and God the mind,
> And one is One, free in the tearing wind.

Such extreme fluctuations of mood, from despair to exaltation, or from exaltation to despair, are not unusual in Roethke's poems.

His later verse, in the years before his sudden death in 1963, reveals a further development in skill as he turned to freer measures encouraged by the times. "Meditations of an Old Woman," a four-part free form poem, is remarkable for the freshness and aptness of its imagery, as when the speaker says of herself:

> I've become a strange piece of flesh,
> Nervous and cold, bird-furtive, whiskery,
> With a cheek soft as a hound's ear.
> What's left is light as a seed . . . .

Aware always of imminent death as a link to the animal world, the old woman still feels the movement of a spirit trying for "another life," like a tired salmon pushing upstream, striving against the current. Through her sense of this impulse and of her bond with nature, it is still possible for the woman, "lacking a god," to be happy.

The impulse toward transcendence is as persistent in Roethke's work as in that of the Romantics and the later Yeats. But there is a difference. Lacking access to the confident supernaturalism of an Emerson, Roethke will not fall back, like Yeats, on magic and a religion of his own devising. In this resistance, he is like other members of his generation who could find little sustenance in the synthetic myths of the moderns. Though their refusal may represent an intellectual advance (a fuller acceptance of a naturalistic world view), it may also help to explain their neglect of the epic or culture poem.

Roethke also does not share the Spenglerian pessimism of Eliot and Yeats. Despite the painfulness of the struggle between the physical and spiritual life (a conflict with Freudian as well as religious implications) and despite the admission of despair, there remains an irresistible gusto and impulse toward joy in Roethke's verse—even an afflatus reminiscent of Whitman, but without Whitman's tendency toward diffuseness. Writing about an early group of poems entitled "The Lost Son," Roethke remarks:

> Some of these pieces, then, begin in the mire; as if man is not more than a shape writhing from the old rock. This may be due, in part, to the Michigan from which I come. Sometimes one gets the feeling that not even the animals have been there before; but the marsh, the mire, the Void, is always there, immediate and terrifying. It is a splendid place for schooling the spirit. It is America.
>
> None the less, in spite of all the muck and welter, the dark, the dreck of these poems, I count myself among the happy poets. "I proclaim, once more, a condition of joy!" says the very last piece.

Richard Eberhart (born in 1904) also recognizes that poetry is both sensuous and (as an expression of aspiration) spiritual. Unlike Roethke, he has striven to resolve the conflict through intellectual apprehension rather than mystical revelation. One of his best-known poems, "In a Hard Intellectual Light," describes his role as poet as the painful effort to see and express the painful beauty of experience in

> . . . the hard intellectual light
> That kills all delight
> And brings the solemn, inward pain
> Of truth into the heart again.

The truth the poet seeks is neither easily come by nor absolute. The word *truth*, Eberhart has said, remains "still consanguineous to ultimate perfectibility, strife, and aspiration." "One would not write poetry if one had perfect understanding . . . . If the mind were clear it would write logic or mathematics." This difficulty does not make poetry less valid, however, or minimize the poet's responsibility. He must try to define the truth of his experience as he sees it, at the height of his power, from moment to moment of his changing life. That the poet's definitions are never absolute enhances rather than cheapens their value: "A one-to-one relationship would devastate the impeccable rarities." Of dogma, Eberhart has said, "On any topic of poetry one should not be dogmatic. There is greater freedom in the tentative."

Eberhart's poetry represents an intense sustained effort to communicate the truth of his experience over the space of more than four decades. In his metrical patterns, he is among the most conservative of his generation, since he has largely restricted himself to regular four- or five-stressed rhymed quatrains, with, in the later poems of *Shifts of Being* (1968), a growing tendency toward rapid reiterative rhyming, as in "The Rolling Eye":

> How should a poem look? Free?
> My poems should look like me.
> But this is harder than it looks.
> Compounding millennial difficulty.

Yet within these limits, by varying accent and rhythm to forge a style of power and compression, Eberhart has established a mature poetic voice that is one of the most distinguished of his generation. With integrity and intellectual rigor he has insisted on confronting the hard facts of experience that stand in the way of the love and harmony he would prefer to see in the world. While recognizing and affirming these values, he has not attempted by force of will to find them where they are not nor has he taken recourse to mysticism as a substitute gratification. In "The Fury of Aerial Bombardment," he admits widespread violence and murderousness to be deeply rooted in human nature:

166

You would feel that after so many centuries
God would give man to repent; yet he can kill
As Cain could, but with multitudinous will,
No farther advanced than in his ancient furies.

"The Human Being Is a Lonely Creature" recognizes the pain and mortal loneliness of the human situation and the requirement of a countervailing courage if life is to be affirmed:

Life is daring all our human stature.
Death looks, and waits for each bright eye.
Love and harmony are our best nurture.
The human being is a lonely creature.

Although Richard Eberhart has been preoccupied with self-definition, he has pursued the enterprise with full respect for his relationship to the world of nature and other individuals. Avoiding the narcissistic self-regard of confessionalism and the opportunities for ambiguity provided by the use of dramatic personae, he has borne witness to the modern world in his own person, with integrity and authority. For these and other virtues, his work should stand as a solid contribution.

12. The Revolution Renewed: Contemporary Poetry

THE ENDLESS PROCESS of innovation and change, of actions that beget reactions in literature and society, has brought a profound shift in sensibility among the poets of the Third Generation. The work of these men and women, born in the 1920s and 1930s, makes it clear that the modern period in poetry has ended and that another, not yet fully realized, has begun.

The younger poets have almost totally rejected the example and precepts of T. S. Eliot, who stood as the leading arbiter of poetic taste during the years between the wars. Besides disliking Eliot's social and political conservatism as a defender of the Establishment, they disagree with his impersonal theory and his idea of the objective correlative. The extremity of their opposition can be most simply understood if one considers that, for a large majority of the younger poets, Eliot's well-known characterization of himself in *For Lancelot Andrewes* (1928) as "a royalist in politics, a classicist in literature, and an Anglo-Catholic in religion" represents the antithesis of their own political, aesthetic, and religious ideals.

The younger writers have also resisted the influence of modern symbolism. Because they have seen this tradition harden into symbological systems in the work of poets like Eliot and Stevens, they have attempted to renew the language of poetry by using images in new ways.

Yet the break from the older generation has not been complete. While denying Eliot, they have turned to Ezra Pound and William Carlos Williams as champions of freer aesthetic views. Alining themselves with the more radical wing of the earlier modern revolution, and with Walt Whitman as its Romantic pioneer, they have tended to affirm the social relevance of poetry. They have shunned the kind of irony and ambiguity admired by the New Critics as a technique of self-containment that divests poetry of social meaning. Many have gone beyond the earlier modern poets in their social rebellion and their insistence that the writer be personally committed or "engaged" in his work. They speak in their own persons rather than indirectly through dramatic personae like Prufrock or Mauberley. Most important, they have accepted the formal theory of the Romantics and the Imagists and attempted to carry forward the principles and practice of organic free verse.

The main stream of organic theory has long embraced two chief principles. One, the idea that form is determined by the nature of the subject and by the artist's perception, is basic to the whole modern movement in the arts, including architecture, stagecraft, and industrial design. Well understood by the American Romantics, it was most concisely set forth in Emerson's observation: "For it is not metres, but a metre-making argument that makes a poem—a thought so passionate and alive that like the spirit of a plant or an animal it has an architecture of its own, and adorns nature with a new thing."[1]

The other principle, which goes back to Aristotle, asserts the interrelatedness of parts and the indispensability of any one to the *whole*, as that from which a part cannot be removed. The idea stresses the unity of the parts of a work and the functional

[1] See above, pp. 7–8.

relationship among them, but it has sometimes been overemphasized to support a puristic formalism that defines the poem as a hermetic language system divorced from its environment. The tensional theories of the New Critics[2] pushed this idea of unity and autonomy to an extreme and did much to inspire the conservative reaction among poets of the Middle Generation.

Reacting in differing ways against the ideas of both the first generation of modern poets and the Middle Generation poets, the members of the Third Generation have shown a variety of interests in subject and technique in their efforts to carry forward the organic tradition. Some, inspired by Charles Olson's theory of projective verse, have engaged in metrical experiments and in theoretical discussions of free verse measure. Some, like the postwar Beat poets, have been less interested in poetics than in unrestrained expression of their feeling of alienation and their protest against the conditions of modern life. Some have carried forward the more personal confessional tradition of Robert Lowell. The extreme psychological alienation of a poet like Sylvia Plath reveals an impulse to push the use of language and imagery beyond the limits of rationality. In its most extreme form, this impulse has been deliberately supported and extended by poets wishing to renew the metaphoric resources of poetry by violating conventional symbolism and meaning—sometimes by attempting to approximate in poetry the effects of such other arts as music, painting, and even sculpture. Through all these currents of change and innovation, there has persisted, as a central stabilizing tradition, a concern for Whitman's conception of the poet as a democratic spokesman for his society and its values.

The following selection of individual figures is intended to represent distinctive tendencies rather than to be comprehensive. Within the limits of a chapter, justice cannot be done to the great number of admirable younger poets who have already gained recognition. Nor is it possible—if form is recognized to be a complex of interrelated patterns of sound, syntax, image and event, and meaning—to discuss the full range of formal interest of the poems chosen to represent the poets who are included.

[2] See above, pp. 152–55.

I

The most influential theoretical statement by a Third Generation poet (chronologically a member of the Middle Generation) is Charles Olson's "Projective Verse" (1950), an essay calling for an open poetic form determined by the dynamics of the subject and, most distinctively, by the breathing of the poet. Olson's models are unmistakable. The beginning of his essay not only cites Pound and Williams but even reproduces the typographical peculiarities of Pound's prose style:

PROJECTIVE   VERSE
        (projectile   (percussive   (prospective
                                vs.

                        The NON-Projective

> *(or what a French critic calls "closed" verse, that verse*
> *which print bred and which is pretty much what we*
> *have had, in English & American, and have still got,*
> *despite the work of Pound & Williams:*
>
> *it led Keats, already a hundred years ago, to see it*
> *(Wordsworth's,Milton's) in the light of "the Egotistical*
> *Sublime"; and it persists, at this latter day, as what you*
> *might call the private-soul-at-any-public-wall)*

Verse now, 1950, if it is to go ahead, if it is to be of *essential* use, must, I take it, catch up and put into itself certain laws and possibilities of the breath, of the breathing of the man who writes as well as of his listenings. (The revolution of the ear, 1910, the trochee's heave, asks it of the younger poets.)

Olson speaks of an "open" form or "composition by field" that is determined by the "kinetics" of the subject and the pattern of the poet's perception, a sequential process which supplies a necessary dynamic and movement. In any given poem, Olson insists, "one perception must MOVE, INSTANTER, ON ANOTHER!"

Together with the movement of perception and, it would seem, even more basic as a determinant of metrical form, is the rhythm of the poet's breathing: "And the line comes (I swear it) from the breath, from the breathing of the man who writes, at the moment that he writes, and thus is, it is here that, the daily work, the WORK, gets in, for only he, the man who writes, can declare, at every moment, the line its metric and its end— where its breathing, shall come to, termination." The rhythm of Olson's own prose line (if it is "measured" by his punctuation) is not only distinctive but highly idiosyncratic.

Like Williams and Cummings before him, Olson is interested in the function of spaces as a measure of verse:

> If a contemporary poet leaves a space as long as the phrase before it, he means that space to be held, by the breath, an equal length of time. If he suspends a word or syllable at the end of a line (this was most Cummings' addition) he means that time to pass that it takes the eye—that hair of time suspended—to pick up the next line. If he wishes a pause so light that it hardly separates the words, yet does not want a comma— which is an interruption of the meaning rather than the sounding of the line—follow him when he uses a symbol the typewriter has ready to hand:

> "What does not change / is the will to change"

Olson feels that the typewriter, because of "its rigidity and its space precisions," is an instrument which makes it possible for the "sons of Pound and Williams", to "indicate exactly the breath, the pauses, the suspensions even of syllables, the juxtapositions even of parts of phrases, which he intends. For the first time the poet has the stave and the bar a musician has had."

Although, except by Olson, little has been said about the typewriter as a metrical instrument, both William Carlos Williams and Denise Levertov have discussed the function of spacing. Of the two, Miss Levertov has been the more specific. She regards a line-end pause as "equal to half a comma," while the pauses between stanzas, which are also important, "are much harder to evaluate." In more general terms she has said, "I believe every space and comma is a living part of the poem and has its function. . . . And the way the lines are broken is a function-

∧ & The daughters of H. D. & Moore

ing part essential to the poem's life." She has discussed her sense of the pauses within a poem and of its spacing in relation to "The Tulips," one of her shorter pieces.

The idea of breath-spaced lines is more problematical. Olson's insistence upon the importance of breath has been taken seriously by a number of younger poets, most notably by Robert Creeley in laconic short-line poems like "I Know a Man," which begins:

> As I sd to my
> friend, because I am
> always talking,—John,I
>
> sd, which was not his
> name, the darkness sur-
> rounds us . . .

Creeley's idiosyncratic poems are often disturbingly spasmodic in movement—an effect exaggerated in the poet's reading of his own work, with a too generous respect for the pauses that separate his short lines. In some pieces, however, the lines follow each other smoothly in functionally measured verses like those of "The Rain," which opens:

> All night the sound had
> come back again,
> and again falls
> this quiet, persistent rain.

Protesting so literal an acceptance of Olson's theory, Denise Levertov has observed that "the breath idea is taken by a lot of young poets to mean the rhythm of the outer voice. They take that in conjunction with Williams's insistence upon the American idiom, and they produce poems which are purely documentary." She believes that the rhythm of a poem is more properly and basically determined by the rhythm of the "inner voice" (not identical with the spoken language) which reflects the flow of consciousness as it continuously works to grasp and evaluate, in words, the flow of experience.

Charles Olson's effort to realize his theory in practice can

173

best be seen in his *Maximus Poems* (1960), an ambitious work reminiscent in various ways of *Paterson* and *The Cantos*. Assuming the persona of "Maximus" (perhaps a designation of the heightened consciousness of the poetic self or, in his own terms, of the "man in the Word"), Olson uses the seaport setting of Gloucester, Massachusetts, in ways that recall Williams's treatment of his New Jersey city. Through a sequence of "letters" or separate poems by Maximus, Olson attempts to find an appropriate form by evoking the past and present life of Gloucester and by merging his identity, in the manner of Whitman and Williams, with both his local environment and the larger cosmopolitan world in which he lives imaginatively. The treatment of the life of Gloucester fishermen and of the town life Olson knew as a boy is often effective. So too are the complementary imagistic passages which capture the beauty of the common harbor:

> when the water glowed,
> black, gold, the tide
> outward, at evening
>
> when bells came like boats
> over the oil-slicks, milkweed
> hulls
> And a man slumped,
> attentionless,
> against pink shingles
>
> o sea city)

But these imagistic interludes do not seem integral to the larger work because Olson's viewpoint is not so firmly established or coherently developed as that of Pound or Williams: there is not the sense of a firm overview of the kind that gives integrity to *Paterson* or *The Cantos*. Olson imitates without fully assimilating many of Pound's attitudes (his anticapitalism, for one) and mannerisms (his fondness for esoteric allusions), and these features of his work jar with the neutral and straightforward presentation of the life of Gloucester and its inhabitants. The general effect of *Maximus* is that of a collection of separate poems without the structural continuity or cumulative impact of Pound's or Williams's major poems. Despite Olson's prescription for a dynamic poetry in which perception follows perception with sustained kinetic thrust, his own verse too often reveals a relaxed poetic line with unassimilated particulars and echoes of the masters. Its chief weakness is a lack of concentration and intensity.

These deficiencies do not detract from the importance of Olson's critical influence on postwar poetry. In "Projective Verse," his was one of the first voices to proclaim the leadership of Pound and Williams among younger poets and to encourage the renewal of formal experimentation discouraged during the years of the conservative counterrevolution. It is true that poets other than Olson, including some of the earlier Objectivists, had been carrying forward the tradition of Pound and Williams during the 1930s and 1940s. But it was primarily Olson, speaking out at a crucial time, who provided a catalyst for the work of the rising generation of poets.

One of these young poets, equally committed to the organic principle but less theory-bound in her work, is Denise Levertov, who has been most closely associated with Robert Creeley and Robert Duncan among her contemporaries. Born in England to a Welsh mother and a Russian Jewish father who became an Anglican priest, she married an American, Mitchell Goodman, shortly after the war. She found moving to the United States in 1948 a stimulating experience that "necessitated the finding of new rhythms of life and speech." In this effort, she was helped by the stylistic influence of William Carlos Williams, which she has acknowledged as necessary, for without it she "could not have developed from a British Romantic with almost Victorian background to an American poet of any vitality." Miss Levertov quickly absorbed the rhythms of American life and speech. Her first book of verse as an American poet, *Here and Now*, was published by Lawrence Ferlinghetti in San Francisco in 1956.

In numerous prose statements and in her poems, Miss Levertov has supported and further elaborated the theory of organic form. She has said that her general view is "really based on the idea that there is form in all things—that the artist doesn't impose form upon chaos, but discovers hidden intrinsic form— and on the idea that poems can arrive at their form by means

175

of the poet's attentive listening, not only his listening but also his feeling, his meditating upon his experience, and by means of his accurate transcription of that experience into words."

In "Illustrious Ancestors," an early poem, she identifies herself with two of her forebears—the "Rav of Northern White Russia," who came to understand the language of birds through attentive listening, and Angel Jones of Mold, the Welsh tailor and mystic—and through this association suggests her own ideal of poetic form:

> Well, I would like to make,
> thinking some line still taut between me and them,
> poems direct as what the birds said,
> hard as a floor, sound as a bench,
> mysterious as the silence when the tailor
> would pause with his needle in the air.

Another heritage is a joy in the creation fostered by the tradition of mystical Hasidic Judaism. In "Come into Animal Presence," Miss Levertov regards the world of creatures with a respect that is not only humane, like Marianne Moore's, but reverential. Her conclusion:

> What is this joy? That no animal
> falters, but knows what it must do?
> That the snake has no blemish,
> that the rabbit inspects his strange surroundings
> in white star-silence? The llama
> rests in dignity, the armadillo
> has some intention to pursue in the palm-forest.
> Those who were sacred have remained so,
> holiness does not dissolve, it is a presence
> of bronze, only the sight that saw it
> faltered and turned from it.
> An old joy returns in holy presence.

This sacramental feeling has led her to reverse the sentiment of Wordsworth's sonnet "The World Is Too Much with Us." "O Taste and See" (a title taken from a subway Bible poster) begins with the proclamation, "The world is / not with us

176

enough." Miss Levertov accepts the religious principle of communion achieved through a symbolic tasting, but extends the idea of the sacrament to embrace a communion not only with the Lord, but, like Williams in "The Host," with "all that lives / to the imagination's tongue":

> grief, mercy, language,
> tangerine, weather, to
> breathe them, bite,
> savor, chew, swallow, transform
>
> into our flesh our
> deaths, crossing the street, plum, quince,
> living in the orchard and being
>
> hungry, and plucking
> the fruit.

In keeping with this desire, like Williams's, for immediate contact with the world of experience, Miss Levertov's poems are often sensuous and intensely personal. A repeated theme is the joy afforded by the perception of uncommon formal beauty in common subjects. "Pleasures" begins:

> I like to find
> what's not found
> at once, but lies
>
> within something of another nature,
> in repose. distinct.
> Gull feathers of glass, hidden
>
> in white pulp: the bones of squid
> which I pull out and lay
> blade by blade on the draining board—
>
> > tapered as if for swiftness, to pierce
> > the heart, but fragile, substance
> > belying design.

Suffering, more than joy, and a growing social awareness have emerged in later poems. Although Miss Levertov worked as a young hospital volunteer in wartime London, she has spoken of herself as relatively untouched by the war and the horrors of Nazism. Subsequent events have brought fuller realization. The trial of Adolf Eichmann in Jerusalem for crimes against the Jewish people provided a poetic focus for the phenomenon of German racism. The mystery of Eichmann's perversion and the terror of the Nazi persecution of the Jews are treated with intensity of feeling and sensitive intelligence in a group of poems published under the title "During the Eichmann Trial" in *The Jacob's Ladder* (1961).

The Sorrow Dance (1967) contains six "Olga Poems" devoted to the memory of an older sister who died in 1964. Among the traits noted by Miss Levertov in her effort to realize her sister's complex personality is a fanatic commitment to a doctrinaire idea of political revolution which she contrasts with her own impulse toward the acceptance and celebration of the world. But Miss Levertov was to appreciate and even share some of her sister's zeal. "Life at War," the last section of poems in *The Sorrow Dance*, reveals deepening concern over the Vietnam war and a commitment to the antiwar cause.

The pressures of the war and of social injustice dominate the poems of *Relearning the Alphabet* (1970). The waste, irrationality, and inequities of the war and a war-waging society are brought home by many experiences: the loss of the children of friends, the suffering of the civilian victims of the war, and the involvement of her husband (a defendant in the Spock trial) and others in the antiwar effort. The common language itself, the poet's medium, seems threatened by a perversion and corruption even greater than that observed by Williams in *Paterson*. The report of an American army officer that "it became necessary to destroy the town to save it" moves Miss Levertov to reflect: "O language, mother of thought, / are you rejecting us as we reject you? / . . . you are eroded as war erodes us."

Under the stress of a predicament that requires a choice between commitment to social revolution and acceptance of a murderous system, the poet's course seems clear: "Of course I choose / revolution." But the prospect of total absorption in a cause—difficult for one temperamentally attuned to personal feelings and perceptions—arouses misgivings and self-distrust: "I choose / revolution but my words / often already don't reach forward / into it—"

Such misgivings lead to an examination and reappraisal of personal attitudes and values, the subject of the title poem, "Relearning the Alphabet." Cast in the form of observations about the associations of the successive letters of the alphabet, the poem rejects the struggle of the "vain will" (which is, however, a condition of political life) and celebrates *caritas* (selfless love), pure contemplation and perception (also selfless), and joy in the beauties of the world revealed to the imagination. The poet's search for the essential "I-who-I-am again" leads away from the rush of events in time, "the unabridged rush of waters," and toward " 'Imagination's holy forest. . . .' "

"Relearning the Alphabet" suggests a desire to withdraw from social involvement and to reconfirm the kind of devotion to contemplation and personal perception that marked Miss Levertov's earlier poems. Yet her recent volume *To Stay Alive* (1971) renews and carries further the revolutionary commitment of the preceding two books, portions of which are included in this volume. In the long poem "Staying Alive," Miss Levertov's opposition to war is extended to "the whole system of insane greed, of racism and imperialism, of which war is only the inevitable expression." Although she recognizes the opposing pulls of the "*private life* I left" and the "tragic, fearful / knowledge of *present history*," she feels that the "singing begins" only when the "pulse rhythms / of revolution and poetry / mesh. . . ." It seems that these pulses have not, as yet, fully meshed in the work of Denise Levertov (thus leaving in some doubt the direction of her poems to come); yet it is clear that *To Stay Alive* is the most important and serious volume of revolutionary poetry by a contemporary American poet.

This achievement has been at some cost, as Miss Levertov acknowledges when she accepts for the first time the principle of violence as a tool of revolution. Also, her usually sensitive and meticulous sense of diction lapses in her use of the propagandistic *Amerika* to designate her adopted country.

The best of Denise Levertov's poems possess a lyric *élan*, appropriate organic form, and an elegance of diction and phrasing that does not call attention to itself. Her friend Robert Duncan has dated his awareness of "a new generation in poetry" from his first encounter with a poem by Miss Levertov in 1952, together with his reading of Robert Creeley's early poems and Charles Olson's essay on projective verse and the *Maximus Poems*. Duncan has also listed, as his models among the moderns, Gertrude Stein, D. H. Lawrence, Ezra Pound, H. D., William Carlos Williams, Marianne Moore, Wallace Stevens, and Edith Sitwell. He then points out, as an indication of the change in the literary climate, that "the two *sure* things—Frost and Eliot—are not there." Yet as a poet who came of age in 1940, Duncan could not easily have escaped the influence of Eliot. In commenting, more recently, that Ezra Pound alone of his old masters was still alive, he acknowledges that "Eliot was one of them."

Duncan's own poetry is most fully and accessibly represented by his collections *The Opening of the Field* (1960), *Roots and Branches* (1964), and *Bending the Bow* (1968). He is among the most "literary" of the poets of his generation. His work, like Pound's, abounds in echoes of and allusions to a wide range of classical, European, and English and American poets. In contrast to Pound, however, a strain of cabalistic mysticism, supported by references to Zen Buddhism and the theosophical mystic Jacob Boehme and to obscure self-devised beliefs and attitudes, stands as something of an obstacle to full imaginative acceptance for many readers.

If Eliot was the most important early influence of the modern generation on Duncan, as in "The Venice Poem" (1948), he has been supplanted by Pound in Duncan's later work. A number of poems, like "Passages 30" of "Stage Directions," recall the manner and imagery of *The Cantos*, though in a more reflective strain. The poem concludes:

> And from the dying body of America I see,
>   or from my dying body,
>   emerge
>   children of a deed long before this deed,
>   seed of Poseidon, depth in which the blue above
>   is reflected

released

huge Chrysaor and Pegasos   sword and flash

Father of Geryon,   of him

who carries Dante and Virgil into Hell's depths,

and Steed of Bellerophon

beneath whose hooves   once again

new springs are loosed on Helicon.

Among earlier American poets, it is Whitman to whom Duncan feels the closest affinity in both his sexual and social attitudes. Concerned like Denise Levertov with the corruption and violence of modern America, Duncan points to Whitman's prose satire of *The Eighteenth Presidency* (1856) and cites Whitman's poetic conception of a libertarian America as an ideal to be renewed in the present.

But Duncan is not a "social poet" in the usual sense of the term. He is primarily a technician interested in poetics and the aesthetic effects of his measures. His adoption of Olson's idea of "composition by field" has been reinforced by an interest in the art of collage in painting. Many of his poems reveal a preoccupation with spatial patterns consisting of a collocation of images and allusions which may have emotional but lack rational coherence or connectedness. For this technique, Pound's ideogrammatic method must have provided a model for Duncan, as it had for Olson.

Duncan has profited from a study of Pound's lyrical style. He often succeeds in achieving a lightness and grace of movement in his lines, as in the early pieces "The Dance" and "A Poem Beginning with a Line by Pindar," that compares favorably with Pound at his best. But Duncan's verse lacks the virility of Pound's. His delicacy of manner is more effective in the treatment of distanced subjects than of personal emotions. In his poems dealing with love, and especially homosexual love, there is often a lushness and effeminacy that puts the reader off as he is not by the *Calamus* poems of Whitman.

II

The most violent postwar reaction against the older generation and established society was expressed by the writers of the Beat

181

movement, represented most prominently by Allen Ginsberg in poetry and Jack Kerouac in prose. Other poets associated with the movement included Gregory Corso, Ginsberg's publisher Lawrence Ferlinghetti, and several writers more or less closely associated with the central figures. The movement originated in New York City in the early 1950s and flourished in San Francisco and other cities, including Denver and New Orleans, among which its members shuttled in beat-up automobiles in frenetic nonstop journeys of the kind celebrated in Kerouac's *On the Road* (1957). Rejecting the mores and folkways of middle-class "square" society, the Beats advocated a withdrawal from reality into an inner world of surrealistic vision induced by drugs, homo- and heterosexual adventure, and the rudiments of an eclectic mysticism drawn from the teachings of Zen Buddhism and the sacred books of India.

The word *Beat* suggests the exhausted condition of the members of a group who felt that they had "had it" as far as the demands of conventional society were concerned. More positively, it represents a belief in the possibility of a beatified experience attainable through mystical vision.

The Beat tradition was largely superseded by the civil rights movement of the 1960s, which demanded an activist, politically engaged position for the writer, as opposed to the regressive withdrawal advocated by the Beats. But the two movements have not remained entirely separate. The younger generation of hippies, who took over the drug mystique and many of the attitudes of the alienated Beats, have paradoxically combined the impulse toward withdrawal and escape with a political activism channeled most strongly into the protest against the Vietnam war. That this cause has not yet produced much poetry of consequence may be explained by the fact that many of its supporters have preferred the indulgence of slogans to the discipline of writing.

The best-known poem of the Beat movement is Allen Ginsberg's "Howl" (1956), the title piece of a collection issued by Lawrence Ferlinghetti's City Lights Bookshop in San Francisco. It opens with a brief introduction by William Carlos Williams, who had known Ginsberg in his boyhood in Paterson, New Jersey. Written in long-line parallel verse-clauses that pile up into huge sentences, "Howl" invites comparison with the "Song of Myself" of Whitman, whom Ginsberg claims as a father. But unlike Whitman's poem of praise, "Howl" is a frenzied protest against the indignities of life in Ginsberg's America. Much shorter than Whitman's 52-part "Song," it consists of three sections supplemented by a brief "Footnote to Howl." Also unlike Whitman's poem, which is addressed to all men and proclaims the universality of human experience ("And what I assume you shall assume"), "Howl" is addressed to Carl Solomon, Ginsberg's former friend and lover, who had been committed to the state hospital at Rockland, New York. In its appeal to the special attitudes and experiences of an alienated group, rather than to mankind at large, it is an in-group poem. To vary Pound's phrase for his *Cantos*, it is not so much the tale of the tribe as the tale of a clan. The poet's role of spokesman for the apocalyptic vision of a chosen rejected few is established in the opening lines of the poem:

I saw the best minds of my generation destroyed by madness,
      starving hysterical naked,
dragging themselves through the negro streets at dawn looking for
      an angry fix,
angelheaded hipsters burning for the ancient heavenly connection
      to the starry dynamo in the machinery of night,
who poverty and tatters and hollow-eyed and high sat up smoking
      in the supernatural darkness of cold-water flats floating
      across the tops of cities contemplating jazz. . . .

The rest of the first section consists largely of a cataloguing of the Beat ordeal and quest for illumination, although just before its end there is a brief reference to an effort

to recreate the syntax and measure of poor human prose and stand
      before you speechless and intelligent and shaking with
      shame, rejected yet confessing out the soul to conform to
      the rhythm of thought in his naked and endless head. . . .

The desire to reform the syntax sounds like Williams's program for reshaping the language, but the confessional impulse which Ginsberg shares with Lowell and others of his own generation was distasteful to Williams. Williams also disapproved of Ginsberg's long lines, finding them shapeless and undisciplined, although Ginsberg has argued, in line with Olson's theory, that "ideally each line of *Howl* is a single breath unit" of a kind he describes as "a Hebraic-Melvillian bardic breath."

The shorter second section of "Howl" is a sustained diatribe against the "Moloch" of materialistic modern America. Section III, addressed directly to Carl Solomon, carries the reiterated refrain "I'm with you in Rockland"—"where fifty more shocks will never return your soul to its / body again from its pilgrimage to a cross in the void." Ginsberg's "Footnote to Howl," in a tone much different from that of the larger poem, is a pietistic proclamation of the "holiness" of the world, including the machinery of Moloch.

Written at great speed, according to his own testimony, Ginsberg's lines give the impression of an excited outpouring of language rather than a "combing out" or selection from common speech. Because of its sensationalism and frequent obscenity, Ginsberg's verse often makes a considerable initial impact upon readers or listeners. Despite his frequent protestations of cosmic piety and disinterested benevolence, "Howl" is largely a tirade revealing an animus directed outward against those who do not share the poet's social and sexual orientation.

One of the founders and supporters of the San Francisco group of poets is Lawrence Ferlinghetti, a painter, poet, and publisher whose City Lights Bookshop Pocket Poet Series helped establish, during the 1950s, the work of Allen Ginsberg, Ferlinghetti himself, and other poets associated with the Beat movement. Strongly influenced by painting and music, Ferlinghetti combines in his verse fragmented discontinuous imagery reminiscent of Dada and Surrealism and a syncopated jazzlike rhythm achieved largely through an interraction of grammatical parallelism and interrupted broken lines. His short staggered lines often suggest a debt to Williams, while the longer parallel verses of his later "visionary" poems reveal his identification with the tradition of Whitman—though with a difference.

The best known of Ferlinghetti's early books are *Pictures of the Gone World* (1955) and *A Coney Island of the Mind* (1958). Art and artists provide the subjects of many of the poems. The first in *A Coney Island* describes Goya's vision of humanity and asserts its validity for the present as well as the past:

In Goya's greatest scenes we seem to see
                              the people of the world
            exactly at the moment when
                  they first attained the title of
                              'suffering humanity'
            They writhe upon the page
                        in a veritable rage
                                    of adversity
                  Heaped up
                        groaning with babies and bayonets
                                    under cement skies

            .   .   .   .
                        it is as if they really still existed
      And they do . . . .

In the fifth poem of *Pictures of the Gone World*, Ferlinghetti
makes much the same point, on a different subject, when he
comments on Joaquín Sarolla's paintings of women "in their
picture hats / stretched upon his canvas beaches" as beguiling
the Spanish Impressionists. "And were they fraudulent pictures
/ of the world / the way the light played on them / creating
illusions of love?" No, the speaker answers: their "reality" is
almost as real as his own memory of "today."

In these appeals to art, Ferlinghetti does not make use of the
paintings of an earlier time as a resource for his own poetic
technique. Instead, he extracts "meanings" that square with his
own outlook and uses his characterizations of the paintings to
enforce statements that are essentially didactic.

Ferlinghetti explains that his title *A Coney Island of the Mind*,
taken from Henry Miller, expresses the way he felt about the
poems when he wrote them—"as if they were, taken together,
a kind of Coney Island of the mind, a kind of circus of the soul."
The general effect is of a kaleidoscopic view of the world and
of life as an absurd carnival of discontinuous sensory impres-
sions and conscious reflections, each with a ragged shape of its
own but without any underlying thematic unity or interrelation-
ship. To this extent the collection suggests a Surrealistic vision.
But it differs in that meanings and easily definable themes can
be found in most of the individual poems, even when the idea
of meaninglessness is the central concern.

In poem twenty-three of *Pictures*, the emphasis is on the

unreality of art and experience (in contrast to the theme of the poems on Goya and Sarolla):

> Dada would have liked a day like this
> > with its various very realistic
> unrealities

The poem ends with an impression of the funeral of a dancer which gives the poet the opportunity to play on the word *Dada* in ways that suggest associations with the aesthetic movement of that name, with a child's prattle, and with Hemingway's nihilistic *Nada*:

> > and her last lover lost
> in the unlonely crowd
> > and its dancer's darling baby
> about to say Dada
> > and its passing priest
> about to pray
> > Dada . . . .

The idea of this poem is more consistent with Ferlinghetti's basic viewpoint than those on Goya and Sarolla, since its appeal to Dada implies the failure of communication and meaning in both social forms and language. In poem ten of *Pictures*, Ferlinghetti comments on the failure of language to approximate reality and gives his opinion that the correspondence of word and thing is an impossibility—an attitude in keeping with the premises of his later "visionary" poetry.

Ferlinghetti is a lively and often interesting but uneven poet. He has a weakness for puns that sometimes leads to a cuteness like that of Cummings's less successful poems. Ferlinghetti also has difficulty in maintaining intensity. Some of his more prosaic verse has a Sandburgian flatness, as when, in poem five of *A Coney Island*, he writes about Jesus in hip slang.

In the more recent poems of *Starting from San Francisco* (1961; revised, 1967) and *The Secret Meaning of Things* (1969), there is a deepening sense of social and political disillusionment, in keeping with the mood of the decade, and a compensatory impulse toward drug-induced visionary experience.

The Secret Meaning of Things begins with "Assassination Raga," inspired by the horror of the political murders of the 1960s, and proceeds through five other long poems often marked by a disillusioned treatment of a number of Whitman's visionary themes. In "Through the Looking Glass," Whitman's "Passage to India" becomes a flight on "LSD Airlines" into a realm of "ecstatic insanity." "After the Cries of the Birds" combines the judgment of the bankruptcy of the progressive American dream with the observation that when the "Westward march of civilization" comes to a dead stop on the shores of the Pacific, there is "no place to go but In." The idea of an enforced introversion points to what Ferlinghetti seems to regard as a necessary connection between an unendurable social and political reality and an escapist art focused on an inner world of psychedelic vision. Though not generally shared by contemporary poets, this view is typical of the Beat writers and their followers. It is perhaps the most completely pessimistic modern expression of the Romantic visionary tradition, because the inner world of psychedelic hallucination, in contrast to that of the earlier Romantic vision, is essentially meaningless and solipsistic.

One somewhat older poet has provided a direct tie between the first generation of moderns and the Beat and other contemporary poets. Kenneth Rexroth, a native Midwesterner long associated with the San Francisco scene, has been writing free verse since the 1920s. He has combined in his work the aesthetic concerns of Pound and Williams with the proletarian sympathies of Whitman and Sandburg. He especially admires Williams for his craft and human sympathies. Like Pound, he has devoted much time to renderings of Japanese and Chinese poems, and much of his own verse reveals a sensitive perception of nature imagistically portrayed. Some of his poems also express an enthusiasm for outdoor life in the mountains that has a special appeal for younger back-packing poets of the Third Generation.

A substantial number of his poems are reflective and personal, in a vein he has characterized as a kind of "interior autobiography," looking back to Whitman but expressing a more idiosyncratic and opinionated self than Whitman's universal man. One of Rexroth's longer narrative poems, which describes a journey through England and Europe bracketed by two crossings of the American continent, is *The Dragon and the Unicorn*

(1952). It includes a mixture of imagistic landscape description, travel narrative, philosophical reflections, and offbeat personal judgments, such as the observation that one can find more communion and love in an hour "In the arms of a pickup in / Singapore or Reykjavik" than "in a lifetime / Married to a middle class / White American woman." This and similar specimens are balanced, however, by more reasonable pronouncements and by lyrical imagistic passages such as the description of Catullus' Sirmio:

> Sirmio, a dark blue grey sky
> Above the grey blue lake, the sun
> Breaking through the mountains at the
> Far end, its light a pale, soft orange;
> Dull red leaves on the hillsides,
> Bright yellow poplars on the shores;
> Everything else wet brown, dusky
> Blue, and chalky white . . . .

Rexroth's work is most fully represented by *The Collected Shorter Poems of Kenneth Rexroth* (1966) and *The Collected Longer Poems . . .* (1968). His *American Poetry in the Twentieth Century* (1971) is an interesting history and critique of modern poetry from a characteristically personal viewpoint. Its great virtue is that it presents an insider's account of a movement in which Rexroth has been closely involved since his and the century's twenties. It is especially valuable for its intimate account of the distinctive features of the San Francisco scene which encouraged the development of a public poetry to speak for the new popular culture.

A younger Western poet who is like Rexroth in his love of nature and proletarian sympathies, Gary Snyder has worked as a logger, a forest ranger, and a seaman. For seven years, he lived in Japan, where he studied Zen in Kyoto. His poems reveal a functional relationship among his work experience, his philosophical outlook, and his idea of poetic language and technique. Like the early Romantics, he believes that the subjects and language of poetry should be rooted in the common life, which he has known intimately. In an essay on "Poetry and the Primitive," he says: "Poets, as few others, must live close to the world that primitive men are in: the world, in its nakedness, which is fundamental for all of us—birth, love, death; the sheer fact of being alive."

In *Riprap and Cold Mountain Poems* (1969), the title of which refers to the laying of stones for mountain logging roads, Snyder sees a connection between this labor and the poet's striving to express the aesthetic and essential facts of his experience. The result is typically, for Snyder, a pattern of images, roughly and irregularly laid down (composed), which represent the poet's perception of his world, with an emphasis on sensuous and instinctual responses.

In "Trail Crew Camp at Bear Valley, 9000 Feet. Northern Sierra—White Bone and Threads of Snowmelt Water," the irregular lines of the opening stanza follow the windings of the trail:

> Cut branches back for a day—
> trail a thin line through willow
> up buckrush meadows,
> creekbed for twenty yards
> winding in boulders
> zigzags the hill
> into timber, white pine.

After another irregular stanza describing movement on the trail as "hooves clang on the riprap," the poem ends with the day's end, and the return to camp and the realities of its life are evoked by five selected images:

> sundown went back
> the clean switchbacks to camp.
> bell on the gelding,
> stew in the cooktent,
> black coffee in a big tin can.

In the eyes of the poet, the objects of this world have an intrinsic value and connectedness, not only as necessities of physical existence but also as parts of a cosmic scheme in which the enlightened Buddhist sees a complete harmony: thus, "the universe and all creatures in it are intrinsically in a state of complete wisdom, love and compassion; acting in natural response and mutual interdependence."

Like Thomas Merton, Snyder recognizes the late nineteenth-century ghost dances of the American Indians as an effort to recapture a lost communal culture. He is, however, more optimistic and revolutionary than Merton in his hope that modern society may be able to reach back to its primitive roots through changes in social organization directed toward the ideal of a tribal or communal family of man. He believes that it may be possible, with luck, eventually to "arrive at a totally integrated world culture with matrilineal descent, free-form marriage, natural-credit communist economy, less industry, far less population, and lots more national parks."

Like Whitman before him, whom he cites in an essay entitled "Passage to More Than India," Snyder looks forward to the possibility of a productive marriage of the traditions of the East and the West. In "Buddhism and the Coming Revolution," he writes: "The mercy of the West has been social revolution; the mercy of the East has been individual insight into the basic self/void. We need both."

In his veneration of nature, his Eastern mysticism, and his revolutionary hopes, Gary Snyder is very much in the current of the times. Whether or not his revolutionary goals are capable of realization (a point on which Snyder is more optimistic than most poets of his generation), his work is a valuable leaven in the process of continuing change in poetic and social forms.

III

The strong confessional impulse of much contemporary poetry is perhaps best represented by the work of Sylvia Plath (1932–63). Born in Boston of German and Austrian parents, she graduated from Smith College with highest honors in 1955. After further study at Cambridge University, she married the British poet Ted Hughes and lived in England until her death by suicide. The somberness and austerity of the poems of *The Colossus* (1960), her only book published during her lifetime, deepened into desperation in the ominously brilliant poems of *Ariel*

(1965). A later collection, *Crossing the Water* (1970), includes poems written during the years between the two earlier volumes.

In a spirit of intensely personal confession, the late poems of *Ariel* reveal some of the sources of inner conflict and self-revulsion. Her dependent love of her German father, who died when she was ten, was countered by her hatred of the Nazism which she associated with him and by her identification with its Jewish victims. Her ambivalence and her drive toward self-destruction are revealed in "Daddy":

> I have always been scared of *you*,
> With your Luftwaffe, your gobbledygoo.
> And your neat moustache
> And your Aryan eye, bright blue.
> Panzer-man, panzer-man, O You——
>
> . . . .
>
> I was ten when they buried you.
> At twenty I tried to die
> And get back, back, back to you.
> I thought even the bones would do.

"Ariel" acknowledges the impulse toward suicide that:

> Hauls me through air——
> Thighs, hair;
> Flakes from my heels.
>
> White
> Godiva, I unpeel——
> Dead hands, dead stringencies.
>
> And now I
> Foam to wheat, a glitter of seas.
> The child's cry
>
> Melts in the wall.
> And I
> Am the arrow

> The dew that flies
> Suicidal, at one with the drive
> Into the red
>
> Eye, the cauldron of morning.

It is not surprising that a heightening and derangement of sensibility should accompany so desperate an impulse and that Miss Plath's language should be evocative but not wholly explicable in terms of either a consistent paraphrasable argument or conventional symbolism. The suggestion of the flaking away and dissolution of the flesh is appropriate, as are the sense of release from human claims ("The child's cry") and the obsessional concentration on death (the arrow speeding toward the red bull's-eye of the target sun). But certain images ("Foam to wheat, a glitter of seas"—"The dew that flies") resist the same kind of logical explanation. And the final image of the "cauldron of morning" remains ambiguous. The destructiveness of the sun's fire and the impulse to merge with the source (like the getting "back, back, back" to Daddy) are consistent with each other. A less appropriate suggestion of rebirth (as well as an appropriate suggestion of grief) is conveyed by the introduction of "morning" (with its reminder of "mourning") into the climactic image of the suicidal plunge into the sun.

The language of Sylvia Plath's later poems reveals a strong impulse toward discipline and control on the one hand (albeit an obsessional control) and a counterimpulse to resist confinement by logic or by any other necessary condition of life. The general effect is of a heightened intensity and precision. But the apparent precision seems determined by neurotic compulsion rather than consistency of meaning. Consequently, the rigorously selected and composed images often vibrate with mysterious suggestions and evocations, as in the poem "Words," which begins:

> Axes
> After whose stroke the wood rings,
> And the echoes!
> Echoes travelling
> Off from the centre like horses.

In the lines that follow, the ax-stroke/hoof-beat association gives way to a composite image of tree sap that "wells like tears" and leads into further imagery of water and dissolution ("A white skull, / Eaten by weedy greens"). The concluding verses reintroduce the images of hoof-beats and water:

> Years later I
> Encounter them on the road——
>
> Words dry and riderless,
> The indefatigable hoof-taps.
> While
> From the bottom of the pool, fixed stars
> Govern a life.

For all the impression of precision and order (an impression enhanced by the appearance of syntactic and imagistic control), the meaning of the poem remains elusive. The affirmation of the evocative power and influence of language (of "words") with which the poem opens leads only to the negation of death. It may even be that the pain evoked by the use of language (the "sap" that "wells like tears") is a cause for the preoccupation with death that pervades the poem. At the end the "words," though "indefatigable," are "dry and riderless," divested of former human associations. It may be that language, the necessary medium of expression, is at last recognized as irrelevant and powerless in the face of the sublinguistic, immitigable irrational forces (the "fixed stars" at the "bottom of the pool") that govern life—or at least this poet's life. What is clearer than any isolable meaning is that Miss Plath is using language untraditionally in ways that serve her peculiar needs.

IV

Whether by necessity or intention, Sylvia Plath was in the current of her time in her resistance to logic and symbolic convention. The poets of the Third Generation have been engaged in an effort to revitalize a language inherited from the moderns but settling, as the speech of each generation tends to do, into stereo-typed conventions and patterns of symbolism. In trying to break through and free themselves from these dying forms, some have even attempted to avoid consistent patterns of meaning in their work and to concentrate on other more abstract aspects of form, in the manner of the nonverbal arts. John Ashbery, an art critic, has been interested in painting and music as well as poetry. He has said that he would like to approximate in his poetry the quality of music, especially its "ability of being convincing, of carrying an argument through successfully to the finish, though the terms of this argument remain unknown quantities." Al-though Ashbery's experimental efforts are interesting and some-times effective, the fact remains that words are words and hence inherently meaningful. Because a sophisticated writer is neces-sarily conditioned by the conventions of literature of the past, it is difficult if not impossible for him fully to exclude patterns of symbolic meaning.

"Rivers and Mountains," the title poem of a collection pub-lished in 1965, establishes an eerie, science-fictionlike atmos-phere in its opening lines:

> On the secret map the assassins
> Cloistered, the Moon River was marked
> Near the eighteen peaks and the city
> Of humiliation and defeat . . . .

The poem continues with an obscure narrative account, inter-spersed with imagistic descriptions of natural and urban land-scapes, of what seems to be a conspiratorial plot to resolve a mysterious, momentous conflict. The equally mysterious con-clusion has the urgency and discontinuity of a dream:

> Your plan was to separate the enemy into two groups
> With the razor-edged mountains between.
> It worked well on paper
> But their camp had grown
> To be the mountains and the map
> Carefully peeled away and not torn
> Was the light, a tender but tough bark
> On everything. Fortunately the war was solved

In another way by isolating the two sections
Of the enemy's navy so that the mainland
Warded away the big floating ships.
Light bounced off the ends
Of the small gray waves to tell
Them in the observatory
About the great drama that was being won
To turn off the machinery
And quietly move among the rustic landscape
Scooping snow off the mountains rinsing
The coarser ones that love had
Slowly risen in the night to overflow
Wetting pillow and petal
Determined to place the letter
On the unassassinated president's desk
So that a stamp could reproduce all this
In detail, down to the last autumn leaf
And the affliction of June ride
Slowly out into the sun-blackened landscape.

Although the meaning of the events of the poem is not clear, there is an unmistakable polarity between the attractive and relatively pure imagery of nature and the repellent imagery of a technologically destructive civilization. To this extent the poem, experimental though it is, conforms to the conventions of nineteenth- and twentieth-century Romanticism.

One obvious cause of the avoidance of logical meaning in the arts can be found in the influence of postwar Existentialism. In fiction and drama, this tradition has stimulated the vogue of the comic novel and the theater of the absurd, both of which exploit irrationality for their main effects. Yet until recently, the deliberate introduction of absurdity into contemporary verse has been rare. One of a very few poets who have written in a comic vein is Kenneth Koch. His verse often seems a frivolous effort at an absurdist abstractionism that complements John Ashbery's more serious work. But the literal meaning of Koch's poems is usually clearer than Ashbery's.

Koch's poems sometimes reveal a strain of critical or satirical humor, often directed against literary subjects, such as effete little magazines or the work of other poets. Examples include

"Mending Sump," a playful parody in brief of the Frostian dramatic dialogue, and "Variations on a Theme by William Carlos Williams," a short poem in four parts that begins:

1

I chopped down the house that you had been saving to live in
    next summer.
I am sorry, but it was morning, and I had nothing to do
and its wooden beams were so inviting.

2

We laughed at the hollyhocks together
and then I sprayed them with lye.
Forgive me. I simply do not know what I am doing.

As the poem proceeds, the speaker apologizes for giving away money "that you had been saving to live on for the next ten years," and justifies himself by explaining,

The man who asked for it was shabby
and the firm March wind on the porch was so juicy
    and cold.

Koch succeeds in parodying in an amusing way the qualities of impulsiveness, inconsecutiveness, and sensuousness of some of Williams's earlier verse. (The relish of March weather is entirely in character.) The irrationality is broadly exaggerated, although it is true that Williams often insisted that the poet must leave room for the irrational in the poem. He himself did, though not to the extent suggested by Koch. The significant difference is that in Williams's own poetry the effects of inconsecutiveness and irrationality usually serve more serious thematic and metaphoric purposes than Koch's view encompasses.

Although Koch's verse does not reveal the integrated vision and seriousness of purpose that underlies effective satire, it is entertainingly humorous and sometimes witty. Whatever the underlying motive of his work, his irreverent absurdity is one way of purging language of usages that have become rigid and oppressive. His poems are also in the current of their time in that they suggest a view of art as a sequence of random events or happenings.

The technique of proceeding not through a logically or chronologically ordered sequence of poetic events but through a process of random juxtapositions resistive to analysis is not entirely novel in modern art or literature. It has antecedents in Dada and Surrealism and in the experiments of Gertrude Stein, James Joyce, and others in automatic or ostensibly stream-of-consciousness writing. The difference is that it is now practiced in the altered context of a post-World War II irrationalistic philosophy and without the symbolic conventions that lay beneath the surface distortions of most of the work of the older generation of modern artists. Although the direction and enduring value of the newer trend is uncertain, it is the appropriate expression of a generation indebted to the ground-breaking of their elders but in need of finding their own ways.

The method represented by the work of Ashbery and Koch has been gaining wide acceptance among contemporary poets. Donald Justice in *Night Light* (1967) and W. S. Merwin in *The Moving Target* (1963) and *The Lice* (1967) have moved successfully beyond the more rationally and symbolically ordered poems of their earlier collections to a distinctive kind of evocative verse involving patterns of dissociated imagery somewhat like Ashbery's. Merwin's "Whenever I Go There" is a typical example of the tendency:

Whenever I go there everything is changed

The stamps on the bandages the titles
Of the professors of water

The portrait of Glare the reasons for
The white mourning

In new rocks new insects are sitting
With the lights off
And once more I remember that the beginning

Is broken

No wonder the addresses are torn

To which I make my way eating the silence of animals
Offering snow to the darkness

Today belongs to few and tomorrow to no one

The somewhat older Thomas Merton (1915–68), responding more directly to European and specifically French literary influences, moved with the same current from the more conventionally ordered free verse of his earlier years to an irreverent antipoetic mixture of sense and apparent nonsense, of sincere protest and ironic satire, to convey his sense of the confusion, the violence, and the accelerating breakdown of modern civilization. In his last two books, completed shortly before his journey to Asia and death in Bangkok, *Cables to the Ace* (1968) and the posthumous *The Geography of Lograire* (1969), Merton also assumed the role of epic or culture poet in the tradition of Walt Whitman, Hart Crane, Ezra Pound, and William Carlos Williams.

The change is proclaimed in the "Prologue" of *Cables to the Ace* (1968) as Merton flippantly greets his readers: "The poet has not announced these mosaics on purpose. Furthermore he has changed his address and his poetics are on vacation. He is not roaring in the old tunnel." Despite an impatient dismissal of the public as a rabble, there is a Whitmanesque acknowledgment of the representativeness of the poet in the closing lines:

I am the incarnation of everybody and the zones of
    reassurance.
I am the obstetrician of good fortune. I live in the social
    cages of joy.
It is morning, afternoon or evening. Begin.
I too have slept here in my stolen Cadillac.
I too have understudied the Paradise swan.

The full force of Merton's satire is directed against a conformist, materialistic society in which the exploitation and abuse of language have resulted in its breakdown as a medium of communication and a cultural bond. To portray this society, Merton uses a fragmented and largely inconsecutive poetic language, rich in irony and absurdity, and echoing, through fre-

198

quent parodies, the false voices of the advertisers, the politicians, and the exploiters of technology. There are also countervailing echoes of the voices of earlier writers to whom Merton is indebted. Conspicuous among these are James Joyce, as a pioneer in modern language experimentation, and William Blake, as both a savage critic of Philistine Britain and a prophet of a visionary New Jerusalem. In his own assumption of a latter-day prophet's role, Merton pessimistically forecasts the future from 1976 (the bicentennial of the American Revolution) to 2000, when "Too many creeps have won," and the doom of modern civilization is sealed.

For all the darkness, there is still the suggestion of a saving order in nature ("I admire the woodpecker and the dove in simple mathematics of flight") and a possible foundation for faith. There are "hidden lovers" in the soil which are "ordered" to reappear as "green plants and gardens tomorrow." There is even, beyond this Romantic hope, the suggestion of a Christ who comes through the garden in search of a lost disciple, "Too literate / To believe words," who can be awakened only when he comes to an understanding of history—an acknowledgement by Merton of the necessity of a social base for religion and for the religious poet in the modern age.

The poet is left with the responsibility of forming his own vision of his world. Although he may invoke the inspiration of "Plato, Prophets, Milton, Blake," he must use his "own numbered line"

> To go down alone
> Into the night sky
> Hand over hand
> And dig it like a mine.

And there is, despite the apparent irreverence and irrationality of the "Cables to the Ace" (cryptic messages to God in a godless world), an underlying reasoned and informing viewpoint.

Merton more fully undertakes the role of epic or culture poet in *The Geography of Lograire* (1969), described in the Author's Note as a "wide-angle mosaic of poems and dreams" in which he has mixed his own experience with "everybody else's." His announced purpose is to carry forward "the common participation of the living and the dead in the work of constructing a world and a viable culture." Disclaiming explicit theological or metaphysical concerns, Merton describes his tactic as that of "an urbane structuralism."

Lograire has something of the sound of a mythical Welsh kingdom. It also may have a link with *logos*, since the poem is a realm of words, and with *logogram*, since it is also a complex verbal symbol. It is the country of the poet's mind and imagination, shaped by his awareness of the conditions of life in the larger world, not simply the world of Western tradition, but the world shared (inequitably) by all its peoples, on the five continents, the islands of the South Seas, and the fastnesses of the Arctic zone. Merton achieves so great a scope through the borrowing and mingling of diverse historical and anthropological documents. Together, these form a mosaiclike pattern organized (as the world is organized in Merton's view of it) by recurrent motifs through which the arrangement of apparently discrete details achieves a metaphoric unity.

The world of Merton's poem is ordered simply by a division into four regions identified by the points of the compass. The four "cantos," as Merton calls them (with an invisible bow to Pound), are entitled "South," "North," "East," "West."

Among the places identified in the first canto, "South," are Kentucky (the setting of Merton's home monastery), Florida, Africa, and sixteeenth-century Mexico and Central America. Images of violence and fratricidal strife, of racial tension, of militarism combined with materialism, of exploitation and inhumanity recur throughout the first and the following cantos. "North" moves from recollections of the poet's New York City youth and residence in Great Britain to historical records of the English persecution of the seventeenth-century religious enthusiasts known as Ranters and finally to an account of the Kane Relief Expedition to the Arctic in 1855. "East" opens with selections from the fourteenth-century diary of Ibn Battuta, a Moroccan Muslim who traveled to Asia, continues with adapted extracts from the South Sea Island journal of Bronislaw Malinowski, and concludes with sections of "Cargo Songs" and other expressions of the modern "cargo" cults of Melanesia in the South Pacific. These cults, which developed especially in the period of the Second World War and its aftermath, express the wishful fantasies of natives that "cargoes" of commodities (rifles, flashlights, fountain pens) may come to them through the sea in white ships or out of the sky by jet planes like those of potent American airmen and provide them with recognition and an identity equal to that of the white man.

The subject of "West," the fourth and last canto, is America past and present, not simply as the poet's home environment but as a region and a civilization, the quality of which concerns the writer.

The opening section, "Day Six O'Hare Telephane," provides a surrealistic impression of Chicago's huge international airport, with its grotesque mechanized creatures ("big slow fish with tailfins erect"; "trains of insect machines"; "Long heavy-assed American dolphin") as a microcosm of Western technological civilization, devoted to populating the world with machinery but basically unreal.

The theme of illusion is continued as a sequence of fragmented vignettes dramatizes the confusion and phoniness of the world of politics and government. "Goody-two-shoes running for Congress," the former child movie star, is represented by her "stand" on the Vietnam war:

> " 'Well I think all of us are agreed and sincerely I myself believe that honest people on both sides have got it all on tape. Governor Reagan thinks that nuclear wampums are a last resort that ought not to be resorted' "

The implied mindlessness of the Hollywood candidate illustrates through an extreme example the inadequacy of political theory and practice to the problems of the modern world. It also dramatizes the disparity between the culture of modern civilization (its values and controlling thought) and its technological achievements.

The last brief sections of the poem—"Ghost Dance: Prologue" and "Ghost Dance"—look back at a primitive American past and its aftermath, as the betrayed and plundered Indians, finally entrapped in reservations by the late nineteenth century, developed compensatory rituals and group fantasies, including ghost dance movements based on the belief that the dead would return, wage war on the whites, and restore their former hunting grounds and homes. As primitive responses to the encroachment of civilization, these beliefs are much like the South Pacific cargo cults. The deprived Indians also believed that status-enhancing things ("gold watches military buttons silver chains and insignia") which would confer equality with the whites might be provided. Unlike the Melanesians, however, the Indians came to be disillusioned and to recognize the futility of their wishes:

> After a while the dreaming stopped and the Dream Dance turned into a Feather Dance. It was just a fun dance. It was mostly a white man's show.

Merton's poem ends with the end of the dreaming and a sense of the failure of civilization as well as of the victimized primitive societies. The modern primitives, both Indian and Melanesian, retain a primeval heritage of myth and ritual, but their capacity for aspiration, or "dreaming," is no longer rooted in a supporting communal economy. Modern civilized society, in contrast, possesses a more than adequate material foundation for cultural values but has lost the capacity for "dreaming," or establishing adequate values for self-realization and fulfillment. In their dilemmas, both societies tend to look to the world of things and to find in objects a support for selfhood and identity, but to Merton the Trappist monk, as to the Buddhist, the world of things is empty and unreal. The problem is one that Merton defines but does not presume to solve or prescribe for. Here he departs from his earlier manner, which implied a religious solution.

As in many other modern epics or culture poems, the sequence of images and events in Merton's final works is fragmented, and the reader's initial reaction is of a greater confusion and discontinuity than this selective discussion may suggest. But the underlying rationale is there, and it is clear that the poems are ordered in ways determined by the mature and largely consistent viewpoint of the writer. In this respect, they are like the major poems of Pound, Eliot, Williams, Hart Crane, and others who have written in the modern epic tradition.

But Merton does not tend to look to the past for a solution, as Pound does in his Confucian-Jeffersonian tradition, Eliot in his Anglo-Catholicism, and Crane in his idealized version of an

202

earlier, more primitive America which he vainly hopes to recapture ("Dance, Maquokeeta! . . . / Lie to us,—dance us back the tribal morn!"). To a greater extent than any of these (more even than Williams in *Paterson*), Merton uses recent anthropology and history as he focuses upon modern society as the only place in which solutions to the cultural crisis may conceivably be sought.

V

Perhaps the most extreme reaction against traditional poetic convention can be found in the efforts of recent "concretist" poets to focus upon the visual qualities of the work as an image or object in the manner of the spatial arts, with minimal recognition—sometimes complete rejection—of sequential language as the necessary medium of poetry.

More broadly international than Imagism, the concretist movement originated in Switzerland and quickly spread to Brazil, the United States and Canada, Japan, and a number of European countries. Largely a phenomenon of the 1950s and 1960s, when it grew to impressive proportions, concretism has strong ties with American poetry and art, especially through the influence of Ezra Pound, E. E. Cummings, Gertrude Stein, Charles Olson, and the painter Jackson Pollock. American publications have done a great deal to promote the movement. *The Chicago Review*'s presentation of concretist poetry eventuated in the useful collection edited by Eugene Wildman, *Anthology of Concretism* (1969). The most comprehensive and scholarly anthology is *Concrete Poetry: A World View* (1970), edited with a critical introduction by Mary Ellen Solt, an American concretist poet. Both of these volumes were preceded by *An Anthology of Concrete Poetry* (1967), edited by Emmett Williams, one of the founders of the movement.

In the introduction to Eugene Wildman's collection, Peter Michelson argues that by becoming his own printer and entirely designing the formal structure and composition of each of his works, the concretist poet "has demechanized the material cause of his poetry" and opened the possibility of a "true organic form" which can be closer than any printed poem to his "pure imagination." His idea of the poem as the expression of the pure imagination is essentially Romantic and closer to the theories of Emerson and Coleridge than to the tenets of the Imagists,[3] who were more concerned with the work as an artifact. Romantic also is Michelson's belief that concretist poetry can circumvent the printing press, through which a machine culture imposes controls upon the writer, and make it possible for the poet and his reader to "come to humanistic terms with our technocratic ethos."

There seems little doubt that the concretist poets are considerably indebted to Pound's idea (inspired by Ernest Fenollosa on the Chinese written character) of the ideogram.[4] As Wildman observes, "Concrete poetry aims, in general, at the ideogrammic state. The poets pattern the letters of the words in much the same way that a Japanese calligrapher patterns the strokes of a character. By no means, however, are all Chinese characters pictures of the things they represent. Language is not all that simple, and this is a too-popular fallacy about ideograms . . . . A Chinese character is not, by itself, a concrete poem. It requires the presence of an artist who will *do something* with the material."

Concrete poems are of many kinds, ranging from ideogrammic patterns in which verbal meaning and visual design interpenetrate for the expression of poetic meaning, through arrangements of words or letters that involve wordplay like punning, through more abstract compositions of letters and visual designs, to completely nonverbal abstractions such as that presented by one "poem" consisting of a black square, with slightly ragged edges, displayed against a white field.

An ideogrammic poem by a Japanese, Seiichi Niikuni, combines the printed forms of the characters for "door," "obscurity," and "sound" (see illustration, p. 206) in a clearly defined composition that integrates the semantic and visual qualities of the words so as to establish among them a relationship involving meaning and feeling as well as sensuousness. The effect is akin to that of the haiku; it is also reminiscent of Pound's definition of the image as "that which presents an intellectual and emotional complex in an instant of time."

[3] See above, pp. 33–34.
[4] See above, pp. 53–54.

An arrangement of letters in a pattern which combines visual representation with verbal associations is Mrs. Solt's "Forsythia" (see illustration, p. 207). The letters of the title, which form the base of the arrangement, are also used anagrammatically as the initials of a close grouping of related words that branch out into upward-reaching stems made up of Roman and Morse code letters. The core group of words, which resembles the stronger, closely alined branches at the base of the plant, itself comprises a kind of telegraphic message: "FORSYTHIA OUT RACE SPRING'S YELLOW TELEGRAM HOPE INSISTS ACTION."

The productions of the concretists, like those of artists in any mode, range from imaginative compositions at one extreme to pretentious and empty ones at the other. At its best, concrete poetry is necessarily lacking in the range of complex associations that makes a literary text so multifaceted and inexhaustible to interpretation. A virtue of concrete poetry, however, is its liberalizing influence upon the form sense of the reader-viewer, who must adjust his perception to the unique structure of each work.

In fairness to modern technology, something should be said about its actual relation to the concretist movement. Although some concretists may think of themselves as resisting the machine in the form of the printing press, they are greatly indebted to recent developments in printing for the means of publishing and circulating their work. Their compositions could be reproduced expensively by photoengraving, but it is the photo-offset printing process, as it has been developed over the past two or three decades, that has made it possible to reproduce and publish work like theirs on a large scale. As artists, the concretists have been not so much the prisoners of the machine's rigidity as beneficiaries of its flexibility and adaptability to the needs of intensely individual expression.

VI

The poetry of random association and concretist poetry both represent liberating efforts toward imaginative freedom in contemporary verse. In the long run, however, it is likely that

door
obscurity
sound

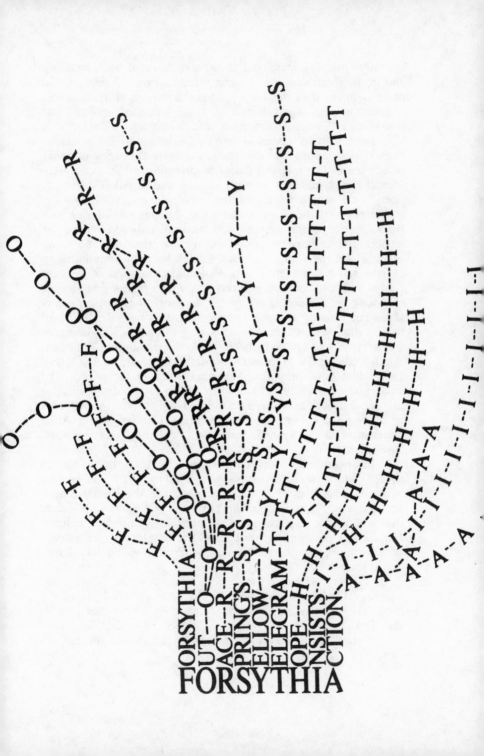

FORSYTHIA

evocative imagery employed in the discovery of fresh meaning and in the illumination of human relationships will prove to be more enduring than that employed in the interest of irrationality.

Extreme innovation has also been balanced by the less conspicuous forces of tradition and continuity. Side by side with radical experimentation, certain persistent strains of earlier poetry have helped to enrich and variegate the work of more recent years. The metrical craft and discipline of Yeats's closely wrought lines, admired by both modern and Middle Generation poets like Roethke, have continued to inspire emulation by some of the poets of the Third Generation. Though out of key with the subjective temper of the times, and officially rejected by the leaders among postwar poets, the metaphysical wit and irony of Eliot and the younger Robert Lowell have also continued to exert a seminal influence. The Objectivist tradition of William Carlos Williams and Louis Zukofsky, which places a modernist emphasis on the autonomy of the art work, has not only survived but actually enjoyed a vigorous recent revival. But of all the continuing strains, the most basic and central for American free verse has undoubtedly been the bardic tradition of Whitman. As in earlier periods, a number of the members of the Third Generation have supported Whitman's idea of the poet as the voice and conscience of American life in all its diversity. The major contributions of Ezra Pound and William Carlos Williams to this tradition have been extended by Charles Olson, Allen Ginsberg, Galway Kinnell, and others, including, most recently, Thomas Merton.

It has been harder for younger poets than for their elders to accept Whitman's optimism (though many share his hopes) when they confront the actualities of life in the United States, and especially in the American city, which Whitman viewed as the melting pot and matrix of an evolving democratic culture. For today's poet and novelist alike, the city looms as a symbol of corruption, repression, and violence in a hypocritically democratic society.

In Galway Kinnell's long poem "The Avenue Bearing the Initial of Christ into the New World," the crowded life of the New York interracial ghetto is detailed in a way that reveals the degradation of the "Maimed, lopped, shucked, and miss-aimed" and the betrayal of the American dream through an inhumane exploitation not greatly different, in the poet's view, from that of the concentration camp. In much the same way, though from the vantage of the black American, LeRoi Jones anatomizes the corrosive features of the life of the city:

> Flesh, and cars, tar, dug holes beneath stone
> a rude hierarchy of money, band saws cross out
> music, feeling. Even speech, corrodes.

The title of the poem, "A contract. for the destruction and re-building of Paterson," with its reminder of Williams's vision of Paterson as the city of man, calls for a radical reformation of the American way of life and hints at the threat of violence that underlies the plea.

But though Whitman's faith may seem to belong to the dead past, it is not entirely forgotten. Even the darkest protest is more optimistic than absurdity and irrationality. In "The River That Is East," Galway Kinnell looks back at two earlier celebrators of New York City, Whitman and Hart Crane (from whom he takes his title), and in "The River of Tomorrow" recognizes the persisting lure of the American dream, despite its perversions. After tentatively identifying the river as the one which "drags the things we love" to extinction, the speaker goes on:

> No, it is the River that is East, known once
> From a high window in Brooklyn, in agony—river
> On which a door locked to the water floats,
> A window sash paned with brown water, a whisky crate,
> Barrel staves, sun spokes, feathers of the birds,
> A breadcrust, a rat, spittle, butts, and peels,
> The immaculate stream, heavy, and swinging home again.

The stream of life flows through a sordid urban setting (much like that of Paterson), but there are saving links with the past in Hart Crane's "high window in Brooklyn," with its view of the harbor and the bridge, and in the "sun spokes" which the poet of "Crossing Brooklyn Ferry" saw reflected in the water of the same river as a token of the divine potential of humanity.

Even Whitman, writing in an expansive age, was aware of the conflict between his democratic ideals and the actualities of American life. In *Democratic Vistas* (1871), he looked out upon the society of the Gilded Age, with the "depravity of the business classes" and the pervasive corruption of government, and saw the "terrible truths" of the life of his time. The democratic revolution seemed to him to be proceeding, too slowly, through three stages—political, economic, and cultural—with the first two largely accomplished and the third as yet unrealized.

Since Whitman's time, the idea of a continuing revolution has become familiar. Despite their burden of pessimism, most modern American writers in the tradition of Whitman—and these include novelists like Dos Passos, Steinbeck, and Wolfe, as well as poets like Pound, Crane, and Williams—have thought of themselves as participants in the process of change. In recent years, the sense of social involvement and responsibility has deepened. In a nuclear age, the pressing consciousness of the interrelationship of societies throughout the world and the shared responsibility for destructive power and questions of public morality will not allow the luxury of alienation. The opposing demands of personal perception and public conscience may often impose a strain upon the poet, as they have in the career of Denise Levertov. But in the long run, the interfusion of social and personal concerns should enrich rather than limit his work if he resists the surrender of his authentic voice to the clichés of the forum.

Looking back at the first generation of the modern revolution, one must be impressed by the extent to which leading poets like Pound and Williams took upon themselves in a period of general disillusionment the role of epic spokesmen in the tradition of Whitman. In major poems, they sought to characterize their age, each in his own way, and to criticize, poetically, its values. The poets of the Middle Generation, influenced by the conservative theory of the New Critics, were less ambitious. They confined themselves for the most part to a more circumscribed realm of personal experience, within which they demonstrated impressive skill. It remains to be seen to what extent the younger generation of poets and their followers, sustained but also challenged by a more liberal theory of organic form, will succeed in realizing their aesthetic and social values in a time of rapid and momentous change.

Whitman saw himself truly as a beginner, a pioneer, in a

process which others would have to carry on. Addressing his successors in "Poets to Come," he said, too modestly, "I myself but write one or two indicative words for the future . . . expecting the main things from you." He actually did much more, but his words reflect a just view of his relation to the poetic and social process. It is to be hoped that today's and tomorrow's poets, involved in the same process at a further stage, will share as fully and consciously in it and see their own works not as finished products but as open, developing forms, integral to the larger life of history in which the poet has his part but which has a life beyond his own.

Notes

Page 6   William Wordsworth, *The Prelude, or Growth of a Poet's Mind*, ed. Ernest de Selincourt, 2nd ed. (Oxford: Clarendon Press, 1959), pp. 409, 407.

Page 7   Ralph Waldo Emerson, *Essays: Second Series* (Boston: James Munroe and Co., 1844), p. 28.

Page 8   Emerson, pp. 10, 26–27, 22.
Emerson, *Poems* (Boston: James Munroe and Co., 1847), p. 118.

Page 9   Emerson, *Poems*, pp. 65–66.
Emerson, *Essays*, pp. 40–41.

Page 10   Walt Whitman, *Leaves of Grass: Comprehensive Reader's Edition*, ed. H. W. Blodgett and Sculley Bradley

(New York: New York Univ. Press, 1965), p. 714. This convenient edition follows the text of the authorized ninth edition of 1892.

Page 11   Whitman, pp. 709, 505, 224.

Page 13   Whitman, p. 59.

Page 14   Whitman, p. 52.

Page 15   Whitman, p. 160.

Page 16   Whitman, pp. 162, 165.
W. C. Williams, *Pictures from Brueghel and Other Poems* (New York: New Directions, 1962), p. 81.

Pages 17–18   Whitman, pp. 246–47.

Page 20   Whitman, p. 300.

Page 21   Whitman, p. 301.

Page 22   Whitman, pp. 307, 534.

Page 26   W. D. Howells, *Criticism and Fiction and Other Essays*, ed. C. M. and R. Kirk (New York: New York Univ. Press, 1959), p. 67.
Henry James, *Partial Portraits* (London & New York: Macmillan, 1905), p. 400.

Page 28   Emily Dickinson, *The Poems of Emily Dickinson*, ed. T. H. Johnson (Cambridge: Harvard Univ. Press, 1955), I, 225; I, 135–36; III, 1010.

Page 29   Stephen Crane, *War Is Kind* (New York: Frederick A. Stokes Co., 1899), pp. 9–10. A convenient inclusive edition is *The Poems of Stephen Crane*, ed. Joseph Katz (New York: Cooper Square, 1966).

Page 30   Whitman, p. 50.
Crane, pp. 40, 54, 55.

Page 35   Edmund Wilson, *Axel's Castle: A Study in the Imaginative Literature of 1870–1930* (New York: Scribner's, 1931), pp. 22–23.
Arthur Symons, *The Symbolist Movement in Literature*, 2nd ed. (London: Constable, 1908), pp. 1–2.

Page 36   T. S. Eliot, *Selected Essays: New Edition* (New York: Harcourt, Brace, 1960), p. 4.

Page 37   Eliot, pp. 124–25, 247.

Page 38   Frank Kermode, *Romantic Image* (New York: Macmillan, 1957), pp. 138–61.

Page 40   Robert Frost, *The Complete Poems of Robert Frost* (New York: Holt, 1949), pp. 230, viii.

Page 41   Wallace Stevens, *Collected Poems* (New York: Knopf, 1954), p. 91.

Page 42   Stevens, pp. 196, 165, 176, 473.

Page 43   Stevens, pp. 35, 250, 59.

Page 44   Langston Hughes, *Selected Poems* (New York: Knopf, 1954), p. 33.

Page 45   W. C. Williams, *Selected Essays* (New York: Random House, 1954), p. 110.

Page 48   Ezra Pound, "Vorticism," *Fortnightly Review*, 96 (September 1, 1914), 463–64.

Page 50   *A Lume Spento and Other Early Poems* (New York: New Directions, 1965). See Pound's "Foreword (1964)," in which he adds, "As to why a reprint? No lessons to be learned save the depth of ignorance, or rather the superficiality of non-perception—neither eye nor ear."
Personae: The Collected Poems of Ezra Pound (1926; New York: New Directions, n.d.), p. 7.

Page 51   *Personae*, pp. 29, 61.
Introduction, *The Oxford Book of Modern Verse*, ed. W. B. Yeats (London: Oxford Univ. Press, 1936).

Page 52   *Personae*, p. 74.

Page 53   *Personae*, p. 64.

Page 54   "Vorticism," p. 469.
            The ABC of Reading (1934; rpt. New York: New
            Directions, 1960), p. 52.

Page 55   *Personae*, pp. 131, 133.

Page 56   *Personae*, pp. 127, 137.

Page 59   *Personae*, pp. 197, 198.

Page 60   *Personae*, pp. 198, 202.

Page 61   *Personae*, pp. 203, 204.

Page 62   With some exceptions, most critics have shared the
            admiration of F. R. Leavis and Hugh Kenner, who,
            though they disagree about Pound's being a man of one
            poem, *Mauberley*, agree on its overall excellence, with
            Leavis going so far as to say, "But *Hugh Selwyn Mau-
            berley*, it must be repeated, is a whole. The whole is
            great poetry, at once traditional and original"—Leavis,
            New Bearings in English Poetry (London: Chatto &
            Windus, 1932), p. 150; Kenner, *The Poetry of Ezra
            Pound* (Norfolk, Conn.: New Directions, 1951), p. 176.

Page 63   *Personae*, pp. 189, 191.

Page 64   *Personae*, p. 193.

Page 67   *Personae*, p. 89.

Page 68   *The Cantos of Ezra Pound* (New York: New Direc-
            tions, 1970), p. 3. Although Pound used Arabic nu-
            merals for some and Roman numerals for other groups
            of cantos, I have for convenience used only Arabic
            numerals in my references.

Page 69   *Cantos*, p. 6.

Page 70   *Cantos*, pp. 10, 11, 28.

Page 71   *Cantos*, pp. 59, 61.

Page 72   See Forrest Read, "A Man of No Fortune," *Motive and Method in* The Cantos *of Ezra Pound,* ed. Lewis Leary (New York: Columbia Univ. Press, 1954), reprinted in *Ezra Pound: A Collection of Critical Essays,* ed. Walter Sutton (Englewood Cliffs, N. J.: Prentice-Hall, 1963), pp. 64–79. In contrast, Noel Stock has found the key to the "underlying nature of the whole work" in Canto 36—Stock, *Reading the Cantos* (New York: Pantheon, 1966), pp. 26–27.
            Cantos, p. 206.

Page 73   *Cantos*, p. 187.
            In *Jefferson and/or Mussolini* (New York: Liveright, 1935), in which he attempts to identify Mussolini, as a pragmatic Fascist reformer, with the ethics and attitudes of Adams and Jefferson, Pound describes himself as "a correct Jeffersonian and Confucian" (p. 46).
            Cantos, pp. 233, 229.

Page 74   *Cantos*, pp. 230, 238.

Page 75   *Cantos*, pp. 414, 265, 264.

Page 76   *Cantos*, pp. 344, 416.

Page 77   *Cantos*, p. 521.

Page 78   *Cantos*, pp. 484, 425, 434.

Page 79   *Cantos*, pp. 426, 430, 503, 513, 533, 527, 488, 427, 436.

Page 80   *Cantos*, pp. 437, 428, 532, 533, 428, 466, 539.

Page 81   *Cantos*, pp. 510, 526, 458, 449.

Page 82   *Cantos*, pp. 457, 466, 520, 522. For Pound's relationship with Wilfred Scawen Blunt, see W. T. Going, "A Peacock Dinner . . .," *Journal of Modern Literature,* 1 (1971), 303–10.

Page 83   *Cantos*, p. 778.

Page 84   *Cantos*, pp. 795, 796, 797.
           Hayden Carruth, "The Poetry of Ezra Pound," *Perspectives USA*, No. 16 (Summer, 1956), 146–47.

Page 85   *Cantos*, pp. 795, 797.

Page 86   I am indebted to James Laughlin for the text of this poem, first printed in America as Canto 120 in the magazine *Anonym* (Buffalo), No. 4 (1969), 1, and for the knowledge of an earlier version, with a different ordering of verses, in the Spring 1962 issue of *Threshold* (Belfast). It is included in the Third Printing (1972) of *The Cantos*.
           "Vorticism," pp. 463–64.

Page 88   E. E. Cummings, *i: six nonlectures* (1953; rpt. New York: Atheneum, 1962), pp. 32–33.

Page 89   Cummings, *Poems, 1923–1954* (New York: Harcourt, Brace, 1954), p. 277.

Page 90   *Poems*, p. 40.

Page 91   *Poems*, p. 333.

Page 92   *Poems*, p. 99.
           Cummings, *95 Poems* (New York: Harcourt, Brace, 1958), p. 1.

Page 93   *Poems*, pp. 284, 301.

Page 94   *Poems*, pp. 154, 252.

Page 95   *Poems*, pp. 373, 208.

Page 96   R. P. Blackmur, *The Double Agent: Essays in Craft and Elucidation* (New York: Arrow Editions, 1935), pp. 1–29.
           Poems, p. 51.

Page 97   *Poems*, pp. 100, 13–14.

Page 98   *Poems*, p. 58.

Page 99   *Poems*, pp. 151–52, 167, 394.

Page 100   *Poems*, pp. 394, 168, 397, 190, 239.

Page 101   *Poems*, pp. 454, 197, 396, 244–45.

Page 102   *95 Poems*, p. 39.

Page 104   Robert McRoberts *et al.*, "Interview with Donald Justice," *Seneca Review*, 2 (1971), 7–8.
Marianne Moore, *The Complete Poems of Marianne Moore* (New York: Macmillan/Viking, 1967), p. 85.

Page 105   Archibald MacLeish, *Collected Poems, 1917–1952* (Boston: Houghton Mifflin, 1952), pp. 40–41.
Wallace Stevens, "About One of Marianne Moore's Poems," *The Necessary Angel* (New York: Knopf, 1951), pp. 91–103.
Moore, p. 99.

Page 106   Moore, p. 119

Page 107   Moore, pp. 120, 121.

Page 108   Moore, pp. 127, 49–50.

Page 109   Moore, pp. 95, 96.

Page 110   Moore, p. 5.

Page 111   Moore, pp. 7, 32.

Page 112   Moore, p. 32.

Page 113   Moore, pp. 32–33, 84.

Page 114   Williams, *Pictures from Brueghel*, p. 29.
Moore, *The Fables of La Fontaine* (New York: Macmillan, 1954).
Moore, *Complete Poems*, pp. 134, 135.

Page 115   Moore, *Complete Poems*, pp. 191, 97–98, 28, 201, 240.

Page 116   Moore, *Complete Poems*, pp. 149–150.

Page 117   Moore, *Complete Poems*, pp. 91, 163.

Page 120   William Carlos Williams, *Imaginations*, ed. Webster
            Schott (New York: New Directions, 1970), pp. 112,
            117.
            *The Collected Earlier Poems of William Carlos Wil-
            liams* (New York: New Directions, 1951), p. 277.

Page 122   Especially by J. H. Miller in his introduction to *Wil-
            liam Carlos Williams: A Collection of Critical Essays*
            (Englewood Cliffs, N. J.: Prentice-Hall, 1966). For
            another intelligent discussion see L. S. Dembo, *Con-
            ceptions of Reality in Modern American Poetry* (Berke-
            ley & Los Angeles: Univ. of California Press, 1966),
            pp. 48–80.
            The Collected Later Poems of William Carlos Williams,
            rev. ed. (New York: New Directions, 1963), p. 7.
            Collected Earlier Poems, pp. 130–31.

Page 123   *Collected Earlier Poems*, pp. 106–7.

Page 124   By J. H. Miller in the introduction cited above.

Page 125   *Collected Earlier Poems*, p. 332.

Page 126   *Collected Earlier Poems*, pp. 67, 80–81.

Page 127   Walter Sutton, "A Visit with William Carlos Williams,"
            The Minnesota Review, 1 (1961), 317.

Page 128   *Collected Earlier Poems*, pp. 81, 3, 126.

Page 129   *Collected Earlier Poems*, pp. 131, 284–85.

Pages   *Collected Earlier Poems*, pp. 270–72.
130–31

Page 132   *Selected Letters of William Carlos Williams*, ed. J. C.
            Thirlwall (New York: McDowell, Obolensky, 1957),
            pp. 312–13.

Page 133   *Selected Essays*, p. 283.
            Paterson (New York: New Directions, 1963), p. 12/3.
            (The pagination was changed in the reset Fifth Printing

of 1969; page references to both versions are given here.)

Page 134   *Paterson*, pp. 30/19, 15/7.

Page 135   *Paterson*, p. 53/40.
Selected Letters, p. 335.

Page 136   *Selected Letters*, p. 326.
Selected Essays, p. 215.
Paterson, pp. 105/86, 100/82.

Page 137   *Paterson*, pp. 118/95, 120/98.

Page 138   *Paterson*, pp. 142–43/118, 145/120, 167/140.

Page 139   *Paterson*, p. 207/176.

Page 140   *Paterson*, pp. 220/188, 222/189, 237–38/203.

Page 141   *The Autobiography of William Carlos Williams* (New York: Random House, 1951), p. 392.
Paterson, p. 241/207.

Page 142   *Paterson*, pp. 244/209.
The initials A. P., as used in the original text of *Paterson, Book Four* (1951) and in the text of the collected *Paterson*, in four books (1951), were changed to A. G. (for editorial reasons explained by James Laughlin) in the complete *Paterson*, in five books (1963).
Paterson, p. 96/77.

Page 143   *Paterson*, pp. 247/212, 268/230, 270/232.

Page 144   *Paterson*, pp. 246–47/211–12.

Page 145   *Paterson*, p. 278/239.

Page 146   *Pictures from Brueghel*, pp. 94–95.

Page 147   *Pictures from Brueghel*, pp. 180–81.
Collected Later Poems, p. 18.

I Wanted to Write a Poem, ed. Edith Heal (Boston: Beacon Press, 1958), p. 76.
Collected Later Poems, p. 161.

Page 148   *Collected Later Poems*, pp. 159–60, 162.

Page 149   Stevens, *Collected Poems*, p. 515.
Collected Later Poems, p. 162.

Page 150   *Collected Later Poems*, pp. 125, 127, 128.

Page 154   I. A. Richards, *Principles of Literary Criticism* (London: Kegan Paul, 1925), p. 259.
Richards, *Coleridge on Imagination* (New York: Harcourt, Brace, 1935), p. 228.

Page 155   This idea supplied the central argument of Ransom's *The World's Body* (New York: Scribner's, 1938).
Allen Tate, *The Man of Letters in the Modern World* (New York: Meridian, 1955), pp. 64–77.
J. C. Ransom, *The New Criticism* (Norfolk, Conn.: New Directions, 1941), pp. 219–20, 280–81.
Tate, p. 337.

Page 157   Robert Lowell, *Lord Weary's Castle and The Mills of the Cavenaughs* (Cleveland and New York: Meridian, 1961), pp. 5, 32.

Page 158   Lowell, *Life Studies* (New York: Vintage, 1959), p. 84.

Page 159   *Life Studies*, p. 86.
Karl Shapiro, *Essay on Rime* (New York: Reynal & Hitchcock, 1945), p. 60.

Page 160   Compare the opening of Eliot's "Burbank with a Baedeker . . .": "Burbank crossed a little bridge / Descending at a small hotel; / Princess Volupine arrived, / They were together, and he fell."—*The Complete Poems and Plays* (New York: Harcourt, Brace, 1952), p. 23.
Shapiro, *Trial of a Poet* (New York: Reynal & Hitchcock, 1947), p. 21.

222

Shapiro, *Selected Poems* (New York: Random House, 1968), pp. 5, 8, 105.

Page 161   *Selected Poems*, pp. 108, 120.

Page 162   *Selected Poems*, p. 213.

Page 163   Theodore Roethke, *The Collected Poems of Theodore Roethke* (New York: Doubleday, 1965), p. 105.
W. B. Yeats, *The Collected Poems of W. B. Yeats* (New York: Macmillan, 1933), pp. 251, 224.
Roethke, p. 107.

Page 164   Roethke, pp. 239, 157.

Page 165   Roethke, "Open Letter," *Mid-Century American Poets*, ed. John Ciardi (New York: Twayne, 1950), pp. 69–70.
Richard Eberhart, *Selected Poems, 1930–1965* (New York: New Directions, 1965), p. 5.

Page 166   Eberhart, "Notes on Poetry," *Mid-Century American Poets*, pp. 226–29.
Eberhart, *Shifts of Being* (New York: Oxford, 1968), p. 24.

Page 167   *Selected Poems*, pp. 29, 41.

Page 171   D. M. Allen, ed., *The New American Poetry* (New York: Grove, 1960), pp. 386–97. Olson's essay, first published in *Poetry New York* (1950), is included in his *Selected Writings* (New York: New Directions, 1967).

Page 172   Walter Sutton, "A Conversation with Denise Levertov," *Minnesota Review*, 5 (1965), 331–32.
Allen, p. 412.

Page 173   Sutton, pp. 330–31.
Robert Creeley, *For Love: Poems 1950–1960* (New York: Scribner's, 1962), pp. 38, 109.
Sutton, p. 332.

Page 174   Charles Olson, *The Maximus Poems* (New York: Jargon/Corinth, 1960), p. 2.

Page 175   Allen, p. 441.
               Sutton, p. 326.

Page 176   Denise Levertov, *The Jacob's Ladder* (New York: New Directions, 1961), pp. 87, 21.

Page 177   *O Taste and See* (New York: New Directions, 1964), p. 53.
               With Eyes at the Back of Our Heads (New York: New Directions, 1959), p. 17.

Page 178   *Relearning the Alphabet* (New York: New Directions, 1970), pp. 22, 92.

Page 179   *Relearning*, pp. 97, 112.
               To Stay Alive (New York: New Directions, 1971), pp. viii–ix, 66, 83, 51, 60, 65, 66, 69.

Page 180   Allen, pp. 434–35.
               Robert Duncan, *Bending the Bow* (New York: New Directions, 1968), pp. 78, 132.

Page 181   Duncan, pp. 44, 113.

Page 183   Allen Ginsberg, *Howl and Other Poems* (San Francisco: City Lights, 1956), pp. 9, 16.

Page 184   Allen, pp. 415–16.
               Ginsberg, p. 20.

Page 185   Lawrence Ferlinghetti, *A Coney Island of the Mind* (New York: New Directions, 1958), pp. 9, 81, 8.

Page 186   Allen, p. 130.
               Ferlinghetti, p. 16.

Page 187   *The Secret Meaning of Things* (New York: New Directions, 1969), pp. 26, 33–34.

Page 188   Kenneth Rexroth, *The Collected Longer Poems* (New York: New Directions, 1968), pp. 195, 223.

Page 189   Gary Snyder, *Earth House Hold* (New York: New Directions, 1969), p. 118.
               Snyder, *The Back Country* (New York: New Direc-

tions, 1968), p. 20/15. (The pagination is changed in the reset Sixth Printing.)

Page 190   *Earth House Hold*, pp. 90, 93, 92.

Page 191   Sylvia Plath, *Ariel* (New York: Harper, 1966), pp. 50–51, 26–27.

Pages
  192–93   Plath, p. 85.

Page 194   John Ashbery, in Paris Leary and Robert Kelly, eds., *A Controversy of Poets* (New York: Doubleday Anchor, 1965), p. 523.
            John Ashbery, *Rivers and Mountains* (New York: Holt, 1965), pp. 10–12.

Page 196   Kenneth Koch, *Thank You and Other Poems* (New York: Grove, 1962), p. 68.

Page 197   W. S. Merwin, *The Lice* (New York: Atheneum, 1967), p. 24.

Page 198   Thomas Merton, *Cables to the Ace* (New York: New Directions, 1968), p. 1.

Page 199   Merton, pp. 6, 53, 58.

Page 200   Merton, *The Geography of Lograire* (New York: New Directions, 1969), pp. 1–2.

Page 201   *Geography*, p. 129.

Page 202   *Georgraphy*, pp. 134, 137.

Page 203   Hart Crane, *Complete Poems and Selected Letters and Prose*, ed. Brom Weber (New York: Liveright, 1966), p. 73.

Page 204   Eugene Wildman, ed., *Anthology of Concretism*, 2nd ed. (Chicago: Swallow, 1969), pp. viii–ix, 162–63, 63.

Page 205   M. E. Solt, *Concrete Poetry: A World View* (Bloomington: Indiana Univ. Press, 1970), p. 243.

225

Page 208 For a valuable recent coverage of this revival, see the special issue of *Contemporary Literature*, 10 (1969), devoted to the theory and careers of Objectivist poets including George Oppen, Carl Rakosi, Charles Reznikoff, and Louis Zukofsky.

Galway Kinnell, *What a Kingdom It Was* (Boston: Houghton Mifflin, 1960), p. 72.

Page 209 LeRoi Jones, *The Dead Lecturer* (New York: Grove, 1964), p. 11.

Kinnell, *Flower Herding on Mount Monadnock* (Boston: Houghton Mifflin, 1964), pp. 4–5.

Index

Joyce, James, 34, 53, 62, 80, 85, 116, 197, 199
Justice, Donald, 104, 197

Keats, John, 88, 119
Kenner, Hugh, 61
Kermode, Frank, 38
Kerouac, Jack, 182
Khayyam, Omar, 81
Kinnell, Galway, 208-9
Klee, Paul, 144
Koch, Kenneth, 195-96

La Fontaine, Jean de, 114
Landor, W. S., 81, 103
Lanier, Sidney, 26-27
Lawrence, D. H., 180
Levertoff, Olga, 178
Levertov, Denise, 172, 173, 175-79, 181, 210
Lewis, P. W., 51, 81
Lincoln, Abraham, 22, 99
Lindsay, Vachel, 43-44, 45
Li-Po (Rihaku), 54-56
Lowell, Robert, 132, 156-59, 161, 162, 170, 183, 208

MacLeish, Archibald, 105
Macpherson, James, 5
Madison, James, 72
Malatesta, Sigismundo, 68, 70, 71, 78
Malinowski, Bronislaw, 200
Masters, E. L., 43
Mathews, Elkin, 47
Melville, Herman, 184
Merton, Thomas, 190, 198-203, 208
Merwin, W. S., 197-98
Michelson, Peter, 203-4
Middle Generation poets, 38, 46, 152-67, 170, 208, 210
Miller, Arthur, 99
Miller, Henry, 185
Milton, John, 4, 149, 171, 199
Monroe, Harriette, 33, 43
Monroe, James, 72
Montaigne, Michel de, 114

Moore, Marianne, 36, 38, 46, 103-17, 121, 152, 156, 158, 176, 180
Moore, Merrill, 45
Mussolini, Benito, 73, 77, 78

Nemerov, Howard, 156
New Criticism, 34, 37, 46, 152-56, 157, 159, 169, 170, 210
Niikuni, Seiichi, 204, 206

objective correlative, 37, 46, 48, 168
Objectivism, 42, 43, 90, 120-22, 124-25, 208
Olson, Charles, 170, 171-75, 180, 181, 203, 208
Orage, A. R., 73
organic form, 7-9, 11, 24, 26, 27, 40, 52, 88, 91, 93, 103, 104, 105, 123, 127, 145, 150, 169, 170-71, 175-76, 210-11
Ovid, 69

Patch, Sam, 134-35, 137
persona, 48-49, 53, 61-62, 169
Petrarch, 84, 94, 95
Picasso, Pablo, 91, 144
Pindar, 63, 181
Plath, Sylvia, 170, 190-93
Plato, 150, 199
Poe, E. A., 34, 147
Pollock, Jackson, 203
Pope, Alexander, 5, 80
Pound, Ezra, 4, 33, 34, 35, 38, 39, 43, 44, 45, 46, 47-64, 65-86, 88, 113, 118, 119, 121, 143, 150, 152, 156, 169, 171, 172, 174, 175, 180, 181, 183, 187, 198, 202, 203, 204, 208, 210

Ransom, J. C., 45-46, 152, 155, 156
Reinach, Salomon, 61
Rexroth, Kenneth, 187-88
Richards, I. A., 153, 154-55
Rihaku (see Li-Po)
Roethke, Theodore, 156, 162-65, 208
Rossetti, D. G., 51, 81